# TO KILL A PRIEST

# TO KILL A PRIEST

*The Murder of Father Popiełuszko and
the Fall of Communism*

by

Kevin Ruane

GIBSON SQUARE

To Waldek Chrostowski
— without whom we might never
have known the truth.

This edition published for the first time in 2004 by

Gibson Square Books Ltd
15 Gibson Square, London N1 0RD
Tel: +44 (0)20 7689 4790; Fax: +44 (0)20 7689 7395
publicity@gibsonsquare.com
www.gibsonsquare.com

© 2004 by Kevin Ruane

ISBN 1-903933-54-4

UK & Ireland sales by Signature
20 Castlegate, York YO1 7EH
Tel 01904 633 633; Fax 01904 675 445
sales@signaturebooks.co.uk
www.signaturebooks.co.uk

UK & European distribution by Central Books Ltd
99 Wallis Road, UK London E9 5LN
Tel +44 (0)845 458 9911; Fax +44 (0)845 458 9912
info@centralbooks.com
www.centralbooks.com

New Zealand, Canada, South Africa, US sales,
please contact
Gibson Square Books Ltd

Printed by Bookwell Ltd

# Contents

# Cast of Characters

| | |
|---|---|
| Grzegorz Przemyk | Murdered schoolboy |
| Fr Jerzy Popiełuszko | Resident priest at St Stanisław Kostka's |
| Waldemar Chrostowski | (Waldek) His friend and driver |
| Cardinal Wyszyński | Primate of the Thousand Years |
| Fr Teofil Bogucki | Parish Priest at St Stanisław's |
| Bishop Władysław Miziołek | Former Rector of the Warsaw Seminary, supporter of Fr Jerzy |
| Fr Zdzisław Król | Chancellor of the Warsaw Curia |
| Cardinal Józef Glemp | Primate of Poland |
| Edward Wende | Lawyer |

### Communist party and government

| | |
|---|---|
| Gen. Wojciech Jaruzelski | Communist Party leader and Prime Minister |
| Gen. Czesław Kiszczak | Minister of Internal Affairs |
| Mirosław Milewski | Former Minister, Politburo member responsible for Internal Affairs |
| Adam Łopatka | Minister in charge of the Office for Denominational Affairs |
| Jerzy Urban | Government Spokesman and Minister |
| (*Izvestiya* | Moscow newspaper) |

### Ministry of Internal Affairs

| | |
|---|---|
| Gen. Władysław Ciastoń | Head of the SB (secret police), a Deputy Minister, |
| Col Zbigniew Pudysz | Head of the Investigations Bureau |
| Gen. Zenon Płatek | Director of Dept Four |
| Col Adam Pietruszka | First Deputy Director, Dept Four |
| Col Zbigniew Jabłoński | Deputy Director, Dept Four |
| Capt. Grzegorz Piotrowski | Head of Section One, Dept Four |
| Lt Leszek Pękała | Junior officer |
| Lt Waldemar Chmielewski | Junior officer |

### Warsaw City Office of Internal Affairs

| | |
|---|---|
| Lt Col Leszek Wolski | Head of Section Four |

### National HQ of the MO (uniformed police)

| | |
|---|---|
| Col Zbigniew Jabłoński | Director, Criminal Investigations Bureau |

### Prosecutors and court officials

| | |
|---|---|
| Leszek Pietrasiński | Lead Prosecutor at Toruń trial |
| Anna Jackowska | Warsaw Deputy Prosecutor (who prepared charges against Fr Popiełuszko) |

### The opposition

| | |
|---|---|
| Lech Wałęsa | Solidarity Chairman (later President) |
| Tadeusz Mazowiecki | Union adviser, editor and publicist (later Prime Minister) |
| Bronisław Geremek | Adviser and historian (later Foreign Minister) |
| Janusz Onyszkiewicz | Union spokesman (later Defence Minister) |

# Polish Pronunciation

Polish names and words look difficult to pronounce, and they are. What follows is an attempt to give the reader a rough idea of how recurring names, words or phrases are normally pronounced.

*Jerzy Popiełuszko* = Yezhee Pop-yeh-wooshko
  This is a particularly useful example indicating several general rules: the letter j, when followed by a vowel, is pronounced as the English y in yes; rz equals zh or the French g in Georges, and sometimes sh; o is always full and upright as in pop or top (never as in open); this ł, with a bar across it, is best pronounced by the non-Pole as w; u is pronounced oo; and sz is sh. The stress in Polish as a rule is always on the next to last syllable, in this case on the woosh.
*Lech Wałęsa* (equally instructive) = Lekh Vawensa
  In Polish, ch is as in Loch Lomond, w is the equivalent of v, a is straightforward as in ah, this ł is the same as in Popiełuszko, and the e has a mark beneath it making it nasalised as in French.
*Wojciech Jaruzelski* = Voychekh Yaroozelski
*Czesław Kiszczak* = Chesswav Keeshchak (cz is English ch)
*Jasna Góra* = Yassna Goora (ó = oo)
*Wyszyński* (Cardinal) = Vyshynski. The y as in bit, the n slightly softened.

*Józef Glemp* = Yoozef Glemp

*Bronisław Dąbrowski* = Broneeswav Dombrovski. The i is ee; the a with a sign underneath is nasalised.

*Władyław Miziołek* = Vwadyswav Miziowek. The z followed by i is softened.

*Grzegorz Przemyk* = Gzhegozh Pzhemyk, or even Gshegosh Pshemyk.

*Wujek* (colliery) = Vooyek

*Katowice* = Katoveetse (c is ts)

*Krakowskie Przedmieście* = Krakovskyeh Pshedmyesche

*Mirosław Milewski* = Meeroswav Meelevski

*St Stanisław Kostka,*

*Żoliborz* = Staneeswav Kostka, Zholeeborzh. The z is like the j in the French joli.

*Teofil Bogucki* = Tayofil Bogootski

*Białystok* = Byahwystok

*Suchowola* = Sookhovola

*Bartoszyce* = Bartoshytse

*Andrzej Przekaziński* = Andzhay Pshekazinski

*Ząbki* = Zombki

*Jarmużyńska-*Janiszewska = Yarmoozhinska-Yanishevska

*Wawrzyszew* = Vavzhyshev

*Piasecki* = Pyahsetski

*Miodowa* Street = Myodova. The io or yo is pronounced as in yacht

*Solidarność* — the accented s is thinner than usual; the accented c is a thinner ch.

# Glossary

MO: Milicja Obywatelska (Citizens' Militia, uniformed police)

SB: Służba Bezpieczenstwa (Security Service), 'secret police'

ZOMO: Riot Police — Zmotoryzowane Odwody Milicji Obywatelskiej (Motorised Reserves of the Citizens' Police)

PRON: Patriotyczny Ruch Odrodzenia Narodowego (Patriotic Movement for National Rebirth) — pro-regime front organisation set up after the imposition of martial law.

Politburo: The Political Bureau or inner cabinet of the Communist Party.

Solidarity NSZZ Solidarność: the independent, self-governing trade union set up under the agreements signed by government and strikers in the Gdańsk Shipyard on 31 August 1980.

SEJM: The Polish Parliament (pronounced 'Same').

KOR: The Committee for the Defence of Workers (Komitet Obrony Robotnikow) set up by a group of intellectual opposition activists in 1976 in response to the authorities' brutal suppression of workers' protests against steep increases in the price of food. Disbanded voluntarily in 1981 after the birth of Solidarity.

Curia: The Church's administrative offices.

*Góra*: Literally, mountain or hill, the top of something, but in common parlance and in the context of this book 'the leadership', 'the bosses upstairs'.

Huta Steel works: Huta Warszawa = Warsaw steel works

# Foreword

One evening in October 1978, I was at my desk in my top-floor flat in Moscow when I heard on the BBC World Service News that the Cardinal Archbishop of Cracow, Karol Wojtyła, had been elected Pope. My first excited reaction was to phone several friends to let them know, and my enthusiasm grew as I wondered what change might be inspired by a Pope who came from a land with a communist government loyal to the Soviet Union but whose feet were now firmly planted in each of the rival camps of the Cold War. It felt like a good omen.

In Warsaw, more than four years later, when Poland was still smarting from the pain of seeing the Solidarity movement outlawed under martial law in 1981, a sense of excitement and hope returned when I heard for the first time a sermon by Fr Jerzy Popiełuszko. I knew then that this seemingly ordinary priest shared with the Polish Pope a special talent for speaking out against political injustice in purely religious terms that people understood.

For me, who had spent three years as the BBC correspondent in Moscow chronicling the struggle of the 'dissidents' and their inevitable punishment under the Soviet system of repression, it was a refreshing experience to go to Fr Popiełuszko's monthly Masses for the Homeland and listen to what he said relayed over loudspeakers to his overflowing congregation. It could never have happened in Moscow. Those were the days when Mikhail

Gorbachev was still waiting in the wings of the Kremlin, when East Berlin and Prague — the scenes of particular jubilation in 1989 — were among the most venomous critics of the Solidarity movement and the Polish Church, and when the West, for all its professed sympathy, showed little confidence that Solidarity could ever come back.

The fact that Solidarity did come back and did form its first government in 1989 has already been attributed, among other things, to the influence of this or that superpower leader or Western politician, and to the overwhelming attractions of the free market system. But as an eyewitness of much of what happened inside Poland during the 1980s, I believe that the credit for Solidarity's moral victory, which preceded and precipitated the revolutions in neighbouring countries, should go rather to the Poles who fought, first and foremost, for justice and refused to give up when martial law was imposed, to the Catholic Church in Poland whose advice was eventually heeded, and, not least, to Fr Popiełuszko who gave his life only to have his good name attacked in a travesty of legal practice at the trial of the secret policemen who killed him.

Two decades after his murder, the story of Fr Popiełuszko and of the Solidarity movement he loved and defended has become almost a footnote in the history of the collapse of Communist rule in Europe. It is my hope that this book will help ensure that the truth will not be erased. It is written it in the spirit of what Milan Kundera once termed 'the struggle of memory against forgetfulness', the struggle, that is, against the misrepresentation of history for political purposes by those in power, a common practice in the former Soviet bloc, but not unknown in democratic countries today.

Kevin Ruane, 2004

# 1
# Death of a Schoolboy

On Thursday, 19 May 1983, tens of thousands of people gathered in Warsaw for the funeral of an eighteen-year-old schoolboy whose name, only a few weeks earlier, had meant nothing to most of them. And yet on this day he was laid to rest in the city's finest cemetery with a solemnity usually reserved for national heroes.

A bishop, assisted by more than twenty priests, celebrated the Requiem Mass on the high altar of the parish church of St Stanisław Kostka in the pleasant district of Żoliborz. As the coffin was carried from the church, bells began to toll. The bereaved mother, walking behind it supported by a young priest, saw the street lined by crowds of people who cast flowers into the path of the cortege and held their hands high above their heads with fingers parted in the sign of victory.

For a large part of the long walk to the Powązki cemetery some miles away, the coffin, bearing just one emblem of the banned Solidarity trade union, was carried by the dead boy's classmates. And it all took place, in response to a request from the altar, in absolute silence. Journalists and camera teams who rushed ahead to secure vantage points looked back to see the broad road leading to the cemetery gates filled from one side to the other by a multitude moving slowly forward like a tide but without a sound.

At the graveside, Bishop Władysław Miziołek spoke of the crime of Cain against Abel and prayed that a brother's blood should not be shed by brother ever again. As the coffin was lowered into the ground, the crowd sang the national anthem.

The Bishop's words provide a clue as to why such homage was paid to Grzegorz Przemyk, an only child who lived with his mother, the poet Barbara Sadowska, in a tiny flat on the eleventh floor of a tower block in the centre of Warsaw.

Everyone believed that he was the victim of police brutality. On the evening of the previous Thursday, 12 May, Grzegorz Przemyk and three friends were larking about on Castle Square, letting off steam at the end of another of their final school exams, when they were approached by policemen who checked their identity documents. Grzegorz and one of his companions were taken to the nearby police station on the street behind St John's Cathedral, where they were separated. Some 45 minutes later, Grzegorz was taken by ambulance to a first aid clinic.

When his mother, alerted by telephone, found him there he was vomiting blood. Rejecting a suggestion that he be placed in a psychiatric hospital, she took him home. There he told her that the policemen had squirted gas into his eyes and beaten him. He had heard one of them saying: 'Don't leave any marks.' On Friday Grzegorz was sent to hospital by the family doctor, who suspected a perforated liver. A surgeon operated in an attempt to save the boy's life, but his internal injuries were far too severe. Grzegorz Przemyk died at lunchtime on Saturday, 14 May.

Word of the boy's death spread privately throughout Warsaw. On Sunday evening, when my assistant, Karol Małcużyński, found me in the BBC office, we decided to visit friends of Barbara Sadowska who had been with her during the weekend. They told us what she had told them.

That night I telephoned a report on the death to London. On Monday morning I sent another after we had talked to Barbara Sadowska herself in her high-rise flat, to which, incidentally, we were accompanied by a very obvious 'secret policeman'. He joined us in the lift going up, got out one floor below our stop but managed to be waiting, without a word, when we got out upstairs. The authorities, no doubt, had heard the overnight report, as Mrs Sadowska had, on the Polish or English broadcasts of the BBC's World Service, and had either guessed or known that we would be visiting the boy's mother.

Any doubts — and there were some in London — about the merits of reporting the premature and painful death of an unknown Warsaw teenager as politically important news were dispelled by the size of the funeral, the biggest seen in Warsaw since that of Cardinal Wyszyński two years earlier, and by the speed with which the government announced an official investigation into the death. But having visited the tiny home the boy had shared with his mother, along with two brown cats and one small dog, and having seen the book-laden desk and above it, on a pin board, the eclectic array of pictures — the Maharishi, St Teresa of Lisieux and Albert Einstein sticking his tongue out — all one could say was that the death of Grzegorz Przemyk was important because he was simply another innocent victim of the system of repression introduced when General Wojciech Jaruzelski imposed martial law in December 1981.

Those who were prepared to defend the General could argue that the costs of his decision in terms of loss of life were relatively small. By May 1983, the government had recognised only 13 fatalities resulting from martial law: nine striking miners shot dead by police at the Wujek colliery near Katowice in Silesia in the first week of martial law; three Solidarity demonstrators who also died from police gunshot wounds in the copper mining town of Lubin in August-September 1982; and a 20-year-old electrician shot in the head by a plain-clothes policeman in Nowa Huta, the steel-making town on the edge of Cracow, in October 1982 during demonstrations against the Act of Parliament making Solidarity illegal. None of those who fired the shots had been considered culpable in any way.

There were, however, other, less publicised deaths, twice as many in fact by May of 1983, and Solidarity classified them without hesitation as acts of murder or manslaughter by members either of the uniformed police (the MO), or the riot police, known as the ZOMO. According to Solidarity, the victims died as a result of being beaten by the police on the streets or on police premises during or after anti-government demonstrations, and in some cases when the victim had been taken into custody for no apparent reason. No one had been prosecuted for any of these deaths and the authorities had offered no official explanation except for the occasional reference to 'unknown assailants' or to 'person or persons unknown'.

The case of Grzegorz Przemyk, though similar in some respects to these others, was different in one crucial feature: his body was not found lying on some street. His mother found him still alive at the clinic and when she took him home he told her what had happened. There were witnesses, his school pals, to say that he had been perfectly fit before being taken to the police station, an hour or so before his mother found him spitting blood. And when he died, she made sure that the truth spread throughout the city. News of Grzegorz Przemyk's death reached the rest of Poland and, indeed, the world, from outside Poland and not from the Polish media. For once, the authorities were not able to ignore it.

The government responded to the outrage and the criticism by claiming that Grzegorz Przemyk had been drunk and violent and had needed to be restrained. It went on to accuse the Solidarity underground resistance movement of seeking to exploit the boy's death for political purposes and complained that the priests had helped to turn the funeral into an anti-State demonstration. This response merely confirmed many people's view that although General Jaruzelski and his senior colleagues did not necessarily instruct police officers to beat political opponents to death, they were unable to bring themselves to expose and punish those who committed murder or manslaughter in their name. It was as if the martial law regime, which relied for its survival on the use of force, felt obliged, out of some corrupt sense of loyalty, to protect those who used violence on its behalf.

The question of where ultimate responsibility lay for crimes committed in the name of the regime was raised repeatedly and

insistently by the democratic opposition in Poland in the first
half of the 1980s, and the month of May 1983 seemed to have
been deliberately chosen by the authorities as an occasion for
demonstrating just how malicious they could be in their efforts
to deter opposition or resistance.

This was not the first time that Grzegorz Przemyk and his
mother had found themselves at loggerheads with the authorities. Like many other women considered by the authorities to be
politically troublesome, Barbara Sadowska had been interned
when martial law was imposed in December 1981 but released
the following March. Since then she had been working with
other volunteers in the Primate's Committee, the charity set up
by Cardinal Józef Glemp to organise and distribute food,
clothing and medicine to poor families affected by martial law.
But on the eve of May Day in 1983, when anti-government
demonstrations were expected in Warsaw, she and her son
Grzegorz were taken into preventive custody and kept there for
48 hours.

Then on the evening of 3 May, Mrs Sadowska had another
unwelcome encounter, this time with unidentified assailants. She
was back working at the Primate's Committee in a building
belonging to the Franciscan Sisters in the grounds of St Martin's
Church in Warsaw's Old Town just as a peaceful pro-Solidarity
demonstration began after Mass in St John's Cathedral nearby.
With a colleague from Reuters, David Storey, I followed the
demonstrators as they made their way up Krakowskie
Przedmieście on their best behaviour, keeping to the pavement
and politely clapping each collection of water cannons and other
riot control machinery that they found lurking in the side streets.

It was while the demonstration was getting further and
further away from the Old Town that the building of the
Primate's Committee was raided by twenty or so men in plain
clothes. They forced their way in through a back door, shouting
at the top of their voices, and picked up chairs to smash the
medicine dispensary. After 10 minutes of mayhem, during
which several of the volunteers were beaten, they left. One was
seen to be carrying a walkie-talkie radio.

This blatant act of thuggery was the subject of baffled speculation. Who could have authorised it? And why? General Jaruzelski was about to preside in Warsaw over the first congress of the Patriotic Movement for National Rebirth, commonly known as PRON (Patriotyczny Ruch Odrodzenia Narodowego), an artificial organisation set up by the government to support its interests and create the pretence of backing martial law in the name of national reconciliation. Could General Jaruzelski, or his trusted lieutenant, General Kiszczak, the Minister of Internal Affairs, even have thought of organising such an unprovoked act of violence on the eve of the PRON congress, which was intended to demonstrate their dedication to national peace and friendship? This seemed hardly likely, especially since the Polish Pope, John Paul II, was preparing to make his second visit to his native land the next month. While organising security arrangements for such a visit, why attack a church charity set up by the Primate of Poland on church premises?

There seemed to be no answers to these questions. Indeed, there was speculation that the raid on St Martin's had been organised and staged by forces inside the police community loyal to General Mirosław Milewski, a so-called hardliner, who had been replaced as Minister of Internal Affairs by Kiszczak the previous summer but still retained a seat in charge of security matters at the Communist Party's Political Bureau. This assumed that Milewski stood for much harsher treatment of opposition activity than that meted out by General Jaruzelski. At any rate a curious incident on the evening of the attack suggested that it was carefully planned and timed.

We did not follow the demonstration to the end of Krakowskie Przedmieście, assuming mistakenly that a demonstration that had continued so peacefully in spite of such an intimidating show of force by riot police would end just as peacefully. In fact, the demonstrators were set upon and dispersed by the ZOMO units which they had previously applauded in the side streets but which had moved ahead surreptitiously to lie in wait for them at the end of the street.

In the meantime, we had retraced our steps in order to pick up my car, which I had parked on Podwale, the street that curves round the fortified walls of the Old Town. We turned left onto Miodowa Street and then right onto Senatorska. There we were confronted by a police van.

A uniformed officer got out and asked us to get in. In those days, this was not an entirely unusual thing to happen to Western journalists going about their ordinary business, but it was difficult to see why it was happening now. The street was deserted. Nothing was happening. Yet there we were sitting in a police van, facing an officer who seemed unable to offer any explanation. He took my small Sony recorder, pressed the play button without first rewinding, recognised the recorded voice of the government spokesman, Jerzy Urban, switched it off and handed it back. 'You shouldn't be here,' he said. Then he let us go.

We were too intent on getting back to our offices to pay much attention at the time to what the officer meant. Looking back, though, it would seem he was giving us good advice, for when we turned left onto Podwale we found ourselves facing a crowd of tough-looking young men, about twenty altogether, coming towards us from the entrance to the Old Town closest to St Martin's. Some of them were pulling hungrily on cigarettes, and none looked at us as we passed between them. They were not talking among themselves. As they turned into the street we had just left, they too seemed intent on getting away.

It wasn't until the following morning that we learned of the raid at St Martin's, but when we did it seemed clear that we had passed through the ranks of the men who had carried out the attack only minutes earlier. It also seemed probable that in the car park across the street from the police van there had been a bus waiting to take the young thugs away, and that the officer in the van had been posted there with orders to keep the coast clear for their departure.

This episode is hardly convincing evidence of who exactly inspired or organised the raid on the premises of the Primate's

Committee but, at the very least, it suggests how much thought went into this deliberate act of violence against those ministering for no reward to the bereaved, the orphaned and the poor. These were the least threatening of the regime's opponents, but the authorities saw them as part of the larger opposition, the underground and those above ground who refused to accept martial law and continued to call for the restoration of their free trade union, Solidarity. This was why the hired thugs attacked the Primate's charity at St Martin's and why Grzegorz Przemyk lost his life. The authorities were picking easy targets and they were doing so because the Poles were not giving up or lying down; they were resisting the repression of a Communist martial law regime in a manner without precedent.

This was 1983, when the Soviet empire betrayed no obvious signs of imminent collapse. Following the death of Leonid Brezhnev, the Soviet Communist Party had a new leader in Yury Andropov, former head of the KGB and the man responsible for the brutally efficient campaign of the late 1970s to crush all internal dissent by sending human rights activists to gaol, to labour camps or into internal exile. Little more than three years had passed since Andrei Sakharov had been transplanted without trial from Moscow to Gorky, the city now known by its old name of Nizhny Novgorod. Two more years were to pass before Mikhail Gorbachev would come to power following the deaths in rapid succession of Andropov and his successor, Konstantin Chernenko, but in 1983 all was relatively quiet in the 'satellite' countries that were Poland's neighbours. The Berlin Wall still looked rather durable. The crowds who were to demonstrate so joyfully in front of the world's television cameras in Prague in 1989 as they enacted the 'Velvet Revolution' were doing little in 1983.

In Poland it was very different. On May Day in 1983 there were anti-government, pro-Solidarity demonstrations in 20 towns and cities during which some 1000 people were detained by the police. Most of these would no doubt have been released shortly afterwards, but the number of arrests gives some idea of how many people were out on the streets demonstrating.

Martial law had been suspended the previous December, but the full rigour of its regulations was applied at will and it was for violating those regulations that more than 200 people were already serving prison terms.

They were to be joined by many others. Many people in Poland refused to be intimidated and believed what few people in the West, even those who earned their living analysing developments in the Soviet Bloc, could bring themselves to believe: that Solidarity could win and that Communism would fall.

Among those believers was the young priest who had organised the funeral of Grzegorz Przemyk and whose voice I had heard requesting from the altar at St Stanisław's that the cortege should pass through the streets of Warsaw to the cemetery at Powązki in absolute silence. His name was Jerzy Popiełuszko.

I heard that voice again when Karol Małcużyński and I went back to St Stanisław's in Żoliborz for the regular Mass for the Homeland at the end of May, celebrated — as always — at seven in the evening on the last Sunday of the month. It was my first Mass for the Homeland and it was a revelation. Even before reaching the church (on foot, because we had to park the car some distance away), I was struck by the sheer size of the crowds converging on it from main roads and side streets like football fans streaming towards a stadium for a big match. The church was full by the time we arrived, so we could not see Father Popiełuszko. But as we stood among the rose beds between the church and the presbytery, we could hear everything that was said inside — the readings, the psalms, poems and prayers — as it was relayed by loudspeakers to the crowds outside. After a year in Poland, I was not surprised by well-attended church services, but this was different. The congregation was huge, made up of people of all ages, and one sensed that they were there not only to pray but also to listen.

On this Sunday evening, Fr Popiełuszko chose to deliver his sermon in the form of a prayer addressed to the Virgin Mary, the 'Queen of Poland', venerated for six centuries in the legendary image of the Black Madonna at the monastery of

Jasna Góra. He recalled how the nation had turned to Mary in times of crisis and survived, as it did in 1920 in the celebrated 'Miracle on the Vistula' when the Soviet Army threatening Warsaw was comprehensively routed by the Poles. But now, he said, after all the pain endured in the 18 months 'since the shameful December night of 1981' when martial law was declared, Mary was needed more than ever as a mother, for 'Satan… through those who serve him, is dealing out fresh suffering'.

To some modern ears, this language may seem unfamiliar, but there was no denying that Fr Popiełuszko was talking of something very real.

> From its very first day, this month of May in Warsaw has been a time when Satan has lorded it in the form of violence, demonstrations of force and hatred, and a torrent of lies and slander. It seems, it was not enough for him to lock up many of our brothers and sisters for forty eight hours lest they ruin the atmosphere of the workers' holiday… It was not enough for him, apparently, to deploy the water cannon on Castle Square and call out the motorised units armed with hate.
>
> On the evening of 3 May, the feast of the Queen of Poland, he launched an attack with the help of a band of thugs on the convent of the Franciscan Sisters and injured people who devote their time and energies to bringing aid to those who have suffered most under martial law and to those imprisoned for their convictions.
>
> But all this was too little for Satan. So he went further and committed a crime so terrible that the whole of Warsaw was struck dumb with shock. He cut short an innocent young life. In bestial fashion he took away a mother's only son. It was not enough for him to have tormented the mother and the son repeatedly in the past, or on 1 May to have placed in detention without cause both the mother and the son, who was due to sit his matriculation exams in only a few days' time. It was not enough for him that on 3 May he had injured her in that brutal attack on the convent.

So silence reigned in the capital, the silence of solidarity which united thousands of hearts in pain and prayer... You know, Mother, that a nation which has suffered so much in history, which has made such a great contribution to the culture of Europe and the world, which has produced and still produces so many wonderful people, the nation which has given a Pope to the world, a Pope who astonishes the world — such a nation cannot be treated with contempt.

Such a nation is not forced to its knees by any satanic power. This nation has proved that it bends its knee only to God. And for that reason we believe that God will stand up for it...[1]

The offertory prayers, read out from the altar by an actor, included one for Grzegorz Przemyk who, it said, had been 'brutally murdered', another for those 'under arrest, under sentence, in hiding or sacked from their jobs', another, in contrast, for 'those who have sold themselves into the service of lies, injustice and violence', that they be granted 'the grace of conversion', and finally one 'for ourselves, that we may be free from fear, intimidation and the lust for revenge'.

On this Sunday evening at the end of May 1983, Fr Popiełuszko was well aware of the dangers of speaking so frankly. In his final announcements at the end of the Mass, he urged the congregation, as usual, to go home in silence, but then he addressed the SB men, the 'secret policemen' of the Security Service (Służba Bezpieczeństwa), whom he correctly presumed to be in attendance.

I have a request for those gentlemen who come to Mass because they have to as part of their duties. I ask you to show a little honesty towards your superiors. Tell them the truth about what you have seen and heard here so that they can avoid making themselves look ridiculous by writing accusations containing things that are fabricated and untrue.[2]

By this time, Fr Popiełuszko knew for sure that his sermons and his Masses for the Homeland were of lively interest to those at the very highest levels of the State.

# 2
# The Priest

Monthly Masses for the Homeland were introduced at St Stanisław Kostka's in Żoliborz by the parish priest, Fr Teofil Bogucki, in October 1981. He was reviving what used to be a feature of church life in Poland between the First and Second World Wars. Indeed, the last Mass for the Homeland had been said by Cardinal Hlond, the Primate of Poland, in St John's Cathedral in Warsaw in the dark days that followed the German invasion of Poland in September 1939. As fate would have it, when Fr Bogucki said the first of the new Masses for the Homeland, assisted by Fr Popiełuszko, he happened to antici-pate by one and a half months the advent of another war, the 'state of war' or *stan wojenny*, better known as martial law.

It was under martial law that Fr Popiełuszko became the regular celebrant and preacher at the Masses for the Homeland. And anyone attending one of those Masses for the first time in the summers of 1982, 1983 or 1984 could be forgiven for assuming that the thousands of people, some from distant parts of Poland, who filled the church, the churchyard and the streets around the church had come to listen to the voice of a born preacher. The truth is, however, that in the first eight years of his priestly life, working in four parishes in and around Warsaw, until his transfer to St Stanisław's in 1980, few detected in Fr Popiełuszko any special talent for delivering sermons. He had a talent, certainly, for making friends but if there was one thing people did remember of those early years it was that he did not seem strong enough for the life he had chosen and was always ailing.

It is a curious fact, though, that the last four years of Fr Popiełuszko's life were devoted to a cause that inevitably entailed a routine that was as gruelling, mentally and physically, as anything he had experienced before. The difference was that he chose to do it. Also remarkable is the fact that coming as he did from a peasant background, he made common cause both with the industrial workers of the big cities and with the intellectual elite.

Jerzy Popiełuszko was born on 14 September 1947, the third child of Marianna and Władysław Popiełuszko. His parents were peasant farmers who worked a small holding in a hamlet called Okopy at the northern end of the province of Białystok, which runs along Poland's north-eastern frontier with present-day Belarus. It would not be unfair to describe Okopy as the back of beyond. When I visited his family home in 1986, I found just one dark dirt road overhung by trees and lined by houses, some of wood, some of brick. The shops and the church were some miles away to the west in Suchowola, which sits on the main road north from Białystok. When I asked what the nearest big town was, Marianna replied without hesitation that it was Grodno, ignoring the fact that this city, which was part of Poland before the Second World War, was then part of the Soviet Union, cut off behind a forbidding frontier. This, it seemed, did not affect her sense of place. She also told me that the Germans had set fire to the barn as they retreated westwards before the advancing Red Army in 1944.

There were five children altogether. Teresa was the eldest and was married to a local farmer. Józef, the second, had become a taxi driver. Then came Jerzy, followed by Jadwiga, who died when she was barely two. The youngest, Stanisław, was helping run the family small holding with his wife, Danusia, a cheerful, smiling woman. They had a baby son called Jerzy.

Oddly enough, Fr Jerzy was never given that name by his

parents. He was christened Alfons, a name he is said to have disliked, possibly because it was commonly used to mean a pimp. At any rate, he dropped Alfons and assumed the names of Jerzy Aleksander shortly before he was ordained priest.

There is little to say about his upbringing except that it was devoutly Catholic. To say this, however, is to say all. When my assistant, Karol Małcużyński, drove to the farm at Okopy in October 1984 (when Fr Jerzy had been missing for a week), Władysław Popiełuszko, who was then in his seventies, spoke fondly about early signs of his son's vocation. 'God has been guiding Jerzy for a long time,' he said. 'When he was five, a daughter of ours died at the age of two. Jerzy stood over the coffin and said: "I want to be a priest. I will pray a lot for her."'

Jerzy Popiełuszko became an altar boy and began most days by walking or trotting through the undulating countryside of sandy gullies and small hillocks that separates Okopy from Suchowola to serve at early morning Mass in the Church of Saints Peter and Paul. When he was eleven, Jerzy said he wanted to begin studying for the priesthood with the Franciscans at Niepokolanów, west of Warsaw. His mother persuaded him to wait. 'I told him he still had his childhood to live.'

Jerzy managed to gain admission to a seminary in 1965 but it required considerable determination. As soon as he had passed his matriculation exams at the grammar school at Suchowola, he applied for entry to the seminary in Białystok only to be told that there was no room for him. To make matters worse, the parish priest at Suchowola refused to support his application for admission to any seminary, on the grounds that his health was simply not up to it. Subsequent events were to show that this judgement was not entirely wide of the mark, but Jerzy refused to accept it.

In June of 1965, when he was still only seventeen, he went to Warsaw on his own initiative and presented himself to the rector of the Metropolitan Seminary of St John the Baptist. As he was to tell close friends later, 'I fell on my knees and begged him to take me in.' The rector — who was to become one of his staunchest supporters in later life as Bishop Miziołek — did so.

Jerzy now found himself in an entirely new setting, in the very heart of Warsaw, in a building set back behind one of several fine churches on one of the city's most beautiful streets. The seminary was also quite close, as it happens, to the premises of the Communist government's Office for Denominational Affairs, which was to be kept busy in later years by the activities of Fr Popieluszko.

In those days, though, the young man from Okopy showed no signs of being difficult. According to Bishop Miziołek, he was a quiet lad who got on well with his fellow students. He was open and trusting and did not trouble his superiors with problems. As for his studies, he was a bit above average without displaying any special intellectual brilliance. It was not until his second year out of home that Jerzy got into trouble with superiors, but that was not at the seminary, it was in the army.

In 1966, Jerzy was one of a group of seminarists who were posted to a unit set up specifically to put 'clerics' through military training. It was at Bartoszyce, a remote spot just below Poland's northern border with the Soviet Union. Only the previous year, the Primate, Cardinal Wyszyński, had written a long letter to the Minister of Defence protesting against the call-up of candidates for the priesthood who had normally been excused military training. The Cardinal alleged that these periods of compulsory military service were used to induce the young men to give up their vocation. He also warned the Minister that one certain outcome would be that those subjected to this treatment would conceive a permanent dislike for the Communist authorities.

In Bartoszyce, Jerzy had good reason to feel aggrieved. It was there that he first learned what the authorities were capable of, but he also discovered his own powers of stubborn resistance. Non-commissioned officers tried in vain to get him to remove the medal of the Virgin Mary which he always wore round his neck. There were several other such arguments and all ended in punishment.

All accounts suggest that Jerzy Popieluszko was not so much punished as persecuted and bullied. However, in letters to his spiritual adviser, Fr Czeslaw Mietek, back at the Warsaw seminary, he gave the distinct impression that in spite of the punishments — such as being forced to parade in full kit but without boots in freezing weather — he actually derived satisfaction from showing open defiance. In one letter, for example, he described how he was given a long talking-to by a lieutenant but then: 'I began to yawn like an idiot. I showed him that all his talk was of little interest to me. That really got him going'.[1]

It is quite possible that when Jerzy returned to the seminary in 1968 he had developed not only a dislike for the Communist authorities but also a taste for standing up to bullies. Unfortunately, he did not have the constitution or the physique to take too much punishment. His vulnerability may well have attracted the attention of bullies, both in the army and in later life.

Soon after returning to Warsaw, Jerzy fell seriously ill. He was rushed to hospital suffering from an over-active thyroid. Part of the gland was removed and his condition was described as critical, although he recovered quite quickly and was back at the seminary in less than a month. Thereafter he was under careful medical supervision for the rest of his life.

The picture of Jerzy Popiełuszko as 'a quiet but ailing' colleague, as one fellow student described him, seems to have been the prevalent image among those who did not know him intimately. But poor health was not the only determining factor in his personality. During his years at the seminary and in the army, a series of events began to create a climate of social and political dissatisfaction to which he could not be indifferent. In March of 1968, when Jerzy was still in uniform, student protests were brutally suppressed at Warsaw University just half a mile away on the same street as the seminary. In August of the same year, the fact that Polish forces took part in the Warsaw Pact invasion of Czechoslovakia to put an end to the 'Prague Spring', when Romania declined to do so, came as a shock to a nation that prided itself on a history of helping other nations fight for their freedom. Then, in December 1970, the nation was shocked again when the army was sent in to crush protests by workers on the Baltic Coast against increases in the price of food. The revolt ended in bloodshed and in the downfall of the Communist leader, Władysław Gomułka.

It seems likely, however, that the greatest influence on the young seminarist was exerted by the towering figure of the Primate, Stefan Cardinal Wyszyński. By the nature of his position, he was obliged to remain a somewhat distant figure, but according to Fr Andrzej Przekaziński, a fellow student at the seminary and later a close friend of Fr Popiełuszko, the Cardinal visited the seminary often and took a personal interest in the progress of every student. Quite apart from that, Fr Przekaziński said 'I think the courage of the Cardinal in speaking out frankly on certain social issues determined the attitude assumed by Jerzy and many others. The Cardinal's involvement in such matters educated us as socially committed people.'[2] Jerzy was 'a disciple' of Cardinal Wyszyński.

An acute sensitivity to the morality of social and political issues as well as the courage to speak out in public came to be recognised eventually as Jerzy Popiełuszko's special contribution to Poland's national cause. It was to take years, however, before he would have the opportunity to show any such talent.

Jerzy was ordained priest by Cardinal Wyszyński in St John's Cathedral in Warsaw on 28 May 1972. He was not quite twenty five years old.

His first parish was at Ząbki, just outside the eastern perimeter of the capital. The parish priest at the church of the Holy Trinity was Fr Tadeusz Karolak. He was still there in 1986 when he gave a frank but generous assessment of the young priest who arrived as curate straight from the seminary in 1972.

Fr Popiełuszko, he said, did everything asked of him but he was simply not up to the job. He wasn't strong enough for the wearing routine that could stretch to a 16-hour day. He was always ailing. His health had been broken during his army service. He always brought medicines of some sort to the dinner table. Fr Karolak also observed that Fr Popiełuszko was no outstanding personality, and nor was he a great preacher. His one great talent was the ability to strike up friendships with people of all ages in a matter of days. His contacts were wide and useful, he said. People were ready to do things for him and he was always trying to do things for others.

After three years at Ząbki, Fr Popiełuszko was transferred to the parish of Our Lady, Queen of Poland in Anin on the eastern edge of Warsaw, and then, after another three years, to the parish of the Child Jesus in the district of Żoliborz closer to the city centre. Neither parish appears to have brought him any appreciable sense of success or satisfaction but in Żoliborz, where he lasted for only one year, his illness was at last properly diagnosed.

Dr Barbara Jarmużyńska-Janiszewska, a parishioner, was asked by one of the priests to have a look at Fr Popiełuszko. Apparently he had been having brief blackouts while saying Mass. The doctor carried out some tests at the hospital where she worked and eventually persuaded Fr Popiełuszko to be admitted to the Institute of Haematology. There his complaint was conclusively diagnosed as Addison-Biermer Disease — pernicious anaemia — an incurable condition but not a killer. It was not, as some reported, Addison's Disease. Fr Popiełuszko was prescribed monthly injections of vitamin B12 and Dr Jarmużyńska-Janiszewska administered them for the rest of his life.[3] She and her husband also became good friends of the young priest.

His next parish was the university church of St Anne's at the foot of Krakowskie Przedmieście where he became Diocesan Chaplain to the medical profession and looked after the spiritual needs of medical students and nurses. He was there when John Paul II paid his first visit to his native land since being elected Pope, surely the high point of his time at St Anne's. He was put in charge of organising first aid services in Warsaw during the visit, so he was able to witness at first hand the almost palpable effect of the Pontiff's inspiring words on what had become a disgruntled and unhappy nation.

Fr Popiełuszko, however, was finding life at St Anne's as difficult as at any of his previous parishes. His close friend Fr Przekaziński explained why: 'Jerzy was a social animal in the full sense of the word... He felt really good only when surrounded by people… In his first parishes access to people was difficult. At St Anne's… he couldn't develop genuine links with people. This went against his nature… In his first parishes he was only a cog in a machine.'⁴

It was Fr Przekaziński who virtually arranged for his friend to move to what would be his final parish, St Stanisław Kostka's in Żoliborz. He had been there himself for some time as a 'resident', a priest who lived at the parish and helped out with parish duties but devoted most of his time to other full-time employment. Fr Przekaziński, who had been a lecturer at the Catholic Theological Academy during his term at St Stanisław's, suggested that Fr Popiełuszko take his place when he moved on; the parish priest, Fr Bogucki, agreed.

On 20 May 1980, Jerzy was appointed resident priest in the parish of St Stanisław Kostka in Żoliborz. He was to be chaplain to what were termed middle-rank medical personnel. The appointment seemed to be a concession to his state of health. He would be excused the full routine of parish duties while being free to arrange his own program of duties in his medical chaplaincy. Such seemed to be the happier prospects for the next three or four years of his life. But before settling in to his new life, he set off by air, for the first time, for a four-week holiday in the United States, paid for by his aunt, Mary Kalinoski of Pittsburgh, Pennsylvania. Fr Popiełuszko left a record of this trip in notes full of wonderment at the richness of the American way of life, jotted down in a small pocket notebook. There was pride, too, on discovering that the U.S. Secretary of State, Edward Muskie, was of Polish origin.

But the carefree days remembered in those notes were but an interval before the start of an entirely new life for him and for Poland. When he returned to Warsaw early in July, an unprecedented series of workers' strikes was gathering momentum throughout the country in protest against sudden increases in the price of meat. The unforeseen outcome of this industrial unrest was to prove a turning point in the history of Communist rule; it would determine the next four years of Father Jerzy's life — and his death.

# 3
# Solidarity

In Poland there is a hint of romantic legend in popular accounts of how Fr Popiełuszko began his association with Solidarity. He and others would claim, for instance, that he was chosen for the job by Cardinal Wyszyński. But it would be truer to say that it was the Primate's secretary and chaplain, Fr Bronisław Piasecki, who did the choosing and that he selected two priests, not one. The fact that Fr Popiełuszko was one of them is seen by some as an act of providence, for the choice was made at what proved to be an historic turning point in the decline of the Soviet empire.

In the final week of August 1980, senior Communist Party and government officials were negotiating with striking workers inside the shipyards of Szczecin and Gdańsk. It was a climactic moment at the end of a wave of industrial strikes which began in the first week of July. It took the authorities about two weeks to admit in public that strikes were even taking place but by so doing they anticipated by several years Mr Gorbachev's much vaunted policy of glasnost, which, in Soviet terms, meant not hiding unpleasant facts from the public. In the dying days of August, the negotiations in the Lenin Shipyard in Gdańsk were also breaking new ground; the workers were demanding the right to form independent trade unions free from government control, something never before permitted in Moscow's 'socialist camp'. And in another example of early glasnost, recordings of the negotiations were broadcast by the local radio in Gdańsk.

It was then that workers at Warsaw's huge steel works, Huta Warszawa, went on strike in support of the strikers on the Baltic Coast. They too occupied the plant and waited. On the following Sunday morning, 31 August, five men left the steel works and made their way to Archbishops' House on Miodowa Street in the centre of town. Received by Cardinal Wyszyński personally, they asked him to appoint a priest to say Mass that morning inside the steel works for the mostly Catholic workers. The Cardinal turned to Fr Piasecki, and asked him to 'find them a priest'.

Fr Piasecki says he set off immediately for the parishes closest to the steel works, St Mary Magdalen in the district of Wawrzyszew and St Stanisław Kostka in Żoliborz. In the first he enlisted the services of Fr Stanisław Ciąpała and at the second he was joined, with the permission of the parish priest, by Fr Jerzy Popiełuszko.[1]

In an interview with a fellow priest three years later, Fr Popiełuszko gave a vivid description of the scene at the steel works.[2]

> I was terribly nervous. The situation was entirely new. What would I find? How would they receive me? Would there be anywhere to say Mass?... But then, as I reached the gates, I had my first big surprise. People, densely packed, forming a lane through which I passed. They were smiling and weeping at the same time. And there was clapping. I thought that somebody important must be behind me. But no, the applause was to welcome the first priest ever to pass through the gates of this enterprise in its history... The applause was for the Church that had been knocking persistently on the factory gates for 30 years and more...

Fr Popiełuszko's anxiety about the arrangements proved to be groundless. An altar had been made ready in the middle of the yard. There was a cross and even a makeshift confessional. Men were selected to read the Lessons.

> You should have heard those voices as they read out the sacred texts with solemnity. 'Thanks be to God!' roared out of a thousand throats like a clap of thunder. And it turned out that they could sing, much better than in church. Before that there were confessions. I sat on a chair with my back practically leaning against some iron structure while these tough blokes in oil-stained overalls knelt on asphalt tinted red with grease and rust.

Curiously, that interview contained no mention of any other priest being present. According to Fr Piasecki, Fr Popiełuszko heard the strikers' confessions and said Mass for them. But there is no record of what the priest from St Mary Magdalen did. There can be no doubt, however, that he was there. In a letter to Fr Popiełuszko in 1983, three of his greatest admirers in the steel works recalled how he had passed through the gates of Huta Warszawa on that August Sunday 'with two other priests'.[3]

The fact is that Fr Popiełuszko stayed with the striking workers for most of the day. One can understand why. After twelve years as a priest, he had suddenly found that he was needed, drawn into a movement of national protest that was about to reach its victorious climax in the Lenin Shipyard in Gdańsk when the Communist government finally conceded the workers' right to form free and independent trade unions.

One can, perhaps, imagine the feelings of the young priest as he realised that he had found his congregation and that they took to him as he took to them. He must also have come to realise that by good fortune or providence he was now part of a new and powerful national movement for reform, and that by being with the strikers that Sunday he had been present, in spirit at least, at the birth of Solidarity. Called in originally because he was a priest, he had stayed on because of his talent for getting on with people.

*

In a measure of Fr Popiełuszko's ability to make friends in widely different sections of society, the claim by a man from the steel works that he was 'one of us' was to be echoed by a Professor of Philosophy at Warsaw University, the late Klemens Szaniawski.

This quality of the priest was also, in a way, the quality of Solidarity. In the months immediately after the signing of the Gdańsk Agreements, which established the independent trade union, Solidarity became more than a union of industrial workers; it developed rapidly and naturally into a social movement and an inspiration for the creation of independent professional associations in all walks of life. The spirit of Solidarity, which was born among workers with the assistance of members of the intelligentsia, spread like an invigorating breeze through professions previously kept under rigid control. Actors, writers, academics, teachers, students, lawyers, doctors, film directors, journalists and broadcasters all welcomed and embraced the new union which had restored something of which they had all been deprived: freedom to breathe normally and make their own decisions. Solidarity, like Fr Popiełuszko, seemed to be welcome in most environments. Within a year, the union was able to have an electrician as its leader and a university lecturer in mathematics as its spokesperson.

It is important to remember that throughout most of the strike in Gdańsk, Mass had been said for the workers and confessions heard inside the shipyard fairly regularly, notably by Fr Henryk Jankowski from the nearby parish of St Brigid. So the precedent had been set well before Fr Popiełuszko set foot inside Huta Warszawa. It is also true that in the fifteen months between the birth of Solidarity and the imposition of martial law which was designed to destroy it, Fr Popiełuszko did not play a nationally conspicuous role.

This, however, was a period of tumultuous change which forms a context essential to any understanding of the priest and of the role of the Church in the Polish crisis. The pronouncements and actions during this time of the Primate, Cardinal Wyszyński, and after his death, of his successor, Archbishop Józef Glemp, tell us not only what the Church was seeking, but also whether the policies of these two very different men were as different as some journalists and historians would have us believe. It was also a period rich in practical examples of the Communist government's resort to its last theoretical line of defence, its Reasons of State, or *racja stanu* in Polish.

It has been claimed, for example, in at least one popular history of the twentieth century, that the Church initially condemned the strikes that led to the creation of Solidarity. It did not. But that was precisely what the Communist authorities wanted people to believe and they set out to achieve this by manipulating the Primate's words.

The tense climax of the negotiations in the Gdańsk Shipyard coincided with the finale of the annual pilgrimages to the shrine of Our Lady of Jasna Góra in Częstochowa, south of Warsaw. Cardinal Wyszyński was there, as usual, to deliver his sermon from the battlements of the monastery to the pilgrims crowding the hillside above the town. The Communist authorities had the sermon recorded and then, without authorisation, broadcast selected excerpts on television. In one of the excerpts, Cardinal Wyszyński said that though man had the right to withdraw his labour in order to make his views known, this was 'a very expensive argument... with negative effects one way or another on the life of the nation, the family and every person... It is never possible to satisfy demands immediately... That has to be spread over a period of time. Talks have to be held... We must always have what in Latin is called *prudentia gubernativa*, the prudence of government.'[4]

As was made abundantly clear from subsequent statements by the Episcopate and the Cardinal himself, he intended his words to be understood not as a condemnation of the strikes but as a caution against asking for too much too quickly. On the evening in question, however, it was asking too much of journalists with imminent deadlines to ignore the sound bite about the negative effects of strikes so conveniently provided by the authorities' editors. Moreover, for effect, the Cardinal's words had been broadcast shortly after a senior Communist Party journalist, Ryszard Wojna, told viewers that the country faced the danger of a national catastrophe as bad as when it was partitioned by Prussia, Russia and Austria at the end of the eighteenth century. Attempts to pit the trade union movement against the Party, he said, were not only wrong but also unrealistic:

> There are issues on which there can be no discussion. They are defined by Poland's *racja stanu* and all its considerations and first of all by the political system and system of alliances to which we belong... Our country lies in the centre of the continent, in the direct security zone... of the Soviet Union.[5]

It would be difficult to find a more perfect example of an appeal to the communists' Reasons of State, if only because the Soviet menace of the warning is contained largely in what is left unsaid.

The authorities' decision to broadcast the Primate's words so soon after Wojna's blatant warning that any challenge to Communist Party primacy could bring Soviet and allied retaliation may have been dictated by a desire to pull off a public relations coup. Perhaps they wanted to suggest, first, that the government had reached the end of the road in the talks in Gdańsk and, second, that the Primate, Cardinal Wyszyński, was of the same mind. Whatever the motive, the decision was clearly intended to mislead.

And some were misled, to judge from the Cardinal's remarks about the foreign press during another crisis more than six months later.

This crisis began in Bydgoszcz, northwest of Warsaw, in the middle of March 1981. Three Solidarity activists who had been lobbying on behalf of farmers who wanted their own union, Rural Solidarity, ended up in hospital after being dragged from the provincial council building and beaten up by SB men in the yard outside. One of them was Jan Rulewski, a national figure. As news of the incident spread, Lech Wałęsa, the Solidarity leader, was quickly on the scene. So too was a team of government investigators and a bishop despatched by Cardinal Wyszyński.

Wałęsa's verdict was that the incident was a provocation not only against Solidarity but against the government of General Jaruzelski, who had called for 90 days of peace when he became Prime Minister only the previous month. Other facts tended to support Wałęsa's view. The Communist Party leader, Stanisław Kania, who had replaced Edward Gierek only six months ago and proclaimed a policy of non-violence, had just left on a visit to Hungary. And to complicate matters further, Warsaw Pact exercises had begun in Poland under the command of a Soviet general on the eve of the incident in Bydgoszcz.

Solidarity demanded an honest investigation and the punishment of those responsible for what it called police brutality. If this was not forthcoming through talks with the government, there would be a general strike on the last day of the month.

Cardinal Wyszyński was, by this time, seriously ill and would die two months later of cancer of the stomach. But in the face of this last serious national crisis of his life, the Primate did not rest. What he said and did in the last week of March 1981 could serve as a lesson on the status of the Primate in Poland even under Communist rule and on the role of the Church in political matters.

At 10 am on Thursday, 26 March, Cardinal Wyszyński began talks with the Prime Minister, General Jaruzelski, at Natolin on the southern outskirts of Warsaw. They were together for three and a half hours. He urged the General to sort out the Bydgoszcz crisis as soon as possible and to let the country's private farmers form their own Solidarity union.

Two days later, shortly before 5 pm on Saturday, 28 March, the Primate received Lech Wałęsa and a Solidarity delegation at Archbishops' House on Miodowa Street in Warsaw. In a remarkable statement, which could easily have been misinterpreted and misreported had it not been made in private, the Cardinal urged his guests to show prudence, postponing for the moment their demand that culprits be punished and concentrating rather on making sure that Solidarity was free to do its work.[6]

> As I parted from the General, I said that I would never forgive myself if even one Pole, if even one young lad, should die as a result of some negligence on my part or of some irresponsible action… So as I think about the situation, I ask myself this: Is it better to risk our freedom, our integrity and the lives of our brothers to achieve our demands, even our most just demands, today? Or is it better to achieve only some of these demands today but to say, as regards the rest of them: Gentlemen, we shall return to this matter later. We are not giving up our demands but we know that at the moment some of them cannot be realised…
>
> Dear Brothers… the most urgent need is to make sure that by wanting much you do not lose what you have now… So give the government a little time.
>
> Don't imagine that I am guided by any wish to avoid trouble or by fear — such as the foreign press might impute to me. Don't suspect me of fear, for I have been head of the Church in Poland for thirty three years now. I have been through a great deal and I am still ready for anything. Sometimes I think it will be my lot to be sent to prison again. And I am not afraid. But that is not the greatest virtue, courage. The greatest of the virtues is love, and also prudence and discretion. The moral philosophers call this the prudence of government, *prudentia gubernativa*… something we all need.

It is, surely, a remarkable thing that the leaders of the first free trade union permitted in the Soviet Bloc, men who had won the right to that union at great risk to themselves by challenging the Communist authorities and organising strikes against them, were now being urged to go easy on the government, to give it 'a little time'.

One reason the Cardinal felt obliged, or able, to talk in this way is that the Primate of Poland, by historical tradition, sees himself and is seen by the faithful as not just defender of the faith, but also defender of the nation, especially in times of crisis. And although one might have supposed that the Communist leaders of modern Poland would have paid scant attention to this traditional status of the Primate, they had already tried to make use of his sermon at Jasna Góra in August 1980 for their own purposes. It was also in recognition of Cardinal Wyszyński's special status as Primate that General Jaruzelski had talks with him at the height of the Bydgoszcz crisis.

Cardinal Wyszyński was able to speak to the Solidarity leaders as he did for two other reasons: because he had an impeccable record of outspoken criticism of the Communists, for which he was arrested and confined in a monastery for three years in the 1950s; and because the overwhelming majority of Poles were Catholics and most of them, including those who rarely went to church, looked on their Catholicism as an indicator of national identity. This attitude was made possible by the fact that Roman Christianity had been a constant feature of Poland's national history since the year 966, the 1000th anniversary of which was celebrated in Communist Poland by Cardinal Wyszyński. Hence his title: Primate of the Millennium.

For all these reasons, the Solidarity leaders listened to the Primate in the crisis of March 1981. After his talks with the Prime Minister, General Jaruzelski, the Cardinal, evidently, was sufficiently worried to urge them to 'refrain from costly steps such as a general strike, which it is quite easy to start but very difficult to end.'

He continued in terms which can only be described as ominous.

At the moment we are still at home, in our own house, but who can guarantee for how long? Who can guarantee that? But we have a duty to go on living in our own home. We have a duty to our homeland, our families, our national culture... Unfortunately, though, we are subject to conditions imposed by blocs and by systems. We have to be aware that these people are quite prepared to defend their systems in their own nations

even at Poland's expense. What's to stop them? ... That cannot
be ruled out... I am no tragedian but I can tell you that the
situation is dangerous. That is why I think that if we were to
stretch the wire too far, we could live to regret very painfully
the consequences we would have brought down upon Poland.[7]

The Cardinal, of course, was using the same argument as that
employed by Ryszard Wojna the previous August, the
Communist government's *racja stanu* or reasons of state. But
whereas the Communist authorities could always refer to *racja
stanu* as a kind of insurance policy — 'Don't try to get rid of us
or we'll be invaded by the Russians' — the Primate saw it as a
form of blackmail and he did so from the point of view of its
likely or potential victims. When he spoke of 'these people'
defending their own systems at Poland's expense, he was
probably thinking of what happened in 1968 when Warsaw Pact
forces invaded Czechoslovakia on the pretext of protecting the
rest of the 'socialist camp' against infection from the reforms of
the Prague Spring. No doubt, his anxiety on that score was
heightened by the convenient presence of Warsaw Pact forces
engaged in exercises in and around Poland at that very moment.

The Primate's meeting with the Solidarity leaders was private,
so his words were not made public immediately and few people
were in a position at the time to judge whether or not he had had
any great influence on the outcome of the crisis. However, the
general strike was called off at the last minute a couple of days
later after Lech Wałęsa and Deputy Premier Mieczysław
Rakowski reached a compromise agreement. As was to be
expected, the agreement did not win total approval either in
Solidarity or in the Party. The Primate, however, seemed to have
got his way. Not only did the government express regret for the
violence in Bydgoszcz and promise to take the culprits to court,
it also agreed to ask a parliamentary commission to study the
possibility of legalising Rural Solidarity.

As for the Cardinal's clear warning of possible Warsaw Pact
intervention, one can only speculate about what might have
happened had the general strike taken place. It's worth noting,

though, that on the eve of the Wałęsa-Rakowski agreement, it did look as though the Soviet news agency, Tass, was preparing readers for the possibility of dramatic developments in Poland. In one report, it alleged that 'anti-socialist forces' had seized a television transmitter for a time in Warsaw. In another, it claimed that a motorway had been closed and road signs destroyed in a province south of the capital. Warsaw Radio simply denied the reports, which were clearly designed to suggest that counter-revolution was about to begin.[8]

Even as the crisis was being resolved, it became apparent that it had brought into the open real divisions within the Communist Party and to a lesser extent in Solidarity as well. As tensions gradually receded, it became increasingly obvious that it was the Party and not Solidarity that had sustained the greater damage.

At a time when it was admitted that many thousands of Party members had joined Solidarity in the seven months since its foundation, some in the leadership of the Party were of a decidedly Soviet mind when it came to determining what should be done to counter the threat from Solidarity. At grassroots level, however, some provincial Party organisations were now demanding democracy within the Party itself.

There were quarrels, too, in the Solidarity leadership, but the union was prudent enough not to emulate the disarray then becoming obvious in the ruling Communist Party. And anyway, it had plenty to be pleased about and to look forward to. Rural Solidarity would be made legal in a matter of weeks. Lech Wałęsa and colleagues would shortly begin a series of foreign trips — to Sweden, Italy, Japan, Switzerland and France — visits that the people of Poland saw as clear evidence that the West, to which they believed they belonged, was on Solidarity's side.

In Warsaw that spring and early summer, there was a palpable sense that Poland was indeed returning to the West, an atmosphere not just of hope but also of excitement and a light-hearted confidence. Back in March, Cardinal Wyszyński had told the Solidarity leaders, at that moment of crisis, that it would be their lot and the lot of their union 'to work in Poland not for one year, not for two, but for many years'. Among Solidarity supporters this belief seemed to outweigh any fear of Soviet intervention. For many Poles, this was an unusually happy time when the freedom granted to Solidarity had spread and was still spreading to other walks of life.

Among the happiest, no doubt, was Fr Popieluszko. He was, first and foremost, pastor to medical personnel. This was the only job to which he had been appointed by the Warsaw Curia, the administrative office of the church in Poland, when he was transferred to St Stanisław Kostka's in Żoliborz. But he was now also recognised as chaplain to the men of the steel works, a position to which he was appointed not by the Church but by the workers themselves.

For the first time he had a superior who seemed to see his qualities before his weaknesses. Fr Teofil Bogucki was a thickset, elderly man with white hair. When encountered walking in the churchyard he was generally unsmiling, sometimes frowning, always apparently deep in his own thoughts. At first glance, he did not come across as the most tolerant or friendly of parish priests. And yet, the young priest who came to him after failing to stir any great enthusiasm in four previous parish priests had no trouble in creating a very good impression with his new parish priest, and went on to earn his support, encouragement and admiration. It was said by some that Fr Bogucki detected the younger priest's potential instinctively. Others said that he created the conditions in which his talent could take wing. Either way, both men were to make it perfectly clear that they considered their association a matter of great good fortune.

Fr Bogucki did not object when it became clear that the men of the Huta Warszawa steel works had also adopted St Stanisław as their Solidarity parish church. In April 1981 Fr Popieluszko was able to organise a special service there, during which the Solidarity standard of the steel works was blessed. Presiding over the ceremony was Bishop Zbigniew Kraszewski. The story goes that Fr Popieluszko had asked the Primate personally if a bishop could attend. Bishop Kraszewski told the congregation with a smile that he had been 'forced' to put in an appearance.

These were the halcyon days of Solidarity's first spring and summer, when humour, more often than not, was the popular response to the sundry dire warnings emerging from the conservative ranks of the Communist Party. When it was alleged, for example, that there were 'anti-socialist elements' in Solidarity, many in Warsaw agreed. They could be encountered on the streets wearing lapel buttons proclaiming 'I am an anti-socialist element'.

This mood persisted in spite of two great shocks. On 13 May 1981, Pope John Paul II was shot in St Peter's Square in Rome by a young Turkish terrorist who had joined thousands of pilgrims at the weekly general audience during which the Pontiff was driven around the square in an open jeep. The Holy Father's chaplain, Fr Dziwisz, gave him the last sacrament of Extreme Unction before the surgeons began operating.

The next day in Poland, a communique from the medical specialists attending to Cardinal Wyszyński's cancer said that his condition was serious; the disease was progressing. Two days later, it was announced that he too had been given the Last Rites.

Within a week it seemed clear that the Pope was going to recover. Cardinal Wyszyński's condition, on the other hand, grew steadily worse. On 24 May, the bedridden Primate received a final gift from the Pope. It was a rosary, delivered by a priest who had just visited the Pontiff in the Gemelli Clinic in Rome. Cardinal Wyszyński asked that it be placed around his neck. He was wearing it the next day when John Paul phoned him from his hospital bed and they talked for the last time.[9]

Stefan Cardinal Wyszyński died in the early hours of Ascension Day, 28 May. From the moment the church bells began to toll and people began streaming towards Archbishops' House, it was clear that the nation was going into mourning regardless of the professed atheism of the country's government, some of whose members began their education in Catholic schools. Flags were lowered to half-mast, places of entertainment were closed, and broadcasts were altered to suit the mood. The Cardinal was described in the official, government-controlled media as a great Polish patriot and a great priest.

After a solemn Requiem Mass on Victory Square, attended by some members of the government and by cardinals, archbishops and bishops from all over the world in a congregation estimated to number hundreds of thousands, the Primate of the Thousand Years was finally laid to rest in the crypt of St John's Cathedral. Attached to one wreath in the mass of flowers was a large ribbon with the inscription: 'To the uncrowned king of Poland'.

Fr Popiełuszko, whose admiration for Cardinal Wyszyński is evident from his sermons at St Stanisław's, could hardly have failed to notice that the Cardinal had died exactly nine years to the day since he had ordained him priest. There can be little doubt either that Fr Popiełuszko could imagine no higher calling than to be judged, as the Cardinal was, to be a great patriot and priest.

In spite of all appearances to the contrary, however, the general mood of confidence was misplaced and within seven months, martial law would be imposed.

They were seven months of turmoil for the Communist Party. First Secretary Kania and Prime Minister Jaruzelski earned some popularity by standing up to criticism from Moscow and its allies as they introduced some elements of democracy to the Party, notably the secret ballot. They also survived challenges to their leadership by hardline colleagues who were clearly encouraged, by their comrades in the Soviet capital. But Moscow's worst fears were confirmed when delegates to the Ninth Extraordinary Communist Party Congress in July elected by secret ballot a Central Committee which returned a mere eighteen members of the sitting committee elected long before Solidarity came into existence.

At that moment, it was probably reasonable to suppose that in Poland the Moscow line had been defeated and that Kania and Jaruzelski, two of only four surviving members of the Politburo, were now in charge of a Party more in tune with the new Solidarity era. It was from that moment, however, that things turned sour.

Within weeks demonstrations broke out in protest against food shortages and price increases. One protest in Warsaw ended up in a 48-hour blockade of the city's largest roundabout by public transport vehicles, after which the government and Solidarity seem to have lost patience with negotiation.

Nobody seems to have paid any attention to an appeal from the Bishops 'to abandon hatred and a desire for revenge'. A call for one month of social peace from the new Primate, Archbishop Józef Glemp, in a sermon at Jasna Góra at the end of August, seems also to have fallen on stony ground. He criticised both sides for ignoring the fact that 'poverty is knocking on the door'.

Solidarity's first National Congress in September did not help matters. Jan Rulewski, the Solidarity leader beaten up during the Bydgoszcz crisis, tried to get Congress to remove from the union's statutes the all-important clause recognising the 'leading role' of the Communist Party in state affairs. The Congress rejected that motion but called for free elections and the removal of the mass media from Communist Party control, moves which would deprive the leading role clause of any meaning anyway. Finally, the Congress saw fit to adopt a message of greeting to the workers of Albania, Bulgaria, Czechoslovakia, East Germany, Romania, Hungary and the nations of the Soviet Union.

> We assure you that in spite of the lies disseminated in your countries, we are a genuine, 10-million-strong representative body of workers, created as a result of workers' strikes... We support those of you who have decided to embark on the difficult path of struggle for a free trade union movement. We believe that it will not be long now before your representatives and ours will be able to meet and exchange experiences as trade unionists.[10]

The calls for free elections and for mass media were tantamount to a call for an end to Communist Party rule in Poland. From the point of view of the Party leaders in Warsaw and their comrades in Moscow and elsewhere, that was bad enough. But the direct message of support and encouragement for workers throughout the Soviet empire was likely to be seen as a provocative challenge to Poland's so-called allies and especially to Moscow, where I personally knew dozens of would-be free trade unionists in the late 1970s who all disappeared into prisons, labour camps or psychiatric clinics.

That was one way of looking at it, a view dictated by acceptance of the Communist *racja stanu*. A second view, based on the advice of the late Cardinal Wyszyński, might have suggested that the Solidarity Congress acted unwisely, not because its calls for free elections and free media and its message to East bloc workers were wrong (on the contrary, the Church could only applaud them), but because of the consequences they could bring down upon Poland.

In the event, the Solidarity Congress had rejected the Communist *racja stanu* regardless of the possible consequences. And it did so, presumably, because it was confident that the danger of serious consequences had now passed. Why was it, they might have argued, that nothing had been done to crush Solidarity long before it reached such a degree of self-confidence?

One answer came only in 1987 when *Kultura*, the Polish language monthly published in Paris, carried an interview with Ryszard Kukliński, who, as a Colonel in the Polish Army, helped draw up the plans for martial law.[11]

According to Kukliński, Poland's Communist leaders conceived the idea of imposing martial law in order to suppress Solidarity even before they had signed the agreements bringing it to life in August 1980. It was under pressure from the Soviet Union, he said, that they set up a small, top-secret team which began drawing up plans for martial law at the headquarters of the Polish General Staff in October of the same year.

But why didn't the Soviet Union intervene itself; why did it wait for martial law? Kukliński, who was a key member of the team, said that the Soviet armed forces came close to intervening in Poland in December 1980 and also in March the following year but had thought better of it for several reasons. One was the fact that Western governments were alert to the possibility of intervention and were warning of the damage it would do to East-West relations. Another reason, according to Kukliński, was the fact that Moscow knew that Poles would do more than spit at invading Soviet tanks (as had happened in Czechoslovakia in 1968); they would set them on fire. General Jaruzelski, meanwhile, had kept responding to Moscow's increasingly impatient demands for action by promising to impose martial law when Solidarity was less strong and the time was ripe.

The odd thing is that martial law came when Solidarity was, if anything, stronger and more confident than ever. Equally odd is the fact that it appeared to come as a surprise, for there were some who had been told it was coming.

The United States had certainly been told. Kukliński himself had passed on precise details of the plans for martial law to a CIA agent in Warsaw. Moreover, in his interview with *Kultura*, he said that General Kiszczak, the Minister of Internal Affairs, had told the National Defence Committee in September 1981 that a large number of Solidarity activists already knew about plans to impose martial law. Five years later, however, Kiszczak would claim that the Americans deliberately withheld Kukliński's information from the Church and from Solidarity.[12]

At the beginning of November, after the revelation that the martial law plans had been leaked to the Americans, Kukliński was placed under surveillance. On 7 November, he left his office at the General Staff for the last time and within days was spirited away to the United States.

It can be argued, with hindsight, that even those who did not know martial law was coming could have sensed that things were taking a dangerous turn. In October 1981, Stanisław Kania resigned as Party leader and was replaced by General Jaruzelski, who was already Prime Minister and Defence Minister and therefore more qualified than most to think of political needs in martial terms. In the Central Committee, there was talk of switching from the force of argument to the argument of force.

At the beginning of November, in contrast, General Jaruzelski had a two-hour meeting with the Roman Catholic Primate, Archbishop Glemp, and the Solidarity leader, Lech Wałęsa. The trio discussed the possibility of what was officially described as a 'front of national accord', an idea which appears to have won no discernible support outside the room where they met. According to Ryszard Kukliński, though, the final decision to impose martial law had already been taken anyway.

As winter set in, the General and the media began to speak the language of Moscow and the hardliners. There were many incidents and occasions for confrontation but the authorities matched their words with action most instructively in an episode in which Fr Popiełuszko played a role.

On 25 November, student cadets at the Fire Brigade Officer Training College in the Żoliborz district of Warsaw began a sit-in strike in support of their demand that the school should no longer be run by the Ministry of Internal Affairs. On the last day of the month, the authorities announced that the school had been closed down. It was surrounded by a tight cordon of police. Nobody could get in or out. But Fr Popiełuszko did get in, as did Seweryn Jaworski, a worker from Huta Warszawa and deputy leader of the Warsaw region Solidarity organisation which supported the strike. In a sermon some years later, Fr Bogucki was to recall with pride how Fr Popiełuszko had slipped through the police cordon that was so impenetrable that 'not even a mouse could get through' and said Mass for the strikers.

On 2 December, when Fr Popiełuszko, it seems, had already departed, squads of riot police quickly put an end to the strike by forcing their way into the building at ground level and by landing on the roof from helicopters. It seems to have been a model operation in which General Kiszczak, the Minister of Internal Affairs, clearly took pride. Several years later he was to say that it was intended as a warning and as a bucket of cold water emptied over the heads of those pushing, he alleged, for bloody confrontation.[13]

The warning was not taken seriously, it seems, by those who

arranged for the leaders, advisers and activists of Solidarity to be gathered together conveniently, all in one place, for a National Commission meeting in Gdańsk on Friday and Saturday, 11 and 12 December.

No one in Solidarity apparently considered the possibility that the raid on the Fire Brigade school in Warsaw could be successfully re-enacted on a much larger scale in Gdańsk in order to achieve a far greater coup, the arrest and internment of the Solidarity leadership. But that, roughly speaking, was what happened.

When General Jaruzelski announced the imposition of martial law in a broadcast to the nation at 6 on the morning of Sunday, 13 December, some sixteen months after Solidarity's formation, General Kiszczak's security police and riot police had already been hard at work for six hours picking up as many Solidarity leaders as they could in the great net they had thrown over Gdańsk. Fortunately for Solidarity and for Poland, some of the union's finest leaders slipped through the net. And in keeping with the best patriotic traditions, they were to form an underground resistance movement, defying the Generals and refusing to accept that Solidarity could ever be defeated.

# 4

# Martial Law

Martial law would make Fr Jerzy Popiełuszko the most celebrated and most loved preacher in Poland, but it was still some time before his voice was heard. It was the Primate, Archbishop Glemp, who had the difficult task of speaking from the pulpit on the first day of the new regime and he did so in the knowledge that what he had to say would not satisfy all his fellow countrymen and could expose him to criticism and even contempt.

The Primate was informed of General Jaruzelski's decision to impose martial law when he was visited at Archbishops' House at 5.30 that Sunday morning by a senior Party leader, a minister and a general. In a radio broadcast twenty years later, Glemp said he was advised by his visitors to be prepared for painful difficulties ahead but that he was not told of the scale of the arrests. At that moment, he said, he did not think that one could be interned simply for belonging to Solidarity.

Having received the news without comment, the Primate set off by road for Częstochowa where he was due to say Mass for students at the Jasna Góra monastery. On the streets of Warsaw he and his driver saw only tanks and army patrols. On the drive south they listened to repeated broadcasts of General Jaruzelski's announcement of martial law. It was only on reaching the monastery, the Primate said, and seeing the dismay on the faces of the Pauline Fathers and the tears of the young people that he realised the depth of the nation's pain. In consultations with colleagues after returning to Warsaw, the Primate said, 'we came to the conclusion that the most rational thing to do was try to calm down feelings of rebellion'.[1]

Hence the sermon he delivered that evening in the Jesuit church of Our Lady the Merciful next door to the Cathedral of St John the Baptist in Warsaw's Old Town. It was recorded and broadcast in full by the country's single surviving radio channel. Towards the end of the first day of martial law, during which thousands of Solidarity activists had been interned, with tanks on the streets and a night-time curfew about to come into force, listeners may well have hoped to hear their own anger given expression in a strongly worded condemnation of the government's actions.

What they heard was an appeal for non-violence in the face of the government's use of force. Martial law, Archbishop Glemp told his congregation, had surprised and stunned them that morning; now what could they do? The answer, he said, was to be found in the teachings of Christ.

> Blessed are they who hunger and thirst after justice. Blessed are the merciful. Blessed are the peacemakers. Blessed are they who suffer persecution for justice's sake.
>
> This sort of answer will not satisfy many people. They will say that it's unrealistic, that it amounts to surrendering one's achievements, accepting defeat...
>
> Fundamentally, the authorities are ceasing to engage in dialogue with citizens; instead, they are equipping themselves with the means of summary coercion and demanding obedience. Resistance to the decisions of the authorities under martial law may prompt the use of violence to coerce obedience, and this could involve bloodshed, for the authorities have armed force at their disposal.
>
> We can voice outrage, we can cry out against the injustice of the situation, protest against the violation of civil and human rights and so on, but this may not produce results... The

authorities think that the extraordinary measure of martial law was dictated by a higher need and that it represents the choice of a lesser evil...

Anyone who accepts that this is correct will acquiesce in the new situation. There are many, however, who will have a painful sense of grievance at having their ambitions and aspirations thwarted, at being pushed aside... Without paying heed to the balance of forces, they will want to resist...

Representatives of the Church will call incessantly... for the release of citizens wrongly detained, for the release of the sick, of fathers of families and so on... But there remains the most important matter of saving lives and preventing bloodshed. In this the Church will be uncompromising. It matters nothing if someone should accuse the Church of cowardice... The Church protects each and every human life, so, under martial law, it will call whenever it can for peace, for the renunciation of violence and the prevention of fratricidal struggle.

There is nothing more valuable than human life. That is why I shall call for good sense even at the price of exposing myself to insults. Even if I have to go barefoot and beg on my knees, I shall plead: Do not start fighting, Pole against Pole. Brother workers, do not give your lives away, for the price of a life cut short will be very cheap, whereas every life and every pair of hands will be beyond price for the rebuilding of Poland which will come and must come after the end of martial law...[2]

That night I studied the translated text of the Primate's sermon at the BBC Monitoring Service and filed a report. For me it came as a surprise to be told later that many people in Poland were deeply displeased with what he had had to say.

Years later, the Primate admitted that he saw their 'tears of disappointment'. They thought, he said, that the Church was abandoning them, when in fact it was 'with the people precisely at that moment' as much as it had ever been.[3] His audience might have reacted more favourably if only he had stated that explicitly in his sermon, and made clear his disapproval of martial law instead of enumerating its implications. Though the Archbishop's martial-law sermon may not have been as eloquently delivered as those of his illustrious predecessor, it would be difficult to demonstrate that its message differed greatly, if at all, from the line pursued by Cardinal Wyszyński. Both aimed to prevent bloodshed and the sacrifice of Polish lives in reckless acts of defiance. As it was, less than six months after being inducted as Primate, Archbishop Glemp was already suffering from the grave disadvantage of being the successor of Cardinal Wyszyński, with whom few could bear comparison. A specialist in canon law, the new Primate was perceived to be lacking in the qualities required for dealing with people — charm, warmth and style. He was also imagined to be more accommodating in his dealings with the Communist authorities than Cardinal Wyszyński had been.

The Primate knew there would be resistance, but he may not have expected his fears to be realised so quickly. On 16 December, armed riot police attacked the Wujek colliery near Katowice in Silesia where the miners had been on strike since the imposition of martial law. According to official radio reports, the strikers fought back with stones, crowbars and pickaxes. The police opened fire, killing seven.

On the eve of the Wujek shooting and after just two days of martial law, the Main Council of the Episcopate meeting under the chairmanship of the Primate had issued a warning about growing bitterness and hatred. The Bishops said they shared 'the pain of the entire nation terrorised by military force'. Many trade union activists had been interned, they said, but the internment net was widening, taking in representatives of culture and learning and also students. Martial law had dealt a blow to the hopes and expectations of the nation. The Church and society should, therefore, concentrate on two aims: the release of those interned and the restoration of trade union activity. 'The Solidarity union... is needed for the restoration of social stability.'

On 6 January, the Feast of the Epiphany, Archbishop Glemp issued a statement condemning the widespread practice under martial law of requiring employees to sign *lojalki* or loyalty state-ments renouncing membership of Solidarity on pain of being sacked from their jobs. This practice, he said, was unethical, for it confronted people with a crisis of conscience. Human con-science, he reminded the authorities, is a thing of singular sanctity which 'is not violated even by God, who will judge us all in the end according to our conscience'.

On 19 January, some five weeks after the imposition of martial law, the Bishops issued another statement calling on the military government to respect the right to freedom of every person, and, in particular, freedom of conscience and convic-tions. The consequence of that, they said, should be the restora-tion of the normal functioning of the State, the swift release of all those who were interned, and the renunciation of the practice of sacking people from their jobs because of their con-victions or their membership of trade unions. 'In the name of freedom, we state our belief that workers should be given back their right to organise themselves in independent, self-governing trade unions and that young people should have unions suited to their needs.'

During all this time, Fr Popieluszko seems to have said little in public about martial law. During the Mass for the Homeland on the last Sunday of January in the new year, he was reported to have said that martial law had taken away freedom of speech, so his congregation should listen to the voice of their conscience and think of those who had been deprived of freedom.

It is interesting that the priest who became famous for speaking freely from the pulpit should have spoken of being deprived of freedom of speech. It is true that, at the outset, martial law regulations severely curtailed normal means of com-munication. There were heavy prison sentences for spreading information thought likely to damage the country's defences or cause riots. Telephone calls, which were cut off completely during the initial stages of martial law, were monitored openly when they were restored. The use of printing presses and radio transmitters was banned. In the early days, all gatherings in public, whether for entertainment or sport were also banned. But there was one crucial exception: religious services were not prohibited.

At the end of February, Fr Popiełuszko took his cue from the Bishops, prefacing readings from their most recent statements with an introduction of his own:[4]

> The Church is always on the side of truth. The Church is always on the side of people who have been wronged. Today the Church is on the side of those who have been deprived of their freedom and whose conscience is being put to the test. The Church today is on the side of worker solidarity, on the side of workers who are repeatedly treated like common criminals.

Fr Popiełuszko's sermons were to become the most important and memorable feature of his Masses for the Homeland. At this Mass, in February 1982, he was clearly feeling his way, but these four sentences contained the essence of what he would always say and already emerging were several other unusual elements which were to become permanent features.

Mass began and ended with stirring patriotic hymns promising loyalty to the faith and praying for the restoration of national freedom. It included the reading of patriotic poems by actors who were then boycotting radio and television in protest against the imposition of martial law. The Offertory prayers were devoted to intentions of immediate, topical interest; they were said for 'those deprived of freedom: sentenced, arrested and interned', for 'those sacked from their jobs', for 'Solidarity activists facing trial', and 'for ourselves, that we may create a solidarity of hearts which no one and no thing will be able to subdue'.

The Masses for the Homeland, which were to attract larger congregations from other parishes and then from other towns, gave everyone attending a sense that they were close to the heart and soul of the Polish nation. Many of the hymns sung and the poems recited had been composed more than 100 or 150 years earlier at times of national resistance to foreign occupation. Now there would be new hymns sung and newly composed poems read out by some of the country's most celebrated and most popular actors at Masses attended by people of all ages and callings. The theme would be the same; the patriotic resistance of the previous century would be as real as that of the present.

Fr Popiełuszko's theme of patriotic survival against all odds coincided with the birth of yet another Polish resistance movement. Among Solidarity leaders who escaped capture on the night martial law was imposed were three of the most popular and charismatic: Zbigniew Bujak from Warsaw, Władysław Frasyniuk from Wrocław and Bogdan Lis from Gdańsk. These men and others like them had been on the run from the police since 13 December, hunted as outlaws but admired by the great majority of the people as true recusants, faithful to the Solidarity union and determined to keep it alive.

In the early months of martial law, Solidarity's most confident response to the authorities was in the slogan 'The winter is yours, but the spring will be ours'. It was, perhaps, too optimistic but by the time the spring of 1982 arrived, Bujak, Frasyniuk, Lis and others had announced the formation of a nationwide underground resistance movement with a national leadership. The announcement reached the public in the form of small leaflets or 'information bulletins' produced on illegal printing presses. They were virtually identical in format to news sheets prepared by the underground resistance during the Nazi occupation in the Second World War. History was repeating itself.

Fr Popiełuszko's sermon during the Mass for the Homeland at the end of April suggests once again that he was still searching for the right formula. Composed entirely in the form of a prayer it made several points which some might find banal but which were, nonetheless, telling: it was the fifth month of martial law, the 134th day of 'national anguish', and the first anniversary of the consecration of the Warsaw steelworkers'

Solidarity standard 'which today must hide from the eyes of people who fear the word Solidarity'.

Solidarity, he continued, 'allowed us to discern evil and the mechanisms of its activity. To the younger generation it revealed many truths about the history of our country which had been suppressed.'

Then came the prayers for people on both sides: 'for those who know not what they do as they cause their fellow country-men suffering, anxiety and fear'; 'for those employed in the system of justice who do not have the courage to contradict lies but accept falsehood as truth'; and, in contrast, 'for those imprisoned and facing trial' and 'for those in hiding, pursued to this day like criminals — grant that they encounter people with warm hearts'.

At the end of Mass, Fr Popiełuszko invited everyone to attend Masses for the 'world of work' at 10 am the following Saturday, 1 May, at St Stanisław's and at churches in three other places: on Krakowskie Przedmieście, in the Old Town and on Three Crosses Square. Oddly enough, the Solidarity under-ground, which had just announced the formation of its Provisional National Committee, issued a similar call in one of its leaflets.

Saturday, of course, was May Day, the traditional workers' holiday, and with so many workers' representatives in prison or internment, the authorities felt obliged to announce the release of a thousand internees and the lifting of the nightly curfew in a matter of days. But the weekend, which was to include the Constitution Day holiday on Monday, 3 May, was to be remem-bered more for the strength of Solidarity resistance and the violence of suppression.

On the eve of May Day, a brief but abortive attempt by the clandestine Solidarity radio to broadcast a statement by the local leader, Zbigniew Bujak, led to surprising scenes in Warsaw as hundreds of police vehicles sealed off one large district close to the city centre in an apparently fruitless search for the pirate broadcasters. Public support for Solidarity and its underground was demonstrated unmistakably on the morning of May Day itself. Thousands of people, who had filled St John's Cathedral and neighbouring streets including Castle Square for the 10 am Mass, staged a march through streets surrounding the Old Town. On a bright, sunny day, it was an impressive act of defiance, the first large-scale protest in Warsaw since martial law was imposed and one made all the more challenging by the fact that the regular, officially sponsored parade attended by General Jaruzelski and colleagues was taking place at the same time only a mile or two away. But in spite of the improvised banners proclaiming 'No to Dictatorship, Freedom for Lech' and the chants of 'Down with the Junta', the police did not intervene; they merely steered marchers away from a collision with the official parade and guided them back towards the Old Town. Here they dispersed peacefully after agreeing to meet again on 3 May, the national holiday commemorating the signing of the Constitution of 1791.

There was obvious satisfaction among Solidarity supporters at the success of their May Day march, but on 3 May, it was the ZOMO riot police who demonstrated what they could do when let off the leash.

Some 15,000 would-be demonstrators assembled at 4 pm in the vicinity of the Cathedral before moving out with banners raised onto Castle Square and up the cobbled slope towards the tall column bearing the statue of King Zygmunt. Beyond that stood an impenetrable barrier of armoured police vehicles, water cannons and helmeted riot police carrying shields and truncheons. For twenty minutes or so there was an exchange of taunts and shouts of 'Gestapo' from one side and loudspeaker warnings from the other, before the order was given for the police to attack. Within seconds, the water cannons and tear gas launchers descended into the beautiful old square and the demonstrators were driven back blindly into the side streets by powerful jets of water amidst clouds of acrid blue smoke, while riot police with flailing truncheons followed. Crowds of people of all ages watching behind police cordons hissed, booed and also shouted 'Gestapo', until the police turned on them as well.

Thus began an evening of violence on the streets which

spread throughout the city. This moment was to determine the mood for the rest of the year. That day there were disturbances in twelve places, including Gdańsk and Cracow, but the worst were in Warsaw where some fifty policemen were said to have been injured. Nearly 1400 people were detained throughout the country.

In a speech to the Sejm (Parliament), General Kiszczak noted that demonstrations often began when people left church after Mass. He said he did not believe it was the intention of the Church hierarchy to encourage such activities. Nonetheless he suggested that street disturbances did not serve the Church's interests.

In a statement the following day, the Bishops did not respond to Kiszczak's remarks but said that disturbances delayed steps towards normalisation and that without peace there could be little chance of the talks needed to achieve what they called a social covenant. In remarks clearly addressed to the authorities, the Bishops stressed that society should not be treated as an object or a tool; there must be respect for the human person.

During his Mass for the Homeland at the end of May, Fr Popiełuszko spoke of 'a new wave of hatred passing over the country during the month... another wave of human suffering especially in its early days.' His sermon once again was composed in the form of a prayer and most of it was taken up by what he called 'a litany of our days'. This was an adaptation, supposedly composed in one of the internment camps, of the traditional Litany of Loreto, in which the usual invocations addressed to the Virgin Mary prompting the response 'pray for us' were replaced by new ones more suited to the moment.

Mother of those who have hope in Solidarity... Mother of those taken in the night, Mother of those in prison, Mother of the shot miners... Mother of those under interrogation, Mother of those wrongly sentenced... Mother of those who act steadfastly... Mother of the incorruptible... Mother of the orphaned... Mother of those sacked... Mother of those

forced to sign statements against their conscience… Mother of
your servant, the imprisoned Lech… Queen of suffering
Poland, Queen of independent Poland, Queen of Poland ever
faithful… pray for us.[5]

All this may seem banal to those who do not believe in prayer.
But these prayers were certainly of great immediate relevance in
a nation without free speech. They are also a perfect example of
how it was possible to say in public all that needed to be said
about martial law without any obvious violation of regulations.

Demonstrations continued on and off for the rest of the
summer but they proved to be very costly when measured
against the increasing number of people arrested, imprisoned,
interned, sacked from their jobs or burdened with impossibly
heavy fines. The Solidarity underground and its supporters
wanted and needed to make their presence felt, if only to make
it absolutely clear that they were not giving in.

But by the time of the May demonstrations, the underground leaders had said they were ready for talks with the government on the basis of proposals put forward by the Church.
These were, however, unlikely to appeal to the authorities; they
called for the release of more internees, for an amnesty for
those sentenced under martial law, for generous treatment of
those in hiding, and for the reinstatement of those sacked from
their jobs. According to the Bishops, the only way General
Jaruzelski could achieve the national accord he was constantly
talking about was by engaging in talks to which the trade unions
were admitted. The Church also reminded the authorities that
the imposition of martial law had come with a promise that the
trade unions it suspended would eventually be able to resume
activity under their own statutes.

At the beginning of June, the Church put aside its previous
doubts about the advisability of the Pope visiting Poland in
August as planned. Addressing the open air crowds at the end
of the traditional Corpus Christi procession, Archbishop
Glemp said that martial law should present no obstacle if the
Pope could visit both Britain and Argentina when they were at

war over the Falkland Islands. Moreover, he noted rather pointedly that Argentina, besides being a Catholic country, was ruled by generals and there was no shortage of internment camps.

This was a curious period of hope in spite of evidence to the contrary. On one day, surprisingly, the Warsaw daily, *Zycie Warszawy*, published a number of readers' letters calling for the Solidarity trade union to be revived and allowed to operate. However, within weeks the Party paper, *Trybuna Ludu*, was hitting back with calls for Solidarity leaders to be tried for treason. Lech Wałęsa, the Solidarity chairman who had been held in solitary detention south of Warsaw, was moved to a place of even greater isolation in Poland's southeastern corner, as far away from his home in Gdańsk as possible without leaving Poland. At the same time, the list grew longer of those sentenced to heavy prison sentences for printing or distributing Solidarity news sheets and leaflets or for taking part in demonstrations.

At the end of June, the four men who formed the leadership of the Solidarity underground signed a statement calling on their followers to desist from strikes and demonstrations as a test of the authorities' goodwill. It was their hope, they said, that this expression of their readiness to reach an agreement would prompt a concrete government response: the release of internees, for instance, and an amnesty for those in prison. They also said they hoped that their appeal would help create conditions for the Pope to visit Poland in August.

The Solidarity leaders had their eyes on 22 July, the Communist National Day, when one could reasonably expect some sort of gesture from General Jaruzelski. They may not have been confident of a favourable response but it was a suitable time for testing the extent of the General's readiness or ability to compromise. It was a time, moreover, when government journalists were 'leaking' suggestions over cocktails that when the holiday arrived martial law could be lifted, Lech Wałęsa could be freed and Solidarity could be restored.

To anyone who read the Party newspapers, however, such

predictions were beyond belief and when the time came General Jaruzelski removed all doubt and all hope. In a speech on the eve of the 'national day', the General announced the release of more than 1200 internees, but this was the only good news. Independent trade unions would be allowed one day, he said, but there would be nothing like Solidarity. The Pope could visit his native land, he said, but not until next year. It was his hope that martial law could be suspended, but not lifted, by the end of the year. As for the Solidarity underground, General Jaruzelski described its members as 'anti-State conspirators'.

Few people had believed that the authorities would respond favourably to the Solidarity underground's initiative but after all the talk of national accord, the General's statement was peculiarly dispiriting. It made clear for the first time that he had not only chosen to ignore all the pleadings of the Church but also that he had gone back on his promise that suspended trade unions would be able eventually to resume work according to their own statutes. If the government were to have its way, Solidarity would have to be destroyed. This could be done by Act of Parliament, and the government was preparing to do that. But the authorities knew that it would not be as easy to destroy the Solidarity underground or silence Solidarity supporters, including priests like Fr Popieluszko who saw support for the union as a moral and patriotic duty.

The leaders of the Solidarity underground responded to the General's speech by accusing the authorities of throwing away a real chance of national reconciliation. They called for peaceful demonstrations on 31 August, the second anniversary of the Gdańsk agreements, and told their supporters in the resistance movement to set about creating what they called 'an underground society', which could develop ultimately into a self-governing society. In a message to those still interned, imprisoned or under arrest, they said: 'We are separated by prison walls and barbed wire, but we are together in a common struggle… We shall not end this struggle which is for your freedom and ours.'

With those final, dramatic words, Solidarity placed itself in the tradition of Polish resistance. And when the crowds flocked as usual to the military cemetery of Powązki in Warsaw on 1 August to honour the memory of the more than 200,000 who died in the Warsaw Uprising against the Nazis in 1944, and of the more than 4000 Polish officers executed by the Soviet NKVD in the Katyn Forest near Smolensk in 1940, they cheered and sang for Solidarity — because Solidarity was seen to be fighting the same fight.

Throughout August, the riot police dealt firmly with demonstrations in places like Gdańsk, Wrocław and Nowa Huta at the edge of Cracow. In Warsaw they used water cannons to sluice away the small groups of people, many of them elderly, who used to gather to pray around a cross made of flowers laid on the ground on Victory Square, where Cardinal Wyszyński's coffin had rested during his funeral the previous year. After removing the cross many times, only to see it reappear (florists were giving a discount on blooms for the cross), the authorities built a fence around the square.

Official propaganda, meanwhile, became increasingly alarmist. The newspapers reported alleged plans for acts of terrorism, bloody rebellion and civil war. General Kiszczak himself went on television for half an hour to warn against these alleged plans to cause bloodshed. Viewers were shown weapons supposedly found in a Warsaw flat along with Solidarity literature. It is doubtful whether many people believed any of this, but the Bishops were concerned, as the Primate had been on the first day of martial law, about the dangers of violence during the planned demonstrations. They prepared a pastoral letter to be read out in all churches calling on government and people alike to avoid violence.

In a sermon from the ramparts of the Jasna Góra monastery on 26 August, the Primate, Archbishop Glemp, spoke out against taking grievances onto the streets, where enough blood had been shed already. He was cheered long and loud by the open-air congregation of some 400,000 when he repeated the Church's proposals for peace in Poland. The authorities, he said, should free Lech Wałęsa and the rest of those interned, restore trade union activity and start work on a general amnesty. The Archbishop also called on the government to name a firm date for a visit to Poland of the Polish Pope, who would have been at Jasna Góra that very day had the government not changed its mind.

The Church could hardly expect that its appeal not to take grievances onto the streets would be heeded. Indeed, as the end of the month approached, Zbigniew Bujak, the leader of the underground in the Warsaw region, said that if Solidarity did not demonstrate on 31 August, it would be admitting defeat. Nobody could expect that to happen either.

It was in an atmosphere, then, of anticipation mixed with apprehension on the part of the Church, and with determination and defiance on the part of Solidarity, that Fr Jerzy Popieluszko prepared for his Mass for the Homeland on Sunday, 29 August, two days before the planned demonstrations. It was at this Mass more than ever before that he and the actors and singers assisting him truly rose to the occasion. And it was his sermon and a reading from a nineteenth-century Polish philosopher that preceded it that seemed to respond perfectly to the national mood. The reading, taken from a work composed at a time when Poland had been removed from the map of Europe by its partition between Russia, Prussia and Austria, had a topical as well as universal application.

> The only mission a government can and should perform is that of serving the people and leading it, without coercion, under the torch of Truth and Justice. No government can be allowed or tolerated on any other conditions. People refuse to give their loyal and spontaneous obedience to the government which abandons its role of loyal and dedicated servant... and they are quite right, for their prime duty is not to yield to the domination of any oppressor...[6]

In his sermon, Fr Popieluszko turned to unimpeachable contemporary sources to continue his theme. The first was Pope John Paul II:

Being in power means being in service. The first love of the person in power is love for those over whom he exercises power. And yet we have witnessed the activity of tyrannical states where the citizen is spoken to in the tones of the prosecutor and the policeman...

The late Cardinal Wyszyński was quoted next:

The biggest enemy of those in power is the citizen. Why? Because the citizen has been robbed of his rights and discouraged from doing his duty. Those in power must not be tyrants. The State must not be an organised prison...

Fr Popiełuszko then spoke of the birth of Solidarity two years earlier, which he described as a 'patriotic outburst' by Polish society.

What can be said today after the agreements signed on the Coast and in Silesia were broken with violence and pain on that December night of last year? When a blow was struck and a wound was inflicted, a wound that still bleeds? It is not a mortal wound for it is impossible to deal a mortal wound to something that is immortal. One cannot kill hope. And Solidarity was and still is the hope of millions of Poles, a hope that is stronger the more it is joined with God through prayer.

He continued with a simile borrowed from Cardinal Wyszyński:

Solidarity grew up in the nation like a mighty tree which when its roots are cut puts out new ones. And though this tree is buffeted by storms and though its crown of glory has been torn away, it still clings tenaciously to its native soil, drawing from our hearts and from our prayers the life-giving sap that enables it to endure and bring forth good fruit in the end.[7]

Before quoting the proposals put forward by Archbishop

Glemp only days earlier at Jasna Góra, Fr Popiełuszko presented his own conclusions:

> In spite of the painful experiences of recent months, the nation is still prepared for self-sacrificing work for the good of the homeland. But only a nation that is respected by those who govern it, a nation that is not beset by constant anxiety and uncertainty about the morrow, a nation that does not feel that it is inside an organised prison, can willingly undertake that task...

Fr Popiełuszko then read out a portion of the pastoral letter issued by the Bishops on the imminent second anniversary of the birth of Solidarity, before the final blessing. 'Out of concern for the good of the entire nation, we earnestly request of everyone that this anniversary be observed in a spirit of national solemnity and peace... We urge all the faithful to pray...'

It is difficult to think of any other Mass for the Homeland at which Fr Popiełuszko succeeded to such an extent in responding to his congregation's need for a faith that in spite of all the dangers and suffering, Solidarity, like the Polish nation, could not be destroyed.

This moment also marked the beginning of a new phase in the priest's life during which he would be the target of repeated complaints from the Communist authorities. This started the very next day. In a memorandum delivered to the Secretary of the Episcopate, Archbishop Bronisław Dąbrowski, the Minister in charge of the Office for Denominational Affairs, Adam Łopatka, said that Fr Popiełuszko's behaviour was a 'glaring example' of how some members of the clergy were failing to apply Church rules on eliminating 'non-religious material' from their services.[8]

> Fr Popiełuszko gave an unambiguously political character to the service held at 19.00 on 29 August. His sermon and the scenario were clearly designed to inspire demonstrative behaviour by the faithful. Fr Popiełuszko allowed into the

church items of decoration which contained elements tending to incite and encourage demonstrations on the anniversary of the Szczecin and Gdańsk agreements of 1980. Without appropriate permission, he had the service relayed by loudspeakers to the area around the church, thus causing nearly 5000 people to assemble and as a result blocking neighbouring streets.

Fr Popiełuszko also allowed several lay people to take an active part in the service and one of them called for prayers for the victims of martial law. There was a collection for those who had suffered as a result of martial law. The attitude and the climate created by Fr Popiełuszko turned a religious gathering into a political demonstration which carried with it a threat to calm, security and public order in the capital...

The memorandum also complained about a Mass said the previous evening at St Anne's Church on Krakowskie Przedmieście (Fr Popiełuszko's previous parish), during which there were prayers for 'the persecuted' and for 'those who fell in the war and after the war in the period of the Communist terror'. The message ended by warning that the continued indiscipline of priests could lead to disturbances of law and order and that the Church could be considered 'jointly responsible' for the possible consequences.

The authorities were clearly being disingenuous, when they accused Fr Popiełuszko of inciting people to demonstrate — a charge they were to repeat to the end. Fr Popiełuszko was no rabble-rouser; his soft, almost hoarse, voice was hardly suited to rallying people to man the barricades. As I stood in my usual place, at the corner of the park facing the church, I never detected in the crowd around me any sign of an excited response to the priest's words, only occasionally an exchange of knowing smiles. His quiet, almost monotone delivery was designed to stir reflection rather than passions. And as the authorities well knew, he usually urged his congregation to go home quietly after Mass, ignoring all attempts to provoke disturbances.

The demonstrations went ahead as planned on 31 August

and proved to be the biggest and most serious since martial law was imposed. General Kiszczak's riot police again proved what they were capable of, as my assistant Karol Małcużyński and I saw for ourselves in Warsaw. We went to one of four starting points chosen by the Solidarity underground, the parade square beneath the towering Palace of Culture in the centre of town. By 4 pm, the appointed hour, it was largely occupied by riot police vehicles. With police checking the documents of people queuing at bus and tram stops along Marszałkowska Street, it hardly seemed possible that any demonstration could take place there. Until one man was taken into custody. People protested. There were shouts of 'Gestapo' and crowds stepped down into the square. As they did, tear gas canisters were fired from behind some trees and rose into the air like a flock of birds startled by the sound of gunfire. So it began.

About an hour later (after I had telephoned my first report to London) we watched as a huge crowd of demonstrators began to march from Constitution Square down Marszałkowska towards the Forum Hotel, filling the street from side to side and waving triumphantly to people shouting encouragement from upstairs windows. For several brief moments, it did seem as though Warsaw belonged to them; they even shouted cheerful greetings to two young soldiers, out on patrol, who hurried by on the pavement, blushing with embarrassment. But as they got closer to the hotel, several armoured personnel carriers danced out of the side streets to confront them, firing tear gas and percussion grenades trailing smoke. The crowd turned only to find more police armour coming up from behind. Everyone scattered into side streets and buildings. In one of these, an elderly woman silently pointed the way for us to escape into the garden and over the back wall.

As the debris of the disturbances was cleared from the streets of Polish cities during the night that followed, Solidarity was obliged to meditate on the sad outcome of the demonstrations for which it had called. Two men had been shot dead by police in Lubin, the copper-mining town in the west of the country. In Gdańsk, the lifeless body of a young man was simply found on a street. The death toll was to rise eventually to five.

The demonstrations of 31 August 1982 were the last of the great nationally organised manifestations of resistance to have any impact. They were undoubtedly impressive. Even the government's own statistics — more than 4000 demonstrators taken into custody in more than a dozen towns — suggested a nationwide protest of a magnitude never seen before in a Soviet Bloc country. And this after eight months of martial law.

The demonstrations did not achieve any of Solidarity's fundamental objectives. The authorities had made it perfectly clear that their ultimate aim was to destroy Solidarity and all it stood for and were setting out to do this methodically and with the wholehearted support of their allies in Moscow, Prague and East Berlin. Years later, however, the citizens of these three cities would have reason to be grateful for the one indisputable achievement of Solidarity and its supporters on 31 August 1982 and on innumerable occasions in the years to come: they were not giving up. Nor, for that matter, was Fr Popiełuszko.

# 5

# Warnings and Dirty Tricks

In the closing months of 1982, the martial law authorities, led by General Jaruzelski, took a series of decisive steps to restore something like the status quo.

On Friday, 8 October 1982, Solidarity and all other trade unions suspended under martial law were abolished and made illegal by a majority vote of the Communist-dominated parliament, the Sejm. A new law provided for new 'free and independent' trade unions, but conditions imposed on their genesis and development — one per enterprise for the foreseeable future — made it unlikely that they would ever be altogether free of Communist Party control. General Jaruzelski thus completed the main assignment pressed upon him and his colleagues by their comrades in Moscow since the day Solidarity was born in the Lenin Shipyard in Gdańsk.

In November, Solidarity's elected leader, Lech Wałęsa, was suddenly released from his place of internment at Arlamów in the southeastern corner of Poland. This was not an act of reconciliation nor was it, as some were encouraged to believe, a sign that Solidarity's democratically elected leader had reached some sort of accommodation with the authorities. Nothing could have been further from the truth. On returning to his home in Gdańsk, Wałęsa said he felt like someone walking a greasy tightrope stretched over a prison yard. In the weeks, months and years to come, Lech Wałęsa was to become the object of insult and scorn, not to speak of slanderous rumour, in the official media. He became 'the former leader of the former Solidarity' or, as one venomous commentator put it, 'a sparrow who thinks he's an eagle'. The policy was clear: humiliation for Solidarity survivors.

The next step came in December. Meeting shortly before Christmas, the Sejm considered an appeal submitted by PRON, the Patriotic Movement for National Rebirth, the front organisation created by the martial law authorities. The appeal bore a striking resemblance to the Church proposals which General Jaruzelski had chosen to ignore earlier in the year: it called for the lifting of martial law, for the release of all internees and for work to start on an amnesty for those in prison. Martial law was suspended, not lifted, from 1 January, so that the authorities could reimpose it wherever and whenever they saw fit. There was no amnesty, just the possibility of clemency to be granted only upon application. Internment, however, was ended. By Christmas Day, on the orders of General Kiszczak, the internment camps had been emptied.

This could have been a welcome Christmas present for the nation had it not been for the fact that seven Solidarity leaders and four prominent Solidarity advisers previously active in KOR, the Committee for the Defence of the Workers, had already been transferred from internment to prison and placed under arrest. They faced charges of trying to overthrow the state system by force.[1]

By the end of 1982, General Jaruzelski and his colleagues had made a start to creating the conditions which they hoped, and maybe even believed, would help ensure the continuation of Communist rule in Poland without serious challenge.

That hope may seem quaintly amusing now, but it is extremely doubtful whether at that time the eventual 'collapse of Communism' was even contemplated by those Western political leaders who were to claim credit for it later. The West's economic sanctions were certainly damaging, but only to the economy; they did not change the minds of the martial law authorities, who were determined to have their way regardless of Western opinion.

The Generals may have thought they had been very clever. There was an undeniable neatness to their work. But if they believed that the nation's sense of commitment to Solidarity would be seriously tested, they were gravely mistaken.

On Sunday, 10 October, Archbishop Glemp made the first public comment on the Sejm vote outlawing Solidarity. Speaking west of the capital at Niepokolanów, home of the Franciscan community founded by Fr Maksymilian Kolbe, who was about to be canonised in Rome, the Primate told a congregation of some 10,000 that any ideal that was just and good could never perish. Structures could vanish, he said, but the idea could not.

In a statement which emerged that same day, the leaders of the Solidarity underground condemned the dissolution of all trade unions as an act without precedent in civilised society. Declaring that the Sejm had forfeited its mandate, they called for a boycott of what they described as the bogus unions planned by the authorities. There followed a week of protest strikes and demonstrations, notably in Gdańsk, Wrocław and Nowa Huta. In Gdańsk, which saw three nights of rioting, the strike at the Lenin Shipyard was brought to an end only when the authorities placed it on a military footing, which meant that strikers could be imprisoned for desertion or for being absent without leave. During the demonstrations in Nowa Huta, the steel-making town on the edge of Cracow, a twenty-year-old steel worker was shot dead by a plain-clothes policeman.

At the end of an awful week, the Primate spoke again, this time from the high pulpit of the parish church of All Saints in the heart of Warsaw. Choosing his words carefully but unambiguously, Archbishop Glemp said that by doing away with the unions, the authorities had taken away something which, since August 1980, had given the people of Poland the sense of being more than mere objects. But the nation should not despair, the Archbishop said. If it was being forced by the authorities to start all over again from scratch, it was not starting from nothing, it was starting from the rich heritage of all that was noble in being Polish. The Polish people, he said, were possessed of a great sense of solidarity in their national feeling, regardless of whether an organisation existed or not. If they believed in themselves, there would always be hope.

At his Mass for the Homeland on the last Sunday of October, Fr Popiełuszko recalled that the Pope had told Polish pilgrims visiting Rome for the canonisation of Fr Kolbe that he had detected tears in their eyes, tears that were not tears of joy. 'Polish society, my own nation,' the Pope had continued, 'does not deserve to be reduced to tears of despair and dejection. It deserves to be able to create a better future for itself.'

Fr Popiełuszko went further:

> The nation which suffered so much in the not too distant past does not deserve to see many of its finest sons and daughters confined in camps and prisons. It does not deserve to see its young people beaten and treated with contempt or to see the crime of Cain taking place. It does not deserve to be deprived against its will of the Solidarity Independent Self-governing Trade Union, the union paid for with the suffering and blood of workers, the union which the late Primate said... did more in a few months than even the most efficient politicians could have achieved, the union for which the present Primate of Poland has urged reinstatement, thus placing his own authority and that of the Church upon the scales...

In this instance, Fr Popiełuszko did more than fill in what the Holy Father had left unsaid. By declaring categorically that the Pope and the Primate stood for Solidarity's return, he was also stating a simple fact: that the Church and Solidarity were on the same side in the war being waged by General Jaruzelski.

One year after he had talked to Archbishop Glemp and Lech Wałęsa about joining him as allies in a 'front for national accord', there could be no doubt now that the General had dispensed with their services. And while he couldn't do to the Church what he had done to Solidarity, there were other, extra-parliamentary ways of trying to undermine the influence and unity of the

Church and silence the troublesome priests in its ranks. From now on, the tactics employed by the authorities against the Solidarity underground and against the Church hierarchy or its priests would be part of a single strategy. First-hand insight into how such tactics worked was provided by Fr Popiełuszko, who started a new diary in an ordinary, sky-blue exercise book on 13 November 1982.[2]

> I'm not too sure why I've taken up my pen today to pour my thoughts out on paper, but for me a lot of interesting things have been happening lately and perhaps it would be a shame to let them be forgotten.
>
> Our authorities — not the Church authorities of course — cannot abide these Masses for the Homeland which I say on the last Sunday of every month. They say they're the biggest rallies to be seen under martial law.
>
> I was in the Cathedral on 1 November. I had an opportunity to compare the atmosphere there and in our church. There one could possibly say that there was a rally. There were shouts of 'bravo' and 'long live'. With us, though, there is always total solemnity in prayer and patriotic feeling. When they leave the church, the people are thoughtful and disciplined.
>
> Last night 'known assailants' sprayed Fr Henryk's car with white paint. But they got the wrong car, for there can be no doubt they were after mine. Still the same old methods, the very same they use to get back at the actors...

It is a measure of Fr Popiełuszko's influence that some of the country's most accomplished and most popular actors of stage, film and television had transferred to his Masses for the Homeland the talented services they had withdrawn from state radio and television and had gone on doing so after falling victim to SB harassment. These were carried out more often than not against their cars.[3]

It is clear from what the young priest wrote that he was now particularly conscious of being the object of hostile attention, even at the highest level. On 8 November, he said, he declined to give a telephone interview to 'a very nice lady' from the Canadian Radio in Toronto because 'alien ears are hanging on the phone lines'. And on 11 November, when visiting the Warsaw Curia, he had been told by the Chancellor that the Communist authorities were not pleased with his Masses for the Homeland.

> Bishop Jerzy Dąbrowski is said to have been told by Minister Łopatka that they will have to arrest three priests in Warsaw in the near future (Frs Kantorski, Prus and Małkowski) and to intern me in the first place... Then, in the evening, Bishop Miziołek was astonished to find on his return from Częstochowa that I was still at liberty. But he also let slip that Jaruzelski had named me as well as the three priests when talking to the Primate.
>
> I recognise that they can intern me or arrest me or stage some scandal, but I can't really give up this activity of mine which is my way of serving the Church and the Homeland.

In view of these menacing circumstances, it is not surprising that Fr Popiełuszko's diary was mainly about himself, paying little attention to the big events of the day. His only reference to the release of Lech Wałęsa, for instance, came obliquely in a somewhat amusing entry describing how Fr Bogucki had reacted to the report that the Solidarity leader had supposedly initiated his release by writing a letter to Jaruzelski.

> Sitting in a confessional, he called me over and showed me a newspaper cutting containing Wałęsa's letter. 'Damn it,' he says, 'I couldn't sleep a wink all night because of this Wałęsa. It must all be a put-up job.' Then at the 8 am Mass, he prayed that the Holy Father would indeed come to Poland — but no funny business. A wonderful man and a patriot, Fr Bogucki...

Fr Popiełuszko's new diary covered only seven months, November 1982 to the end of May 1983, when the authorities' campaign against him really got under way. While most of his entries were concerned with that, he wrote enough about other things to make it clear that he was permanently busy with a routine, largely of his own making, which had both rewards and drawbacks.

One can understand his satisfaction as he wrote shortly before midnight about a young man who had returned to the Church after an absence of several years because of the Masses for the Homeland. But in the lines that follow, the priest who had been considered too frail to cope with the burden of normal parish work was forced to admit that he could not rest.

> I am very, very tired. For practically two years I have not switched off mentally from patriotic affairs. I don't have a day off. I've noticed that I often sit at home when I could be off somewhere, because I would be sorry if someone needed help when I was absent.

Fr Popieluszko was also highly conscious now of the value of time and the uncertainty of the future. On Monday, 15 November, he went home to see his elderly parents. He hadn't been to Okopy for a long time, he wrote, 'and no one can say what my fate will be'. His mother and father had been worried and were pleased to see him, but when he took some pictures of his father, the old man had started crying. 'I have so little time to spend with my parents. And I won't have them for much longer. Dad is seventy two.'

Three days later, when visiting the Curia, he was told that a complaint had been received from Police Headquarters stating that he had been warned about his behaviour repeatedly and unless he changed it, the authorities would treat him in accordance with the decree on martial law. 'But what can be changed in my behaviour? After all I can't stop serving people.'

In contrast, Fr Popieluszko had received more than forty letters that week thanking him for the Masses for the Homeland. Among them, quite probably, was one dated 15 November and sent by an older man who declared himself to be a non-believer but who had been to two of the Masses 'so far', finding them 'moving and uplifting experiences'.

> We differ both as regards our age and our world view... There
> is one thing, however, that undoubtedly unites us both — we
> both feel ourselves to be Poles. I belong to a generation that
> can be justly accused... of allowing itself to be manoeuvred
> onto a road leading to catastrophe and of doing practically
> nothing to avoid that catastrophe... The future belongs to you
> and to your generation, Father, to the generation of my sons. I
> look on you with hope and pride. In spite of everything... in
> spite of the propaganda, a generation has grown up that is
> resourceful and wise, courageously seeking its rights. So one
> can hope that not all is lost.

The writer, who identified himself simply as Andrzej, then quoted from the latest edition of *Tygodnik Powszechny*, the Catholic weekly published in Cracow which said that Poland had regained its independence on 11 November 1918 because there had been 'a sufficiently large number of people doomed to greatness to make the miracle of 11 November possible'. He continued:

> You, Father, belong to those who are doomed to greatness and
> I believe profoundly that at present there is a sufficiently large
> number of those thus doomed to make another miracle
> possible... It is certain, Father, that as a result of your zealous
> work you will meet not only with gratitude and warm approval
> but also with hatred and villainy. I therefore end by wishing
> with all my heart that you keep up your courage and unbroken
> spirit. If I were a believer, I would no doubt write this: May
> God protect you and keep you in his care...[4]

Fr Popiełuszko, it seems, needed all such encouragement, recording in his diary the occasions when he had reason to feel similarly encouraged. One was when he was visited by a man who said he had returned to the Church after an absence of thirty four years because of the Masses for the Homeland and the priest's regular presence in court during the trials of workers under martial law regulations.

In December workers organised a system of night watches to protect Fr Popiełuszko by guarding the presbytery and churchyard. By then it had become clear that he was in physical danger.

On the day Fr Popiełuszko heard of the police warning, he was also informed that a Dr Adynowski, with whom he had worked well in the past through his association with the medical profession, had not only accused him, at an official briefing, of stirring people up but had suggested that this amounted to treason. The practice of denunciation, used to such evil effect in Moscow and elsewhere in the days of Stalin, had been revived.

On 26 November, Jerzy Śliwiński of the Warsaw City Office for Denominational Affairs sent two letters to the Warsaw Curia enumerating the alleged misdemeanours of two local priests — Fr Leon Kantorski of the parish of St Christopher in the village of Podkowa Leśna, just outside Warsaw, and Fr Jerzy Popiełuszko of St Stanisław's in Żoliborz.

In the case of Fr Kantorski, Śliwiński demanded that he be dismissed as parish priest in Podkowa Leśna in accordance with a 1956 decree on Church appointments on the grounds that he was aggressively anti-socialist and had been so since 1976 when he became closely associated with the newly formed Committee for the Defence of the Workers, better known by its initials KOR.

The complaint against Fr Popiełuszko claimed that his Masses had become 'political demonstrations, creating a threat to calm, security and public order in the capital'. Accusing him of manipulating the feelings of the faithful and even of tolerating the raising of hands in the V sign, it also claimed that the Solidarity underground circulated special leaflets with information about his services and placed its symbols inside the church. Śliwiński objected in particular to the August and October sermons and called for 'appropriate dispositions' to be taken as regards Fr Popiełuszko in accordance with the 1956 decree.[5]

Whatever the meaning of 'appropriate dispositions' as distinct from the demand for the sacking of Fr Kantorski, it is clear that the authorities wanted to be rid of both priests and were pressing the Church to act on their demands. The Church never obliged in either case but it did seriously consider the possibility of sending Fr Popiełuszko to study in Rome, in the interests of his personal safety. Indeed, the underground editors of his diaries suggested in a footnote that the priest agreed to such a move initially because of his extreme exhaustion.

It is not clear from Fr Popiełuszko's diary when precisely he learned of Śliwiński's letter to the Curia, because he wrote nothing for more than five weeks, from 20 November to 28 December. And when he resumed writing, he did not appear to attribute great significance to the authorities' demand, merely recording that the letter even alleged that the hymns sung at the Masses for the Homeland were political and anti-State in character.

Catching up with the events of the previous month or so, Fr Popiełuszko gave pride of place to the fact that he had been unable to give his sermon at the November Mass for the Homeland. He had been visited, he said, by Bishop Kraszewski who urged him to go away for a couple of days because there was an order out to arrest him after Mass. Out of concern for Fr Popiełuszko, the parish priest Fr Bogucki had taken his place at the Mass, allowing his younger colleague to assist on the altar.

As we have seen, this was not the first Bishop to relate information from an unidentified source suggesting that Fr Popiełuszko faced imminent arrest or similar. In retrospect, the danger does not seem to have been all that serious, but the Bishop, having heard of it, had to pass the information on in case it was true. The effect, whether intended or not, must have been extremely wearing on the young priest's nerves. In the very next sentence, almost in the same breath, the priest reported a police raid at the home of an acquaintance. Then the fact that 'once again they've sprayed my car with white paint'.

But something far more sinister happened during the night of 13 December. 'At 2 am the door bell rang and moments later there was an explosion. A brick fitted with a percussion cap knocked out two windows.'

The editors of the diaries said that in this entry Fr Popiełuszko was making light of the incident. The brick was fitted with an explosive, not a percussion cap, they said, and it was thanks only to the fact that he was too tired to respond quickly to the door bell that the priest did not sustain serious injuries.

The next night, the diary reports, there were signs of a break-in, probably only a pretence of a break-in judging by the priest's words. It was after this that his worker friends set up their system of night watches and as Fr Popiełuszko was to note in a later diary entry, from 14 December onwards there would always be someone staying with him overnight. The following night, a young man who was disturbed when apparently inter-fering with the priest's car, got into a police car and made off.

The pressure continued on the night of 27 December. 'They tormented me mentally, driving a car like mad up and down near the priests' house from 1 am to 4 am. The lads took about twenty pictures of them...'

The previous evening in his sermon at the last Mass for the Homeland of the year, Fr Popiełuszko had quoted a statement by the Pope that 'a State cannot be powerful on the strength of violence', and added his own thoughts:

> Violence is not a sign of strength but of weakness. It is the person who has failed to win through the heart or through reason who tries to win by force. Every manifestation of violence is evidence of moral inferiority. The finest and the longest struggles known to mankind and to history are those of human thought. The most squalid and the shortest are those involving violence. An idea which needs weapons to support itself dies away of itself. The idea which is capable of life makes its own way and millions follow it spontaneously.

One can only speculate whether this passage was intended as a defiant response to the explosion at his flat nearly two weeks earlier. What is certain is that the diary says no more about any night-time harassment of Fr Popiełuszko, perhaps the result of his worker friends starting their guard duty. And the first month of 1983 passed by almost without mention of attention from the authorities.

On 3 January, Fr Popiełuszko organised a gathering of health workers attended by the Primate himself for the traditional breaking of the Christmas and New Year wafer and he was clearly pleased with it.

> The atmosphere was very good. The Primate spoke very nicely. 'The Church will not abandon the people,' he said, 'just as the doctor does not desert a sick patient. The Church will not go after any privileges, for on earth there is no privilege for the Church apart from Christ.'

This is of particular interest because of a report that had circulated in Warsaw during December. It said that a group of pro-Solidarity priests, including Fr Popiełuszko, had a meeting with the Primate and virtually accused him of collaborating with the Communist authorities. It was difficult to establish the source of this report, let alone whether it was true. The fact that one of the papers reported on 1 December that the Archbishop had asked the actors to give up their boycott of radio and television in time for Christmas might well have been seen as evidence of collaboration.

The facts, however, were different and the authorities had concealed them. The Primate had made his appeal to the actors at the request of those same actors, who expected martial law to be lifted shortly and wanted to give up their boycott in response to a request from someone they could respect. Indeed, the actors' leader had written to the Minister of Culture on 29 November expressing the hope that the boycott could end as civil rights were restored. By concealing the facts, the authorities were able to expose the Primate to suspicion, or as the colourful Polish expression would have it, they 'pushed him into the raspberry bushes'. The Minister of Culture's response to the letter was to have the actors' union abolished.

The actors also had something to do with Fr Popiełuszko's second successful enterprise of the month. When, according to the diary, Bishop Jerzy Dąbrowski let it be known that he did not want actors to take part in the January Mass for the Homeland (for reasons not explained), Fr Jerzy decided to use them instead at a special Mass requested by the History Institute of Warsaw University on 22 January, the anniversary of the January Uprising of 1863.

The church was full to overflowing and for the first time in the diary we read of senior Solidarity figures being present. Tadeusz Mazowiecki, an adviser to the union's National Commission, read the lesson. After the Mass, during which a banner was unfurled proclaiming that 'Solidarity Lives', Klemens Szaniawski, Professor of Philosophy at Warsaw University, 'threw himself on my neck with tears in his eyes and thanked me'. Later, Fr Popiełuszko was joined for tea upstairs by Janusz Onyszkiewicz, Bronisław Geremek, Mazowiecki and Marek Kulerski, the brother of Viktor Kulerski of the Warsaw underground. All four had only recently been released from internment — Kulerski in November, the others just before Christmas. Fr Popiełuszko was clearly delighted to be visited by such celebrities. He was not to know that one day Mazowiecki would be Prime Minister, Geremek Foreign Minister and Onyszkiewicz Defence Minister of the Polish Republic.

The uprising of 1863 was the subject of Fr Popiełuszko's sermon during the Mass for the Homeland on the last Sunday of the month and once again he seems to have been in a state of euphoria in spite of all kinds of difficulties preparing for it. The congregation, he wrote, was 'exceptionally large, blocking the streets and stretching as far as the park'. By then, though, he knew that the police had not forgotten about him.

On the previous Thursday morning he had received a phone call from Police Headquarters asking him to report to the police station on Waliców Street to testify in the case of a Dr Śliwowski, who was said to have claimed that he had received medicines from him. Not knowing any such doctor and suspecting that this was a ruse by the police to get him in for interrogation, Fr Popiełuszko said he would see if he could go in the following Tuesday.

By the time Tuesday came round, he had been told that there was no need for him to report since the case had been dropped. But that afternoon he was visited by a young man of about twenty wearing a light-coloured raincoat who asked if he could talk to him alone about a private matter. The young man turned out to be from the police; his task was to persuade Fr Popiełuszko to accept a police summons to an interrogation. He did not accept it.

At 6 am two days later on 3 February, Fr Popiełuszko set off by car for the mountains of the south on what was intended to be a nine-day holiday at Kosarzysk. With him in the car were Krzysiek O. and Malgosia Z.; others were to join them later. As soon as they had left Warsaw, they were joined on the road by a green Fiat 125 with two policemen inside. The policemen took pictures of them from the rear and the side before signalling them to pull in to the side of the road. There, Fr Popiełuszko and his friends were subjected to a lengthy and annoying search of the car and the examination of all personal documents, initiated by such farcical remarks, as recorded in the diary, as 'What's all this then? An illegally organised group?'

When they were eventually allowed to continue their journey, they were tailed in turn by several other cars. Shortly before reaching Kielce, when their car started to play up and they were being followed, in Fr Popiełuszko's words, by a 'real bulldog', the trio decided to drive into the town to take stock over a cup of tea with Malgosia's parents.

Fr Popiełuszko and his two companions were 'accompanied' all the way to the home of Malgosia's parents and throughout the evening several cars took it in turns to keep watch outside. It was then that he decided to go no further but to stay in the Kielce area, leaving his car on the grounds of the local seminary. The SB, he wrote, watched the gates of the seminary for two days after he had parked the car there. When he eventually drove back to Warsaw, he was accompanied 'in a primitive fashion' by two men and a woman in a brown Fiat. By now it was clear that the authorities were prepared to go to absurd lengths to impress upon Fr Popiełuszko that he could never escape their gaze.

On returning to Warsaw, Fr Popiełuszko was told that a summons had arrived for him from the Prosecutor's Office but that the Sisters had refused to accept it. So once again, the authorities used a Bishop to convey the message of official displeasure. The diary records that on Friday, 25 February, Fr Popiełuszko was called in by Bishop Kazimierz Romaniuk, who was in charge of personnel matters in the diocese, to be told that the Warsaw authorities deplored his behaviour, claiming that St Stanisław's was 'a thorn in the side of Church-State relations'. The Bishop, Fr Popiełuszko noted, 'is under great pressure from the Ministry of Internal Affairs to do something about this'.

For the February Mass for the Homeland two days later, the SB tried something different. The diary account is brief but telling:

> At 6.20 pm, before Mass began, a couple of lorries coming from the direction of Mierosławski Street delivered 'young people' to provoke trouble. During the Mass, Żoliborz was surrounded by the ZOMO, along with amphibious and armoured vehicles. Some people were prevented from reaching the church. We asked the congregation not to allow themselves to be provoked, and they behaved as required, dispersing with decorum. At about 10 pm, after the failure of their operation, the strange people left Żoliborz in the lorries.

This was a significant, even ominous development. After concentrating in the final months of 1982 on waging a war of nerves against Fr Popiełuszko, the SB had now switched their attention to the Masses for the Homeland, the very source of their displeasure, in the hope of provoking the sort of civil commotion which they had falsely claimed was the result of Fr Popiełuszko's sermons. Hence the presence of the armoured ZOMO riot police, ready to restore order. It is also more than likely that the 'young people' of this episode came from the same hard school as the thugs who would raid the Primate's charity at St Martin's months later, on 3 May.

Also significant was the fact that, in spite of rain, the Mass attracted the largest congregation so far, tightly packing the streets around the church and stretching into the park. Among those welcomed at the beginning of the Mass by Fr Bogucki, who had only recently returned from hospital, were 'those from distant corners of our land'. No matter what the authorities did or threatened to do, the crowds flocking to St Stanisław's on the last Sunday of every month were getting bigger and bigger.

Fr Popiełuszko, however, was not getting any stronger. On 8 March, at 11.20 pm, he wrote once again of his tiredness. For two weeks, he said, he had been feeling the onset of flu, but had been unable to find even two free days to go to bed and get warm. Earlier that day he had been visited by friends who had suggested he go away until 13 March; they had learned from leaked information that the SB were out to torment him in a special way.

Here, for the first time, Fr Popiełuszko betrayed a sense of weary frustration. He certainly appreciated 'so much concern' by these 'dear people' but they thought of him, he wrote, in terms of the Masses for the Homeland and his association with the workers.

> They don't know that I do these things at the cost of my contacts with friends, my recreation and sleep at nights. After all, my basic work, the work I've been appointed to do is with the medical profession and, as 'resident', helping out in the parish...

If not exactly a complaint, it was at least recognition that the extra work he had undertaken with enthusiasm and for which he was frequently praised was sometimes a bit much for him. But he couldn't give it up. How could he when the Mass at the end of March was attended by more people than ever? And this in spite of the fact, as he recorded in his diary, that 'the SB had posted notices at other churches announcing that the Mass had been cancelled'. Once again, the police were on hand with water cannons at the ready but were unable to use them because the congregation dispersed at the end of the Mass very quietly, having been urged by Fr Popiełuszko to ignore provocateurs. The priest even had a few words for the SB men present: 'And you, brothers, who are here on the orders of others, if you want to serve the truth and respect your own dignity, allow the faithful to go home in peace.'

Some two weeks later, Fr Popiełuszko took to his bed for several days with what seems to have been a feverish cold. But even then he received visitors and one evening he got up to say Mass in the crypt for those who fell in the Warsaw Ghetto Uprising of 1943, and to hear a twenty-minute lecture on the subject by Jan Józef Lipski, a historian and one of the founders of KOR.

There can be no doubt that in spite of his chronic exhaustion and poor health, Fr Popiełuszko was happy at this time for the simple reason that people needed him and he was able to respond to their needs. He did this, moreover, in more ways than one might have suspected. According to one of the many women who worked as volunteers at the Primate's charity at St Martin's, where a great deal of foreign aid was sorted for distribution, it was not unknown for the priest from Żoliborz to drop in for a chat, but also in the hope of leaving with some small item for a needy family of his choosing somewhere in Warsaw.

However, Fr Popiełuszko was aware almost constantly of the attentions of the SB. At the beginning of April, he knew that the authorities preparing for the Pope's visit in June had written to the Curia stating that his name should not appear on any list of people chosen by the Church to play a role during the visit. The Bishops ignored this demand, insisting that he should again be in charge of their arrangements for first aid medical services for the huge crowds that would gather to see the Pope in Warsaw.

Later that month, when Fr Popiełuszko drove out to the Franciscan community at Niepokolanów for some crucifixes, 'the gentlemen from the SB drove behind me all the way to the monastery to check on what I was picking up there; they upbraided the Prior for having something printed there. How crude. Why should I expose the monastery that way when I have so many other ways of doing things.'

By this time, Fr Popiełuszko may well have felt that he was going through an advanced version of the treatment he once received from the NCOs and Officers during his army service, but with the emphasis exclusively on mental rather than physical chastisement.

He next wrote in his diary on 21 May 1983, two days after the funeral of Grzegorz Przemyk. He was in Częstochowa, at the convent of the Sisters of Charity, attending a retreat for health service personnel. This was a valuable time for him too, he wrote, 'for I seem to be at the limit of my endurance, mentally and physically, after the recent ordeals in Warsaw'.

The pressure was beginning to tell. Fr Popiełuszko wrote that he had driven to Częstochowa in a borrowed car because his own had been regularly followed beforehand by two from the UB (the old name for the SB, or secret police).

I feel more and more hunted down by them, but God is good and He gives me a lot of spiritual strength and also physical strength... though it often happens that my nights are seriously disturbed...

On these last few pages of his exercise book, one can feel not only Fr Popiełuszko's weariness but his growing sense of defiance and no doubt anger at the end of a month of unprovoked violence against the innocent. He revealed that he had organised the funeral service for Grzegorz Przemyk at St Stanisław's in spite of 'the contrary opinions' of Professors Lipski and Szaniawski and thanked God that it had all passed off quietly. After his appeal for absolute silence, he wrote, it had been 'the biggest and the most eloquent demonstration by the Warsaw public'. In the very same breath, he prays: 'God give strength to that suffering mother, who took that blow heroically.'

At this point, anyone reading the diary may feel that Fr Popiełuszko is hurrying to get everything down before it is too late. As usual it is getting late, but there also appears to be a sense of urgency that had little to do with the time of day. There was still no resolution of the argument over his part in the Papal visit in June.

> The State authorities are unwilling to talk to me; it's as if I were some rabid extremist. And Director Adynowski, once again, has turned out to be a scoundrel, to put it mildly. Backing him up has been a certain Śliwiński of Denominational Affairs. I have told Adynowski over the phone that I have not changed; it is he and his supporters who have changed in these past two years.

More complaints meanwhile, came from on high. Bishop Miziołek had received a letter from the Commandant General of Warsaw alleging that Fr Popiełuszko had said Mass in the church of the Holy Cross on 13 May and made use of 'texts not in keeping with the dignity' of that church. 'The General has poor informants. On 13 May, I was hearing confessions in our church. I have never said Mass at Holy Cross.'

A day or so later, Bishop Miziołek told him that General Kiszczak himself had shown him Fr Popiełuszko's sermon from the March Mass for the Homeland. 'The Bishop found nothing wrong with it since it calls for reconciliation and accord.'

Bishop Miziołek, along with Bishop Kraszewski, was a great champion of Fr Popiełuszko. So too was the Chancellor of the Warsaw Curia, Fr Zdzisław Król. It was he, it seems, who went to Częstochowa to give the address at the end of the health service retreat at the convent of the Sisters of Charity.

> Closing the retreat today, the Chancellor devoted to me a couple of sentences which I did not deserve. He said, among other things, that the work which I do requires heroism and discretion. And that both these virtues are embodied in me. It

turns out that people know me, for when my name was mentioned I received loud bravoes.

The Chancellor caused the greatest merriment when he said that the President of Warsaw had talked to him about the funeral of Fr Popiełuszko. 'But Mr President, Fr Popiełuszko is alive.' The President calls Gzresia's [Grzegorz Przemyk's] funeral mine because I organised it.

It's midnight and I'm back from the Stations of the Cross. As always, it's a wonderful religious experience.

Fr Popiełuszko was undoubtedly delighted to receive such praise from Fr Król and to hear the applause provoked by the mention of his name. But there was little joy in the lines, now completed, in the sky-blue exercise book. They were permeated instead by the priest's growing awareness of the forces of the State assembled against him, and by an unspoken premonition that they would make life even harder for him in the time that lay ahead.

# 6

# A Night in Gaol

When Pope John Paul II stepped down from his Alitalia plane at Warsaw International Airport on the afternoon of Thursday, 16 June 1983, he knelt and kissed the ground. He had done it before, but this was a special moment.

Kissing the soil of Poland, he said, was like kissing a mother's hand. For Poland was a special mother, one who had suffered a great deal and kept on suffering anew, and, for that reason, was deserving of a special love. The Pope asked all who were suffering to feel especially close to him. He did so, he said, in the name of Christ who had said: I was sick and you visited me; I was in prison and you came to me. He could not visit all who were sick, imprisoned or suffering but he asked them all to be close to him in spirit.

These were powerful and moving words, coming as they did from the Pope who had watched from afar as Solidarity, the union to which he had given his blessing, was first suspended and then abolished. Now he was speaking directly, in the presence of the Chairman of the Council of State, to those who had become political prisoners and fugitives for the sake of Solidarity.

The Pope's safety during his visit was in the hands of a department of the Ministry of Internal Affairs. But in a remarkable example of the ambivalence of Polish government attitudes in those days, the SB men protecting the Pope came from the same team and in some cases may even have been the same individuals as those engaged in efforts to silence Fr Popiełuszko. In spite of their objections, however, the young priest from Żoliborz, at the Church's insistence, was still in charge of first aid services during the Pope's visit to the Warsaw area.

Later Fr Popiełuszko would write that the Pope's visit had been 'a magnificent national, religious and patriotic plebiscite' which 'strengthened me in my work and confirmed that it is correct'.[1] It was indeed a plebiscite, for the Poles voted with their feet, assembling in multitudes wherever he went. It was difficult to assess the size of the crowds because they always stretched further than the eye could see, but more striking than the numbers was the sense that people were being drawn, individually and collectively, by an exceptional force of attraction.

In Częstochowa, for instance, at 6 am on a dark morning of pouring rain, I woke up to the sound of an organ being played at the shrine on the hilltop above, only to be drawn to my hotel window by another, almost inaudible sound: that of pilgrims making their way softly up the wooded slope to the monastery of Jasna Góra.

In Cracow, as I stood at another hotel window long after midnight, there was the same, barely discernible sound of movement. And it was just possible to make out the figures of people, many people, making their way purposefully through the darkness onto the huge city common where the Pope was to deliver the final sermon of his visit many hours later.

Nationally and spiritually, the Pope's visit was a success, leaving no one in any doubt about the Church's teaching on human and civil rights. But the politics of Poland did not change. The authorities ignored the Church's call for the slate to be wiped clean. And although martial law, suspended since December, was finally lifted completely a month after the Pope's departure, the only amnesty the authorities offered was one that required beneficiaries to give themselves up and admit to wrongdoing. Further restrictions were introduced, including tighter censorship. Political prisoners remained imprisoned, Solidarity remained banned, its underground leaders were still hunted and Lech Wałęsa, who had been allowed to meet the Pope in the hills above Cracow on the last afternoon of the visit, remained the target of insults and harassment.

Fr Popiełuszko, for his part, continued to be followed wherever he went. In August, he went on holiday to Dębki, a little place on the Baltic Coast northwest of Gdańsk, where his lawyer, Edward Wende and his wife Ewa had a holiday home.

On the morning after the priest arrived, the Wendes were surprised to see some men fishing in the stream behind their house where they had never seen anyone fishing before. They assumed they were SB men. There can be no doubt, at any rate, that SB men were in Fr Jankowski's parish church of St Brigid in Gdańsk on 13 August to record a sermon by Fr Popiełuszko at a Mass attended by Lech Wałęsa.

This was an important moment in the young priest's career as spiritual champion of Solidarity. And he seemed conscious of this when I went into the sacristy after Mass had begun and found him standing alone in his vestments, waiting for his cue to enter the sanctuary and preach. We exchanged a glance but not a word. His sermon was of considerable interest to the foreign correspondents who had come up from Warsaw and also to the authorities.

Describing the lifting of martial law as a sham, he said that the introduction of further restrictions on civil rights meant that the manacles removed from the hands had been fixed more tightly onto people's hearts and minds.

Two weeks later, in his sermon at the Mass for the Homeland at St Stanisław's, he said that new regulations recently passed by the Sejm were 'without doubt laws which do not serve the good or the interests of society' but 'strike a blow at freedom of thought'. It took only two days for the Office for Denominational Affairs to deliver to Archbishop Bronisław Dąbrowski, the Secretary of the Episcopate, a protest which was said to have been authorised by the Minister, Adam Łopatka, but was not signed by him.

Complaining that the Church had done nothing to stop churches being used for 'political demonstrations against the State authorities', the letter alleged that Fr Popiełuszko's sermon at St Stanisław's on the evening of 28 August had contained 'social and political elements hostile to the State' and that they had been presented in 'a manner distinctly calculated to incite and excite the assembled faithful'. The letter advised the Archbishop to think of the possible consequences of the involvement of clergymen in political activities designed to disturb public order, and urged the Episcopate to put a stop to 'situations such as those created by Fr Popiełuszko'.[2]

This was not one of the usual protests, taking in the alleged misdemeanours of several priests; it was directed specifically at Fr Popiełuszko. The fact that it was apparently considered too important to wait for the Minister's signature suggests that a decision had been taken to act swiftly and decisively against the priest from Żoliborz. This was confirmed on the same day the letter of protest was sent to the Archbishop.

Fr Popiełuszko set off by car that day, 30 August, for Gdynia, the city next to Gdańsk, in the company of two friends — Fr Bogdan Liniewski and Waldemar (Waldek) Chrostowski. The latter became one of his regular drivers and was described by Fr Jerzy, when he resumed his diary at the end of the year, as someone 'who helps me a lot and protects me'. Fr Popiełuszko was to give a sermon in a local church at the request of Anna Walentynowicz, whose name was as well known as Wałęsa's at the start of the Gdańsk Shipyard strike in August 1980.

Whether he realised it or not, Fr Popiełuszko was becoming a travelling preacher and that was another thing the authorities did not like. At Łomianki on the northern perimeter of Warsaw, Fr Popiełuszko and his companions were stopped by a total of five cars — three ordinary police cars and two belonging to the SB. According to his diary account composed months later, the police searched him and the car but found nothing apart from his last sermon which he said they could keep if they wanted. Fr Popiełuszko was released eight hours later after the appearance of Fr Kalwarczyk from the Warsaw Curia and a Colonel Celak from the SB. He drove to see Bishop Miziołek and then home, in the company of two SB cars. Waldemar Chrostowski was detained for fifty hours at the police station on Żytnia Street in Warsaw.

The SB's preoccupation with Fr Popiełuszko was intense. A day or two later, his diary recorded, he was under non-stop surveillance, with four men in two cars watching his every step. When he visited the Loreto Sisters in the Warsaw district of Bródno, the convent was surrounded by five cars.

What Fr Popiełuszko did not know was that the SB was beginning to collect documentary evidence against him.[3] On 1 September, Lieutenant Colonel Adam Adamski, head of an investigations section at the Ministry of Internal Affairs, sent a copy of his sermon of 28 August to the Censorship Office — the Chief Office for the Control of the Press, Publications and Performances — seeking a professional opinion. The reply came that the sermon was 'a threat to public peace and security'.

On 21 September, Lieutenant Mieczysław Chylkiewicz of the SB secret police at the Mostowski Palace, headquarters of the Warsaw City Office of Internal Affairs, composed an official memorandum detailing evidence that Fr Popiełuszko had abused freedom of conscience and religion in sermons recorded 'in the course of duty' in Warsaw, Gdańsk and Częstochowa. It concluded that the priest's 'anti-State formulations' fitted the crime described under Article 194 of the Criminal Code.

The following day, Deputy Prosecutor Anna Jackowska launched an official investigation into Fr Popiełuszko. Four days later, on 26 September, according to a subsequent diary entry, Fr Popiełuszko learned of the decision from an official telex sent by the Communist Party Central Committee to Party cells in the factories. The message had been 'intercepted'. Anyone convicted under Article 194, he noted, could be sent to prison for terms ranging from one to ten years.

This meant it was official Party policy, known to Party members in the factories, that Fr Popiełuszko (and also, incidentally, Fr Jankowski) was to be investigated on specific charges with a view to prosecution. This was not known, however, to the general public. Nor, indeed, were any of the confidential memoranda that normally passed between Church and State. Fr Jankowski was the first to be subjected to the regular routine of being summoned by the police for interrogation. Never shy of publicity, he rarely let this happen without keeping the foreign press corps informed. Fr Popiełuszko, in contrast, did not take his troubles to foreign correspondents. By this time, I was regularly attending his Masses for the Homeland and Karol Małcużyński and I were at St Brigid's in Gdańsk on 13 August when he gave the sermon that so alarmed the authorities. Even so, we had no idea of the full extent of official moves against him.

Oddly enough, it was still possible to report developments which were, without doubt, ingredients in the largely covert campaign. In August, for instance, an article in the weighty Communist Party journal, *Zycie Partii* (Life of the Party), admitted that quite a number of Party members actually went to church, making a great display of their piety, contrary to their ideology of Marxism-Leninism. There should be no place in the Party, the article said, for 'God-fearing comrades' who kept 'hanging on to the cassocks of priests'.

At about the same time, Leonid Zamyatin, a long-standing member of the Secretariat of the Central Committee of the Soviet Communist Party, who had recently visited Warsaw, went on television in Moscow to speak of the 'dangers' presented by the Church in Poland. The Church, he said, had supported what he called the 'counter-revolution' of August 1980. Moreover, since the visit of the Pope in June, aggressive elements in the Church had been looking for a fight with the socialist State, anti-socialist sermons were becoming more virulent, and anti-socialist atheists were even seeking an alliance with anti-socialists in the Church. Mr Zamyatin's classic view of the situation would have been intimated, at least, to his Polish comrades during his own visit. And this may well have prompted the supposedly liberal *Polityka* weekly to publish a lengthy article in September claiming not only that the Solidarity opposition was sheltering behind the Church but that the Church's main objective was material and political power.

Any hopes that the Papal visit would promote a conciliatory attitude from the authorities had, by now, been conclusively dashed. General Jaruzelski and his colleagues seemed to have opted instead for a course which treated its critics with pugnacious contempt. The best example of this was Deputy Premier Rakowski's visit, with television cameras, to the Lenin Shipyard in Gdańsk, for a stage-managed harangue to the assembled workers at the birthplace of Solidarity. During this visit, he told Lech Wałęsa to his face and in public that 'the time will come when the Western press will lose interest in you and you will be alone and lonely'.

The Primate, now Cardinal Glemp, gave this nauseating performance a sharp response. In a sermon at Jasna Góra shortly afterwards, he said that when an educated man insults a working man, it is the former who will find himself alone, while the worker will have with him thousands like him who feel the insult just as painfully.

At that time, however, the authorities paid little heed to criticism, preoccupied as they were with their latest success — the capture of one of the original leaders of the Solidarity underground, the steelworker from Nowa Huta, Władysław Hardek. Not only had they captured him, they had also persuaded him to appear on television to say that he had surrendered and to suggest to his former colleagues, with whom he had only recently condemned the government's amnesty offer, that they should do the same.

For Solidarity this was a terrible shock. The hope of the authorities, as they let Hardek go free under the amnesty, was that the very idea of underground resistance would be discredited. Within days, however, an eloquent endorsement of resistance, smuggled out of a cell in the SB block of the remand prison on Rakowiecka Street, Warsaw, appeared in an underground Solidarity weekly. Its author was Adam Michnik, the historian who had been in custody since 13 December 1981 and was one of the eleven facing charges of trying to overthrow the State by force.

In what was described as an interview given earlier in August for publication elsewhere (but possibly reproduced now in response to the news about Hardek), Michnik said he used to be opposed to underground, conspiratorial activity, but that now the situation had changed. Leaders who remained in hiding were essential; they were the symbols of the national movement. After all, he said, 'we have been pushed into the underground' and, to all intents and purposes, everyone was a conspirator now. To give up on conditions dictated by the authorities would be tantamount to capitulation. Describing the lifting of martial law as a ritual gesture and the government offer of amnesty as a routine comedy, Michnik said that General Jaruzelski had not yet satisfied his Soviet allies. They would continue to be haunted by the spectre of counter-revolution, he said, until the peasants were driven into collective farms and Catholic priests were forced into the catacombs.

There was never any danger that Zbigniew Bujak from Warsaw or Bogdan Lis from Gdańsk or any of their colleagues would even think of giving up their resistance in response to the Hardek broadcast. But Michnik's words, placing the underground of the present and the catacombs of history in the same context, confirmed Solidarity supporters in the moral and patriotic motives of their cause.

Fr Popiełuszko's sermons did the same. When the authorities closed down the Union of Writers, completing their destruction of the artistic and cultural associations which had followed Solidarity's lead and become self-governing and independent, Fr Popiełuszko responded with a sermon at the end of September. He declared that it was thanks to its largely Christian culture and its connections, through this, with the West that the Polish nation had 'not allowed itself to be destroyed in spite of the partitions, in spite of the uprisings which failed, in spite of Siberia, in spite of the attempts to extinguish national characteristics, in spite of the Russification and the *Kulturkampf...*' But on what elements of the culture being created in 1983, he asked, could the nation nourish itself in future? On lying articles in the official press? On the mud slung at Solidarity or the charges facing its democratically elected leaders?[4]

At the end of October, Fr Popiełuszko was able to respond to something said about those leaders by the government spokesman, Jerzy Urban. At one of his regular press conferences, Urban had suggested that even the eleven men held in remand facing charges of trying to overthrow the State system could benefit from the government's amnesty if they agreed to leave the country until complete stability had been restored. On that score, Fr Popiełuszko simply quoted what the Pope had said on an earlier occasion:

> There must be a place for Poles in Poland. Every man has a right to his own country. No one can be condemned to emigration.

The government's proposal, however, suggested strongly that General Jaruzelski was having second thoughts about putting on trial men accused of the worst crime in the Communists' criminal code. It looked as though he would prefer simply to be rid of them. It was already clear that there had been little response from members of the Solidarity underground to the amnesty offer. In fact, October had proved to be a cruel month for the authorities, bringing as it did the embarrassing announcement that Lech Wałęsa, 'the former leader of the former Solidarity', had been awarded the Nobel Peace Prize. Fr Popiełuszko did not omit to mention this in his October sermon.

At the end of November, after the United States had announced that it was to maintain the bulk of its economic sanctions against Poland — a decision which prompted a bitter outburst from General Jaruzelski — Fr Popiełuszko's sermon not only gave a clear account of what he called the sufferings of the Polish nation since the Second World War; it also flatly contradicted what the authorities wanted to believe.

Let no one say that Solidarity has suffered a defeat. It is moving towards victory. It is moving slowly, but it is becoming rooted more and more powerfully in the nation. Maybe it still has to suffer a great deal, to become tempered like gold in the crucible. But August 1980 demonstrated the right road for people of the new generation, for people who live in the love of truth, sobriety, courage and brotherly love...

It was after that sermon, Fr Popiełuszko wrote in his diary, that 'it began'. The new diary, which he started in a black exercise book on 29 December, provides a detailed, retrospective account of the most determined effort so far by the authorities to get their hands on him. It was Friday, 2 December 1983:

During the 7 am Mass I noticed some men behaving oddly inside the church. It turned out later that they were from the SB and the Prosecutor's Office. Although all the exits were staked out, I somehow managed to slip past them.

After I got back to my flat in the presbytery across the churchyard the door bell began ringing insistently. There were about twelve of the men positioned about the churchyard. Outside it I could see a police van and two SB cars with people inside. They had a prosecutor's warrant to take me in immediately.

At the 9 am Mass, Fr Bogucki told the congregation that some strange people claiming to be from the General Prosecutor's Office were asking for Fr Jerzy. 'Let us pray that God changes their hearts, he said, and intoned a hymn... After the Mass, people gathered near the presbytery and said the rosary. I phoned the Chancellor of the Curia. He told me not to leave the house...

Fr Bogucki refused to accept the summons on the grounds that I was subordinate not to him but to the Bishop. So the police went to the Curia, where the Chancellor Fr Król sent them off to Bishop Miziołek. The Bishop noted that the summons was for 9 am, and that since it was now 12, it was no longer valid.

In the meantime, more and more workers assembled outside the presbytery. The police made two further attempts to hand over the summons, at 3 pm and at 6 pm, this time using a postman to deliver it, but the workers would not let them in.

People guarded the presbytery throughout the night from Friday to Saturday, on Saturday and again on the night from Saturday to Sunday. People really passed the test. At 1 am hot tea was delivered. I received many expressions of sympathy in the form of letters, flowers and sweets...

It is hard to escape the impression that Fr Popiełuszko rather enjoyed writing about this messy episode as well as the reception he received on the Sunday when he said a special Mass for coal miners, after which he had to step outside the presbytery several times to receive the plaudits of the crowd shouting 'God Bless You'. The people believed, he wrote, that this was 'our little victory'. But then, he added, 'Satan became even angrier'.

Indeed, when the SB officers eventually got their hands on Fr Popiełuszko, some ten days after being foiled in their first attempt, they had something special prepared for him to make up for their earlier disappointment.

On 10 December, according to the priest's diary, Minister Łopatka of the Office for Denominational Affairs gave an assurance to Archbishop Bronisław Dąbrowski, Secretary General of the Episcopate, that if Fr Popiełuszko responded to the summons, he would be released after no more than two hours of questioning. And so 'the Archbishop, through the Chancellor, handed me in the Minister's envelope a summons to appear on 12.XII'. Fr Popiełuszko went on to comment, somewhat surprisingly: 'The Archbishop forgot that one mustn't do deals with the devil.'

One has to wonder why Fr Popiełuszko and his supporters had been so determined to stop the police presenting their summons. Fr Jankowski in Gdańsk had responded to a similar summons in November without much fuss, and since he had made sure that people knew what was happening, his case was widely reported by Western correspondents in Warsaw.

At 9 am on 12 December, without the benefit of such publicity, Fr Popiełuszko reported to the Prosecutor's Office in the company of two lawyers, Tadeusz De Virion and Edward Wende. People with flowers were waiting outside the building to wish him well.

Deputy Prosecutor Anna Jackowska opened proceedings by reading her decision to institute investigations. It alleged that Fr Popiełuszko was guilty, under Article 194 of the Criminal Code, of using churches to conduct damaging anti-State propaganda and of slandering the State authorities in sermons that were political. The evidence presented in support consisted of sound and video recordings of the priest's sermons and the scene inside St Stanisław's Church. Video cassettes had been confiscated from the correspondent of the American ABC Network after the October Mass for the Homeland.

Fr Popiełuszko denied the charges and declined to answer questions directly connected with them. According to the diary, this attempt at interrogation ended at noon but they were kept waiting till 1 pm when it was announced that his private flat at 15 Chłodna Street was to be searched immediately, in the presence of his two lawyers if they so wished. Neither of them attended the search, however, and the only witness to go with Fr Popiełuszko was his friend and frequent driver, Waldek (Waldemar) Chrostowski. No one, it seems, expected any sensational outcome, least of all the priest himself.

> I was quite calm on the way to the flat because I hadn't kept even a leaflet there since before martial law. What a surprise, then, when one of the four officers conducting the search... pulled out a pile of incriminating materials within three minutes.

The haul, as listed in the diary, was impressive: 15,000 copies of illegal publications; a message in French smuggled from prison; sixty copies of a fourteen-page report by Fr Małkowski on the meeting with the Primate, allegedly sent from Paris accompanied by a letter from Giedroyc, the editor of *Kultura*, the intellectual Polish-language monthly published in the French capital; thirty six rounds of ammunition for a machine pistol; dynamite with a fuse and an electric detonating cable; four large tear gas canisters; sixty foreign printing matrices and five tubes of printer's ink.

> The Lord, however, gave me strength. I took it all calmly. I began to laugh and told them: 'Gentlemen, you've overdone it.' I added a note of my own to the record of the search compiled by Lieutenant Chylkiewicz. It said: 'I draw your attention to the fact that upon entering the flat one of the officers went straight to the places where he found the incriminating materials, as though he already knew they were there.'
>
> The other three officers, meanwhile, were looking rather delicately through my books. You could tell that only one of them was in the know. I learned later that an SB man from Television News had been living in the flat opposite for a couple of months. All the stuff must have been prepared in his place. I can't see any other possibility. A television crew did turn up and opened up all the cupboards and the refrigerator to film them.

Fr Popieluszko's account ended with an interesting observation. He was surprised, he said, that the police, when it was over, simply gave him back his keys and discarded 'the packaging' (which had, presumably, contained the incriminating materials) down the rubbish chute. He found it strange that they had not 'set a trap', leaving someone in the flat to confront future visitors. His thought, no doubt, was that if the police genuinely believed that the flat was used for storing materials of the Solidarity underground, they would have been keen to lay their hands on other 'conspirators'. As for the packaging, it would have been subjected to expert forensic examination in any genuine investigation. By throwing it away, the police were destroying evidence — evidence that probably led directly to the SB. One of the SB officers conducting the search was called Leszek Pękala. In less than a year, their paths would cross again.

Fr Popiełuszko was taken into custody and driven to the Mostowski Palace, headquarters of the Warsaw City Police. There, he was told to strip naked and subjected to a body search by a policeman aged no more than twenty, who put his hand to his head and muttered: 'It would have to be me wouldn't it.' Fr Popiełuszko was placed in a cell already occupied by five men. As his diary records, one was suspected of murdering his wife and throwing her body into the River Vistula, another of taking part in a murder in a local town. The third was held for killing four people 'with a locomotive'; the fourth for embezzlement. The fifth was a police agent. Fr Popiełuszko said he had no complaints about these five or the uniformed warders, all of whom treated him with kindness. As he lay down for the night on his mattress spread out on the floor, he noticed that the cell had yet another occupant, 'a nice rat who kept emerging from the ventilator searching for bread'.

At lunchtime the next day, Tuesday, 13 December, government spokesman Jerzy Urban announced at his regular weekly news conference for foreign journalists that Fr Popiełuszko was in custody and facing possible arrest after the discovery of a large quantity of seriously incriminating materials during a police search of his flat on Chłodna Street. The spokesman did not say what the materials were — he would mention the ammunition and explosives only a week later — but he gave a definite impression that the authorities had not known, until the search, that the priest had a private flat in addition to the one he occupied at St Stanisław's. The general public did not know, but the authorities did; the police had already sent to the Chłodna address the warrant authorising their search of the priest and his car at Łomianki on 30 August. Whatever the government spokesman said, however, would have made little difference, since most people believed that it was an SB provocation.

Fr Popiełuszko knew this too, but on Tuesday afternoon that hardly mattered. At 2 pm he was photographed in three positions, full face and both sides. Later he was summoned to another meeting with Deputy Prosecutor Jackowska, in the presence of two investigators, presumably from the SB, and his lawyer, Edward Wende. It was then that he was informed of fresh charges against him resulting from the discovery in his flat of ammunition for a 9 millimetre calibre pistol, dynamite, detonators and three tear gas grenades, as well as illegal publications. Because of the publications, Fr Popiełuszko was accused under three linked articles of the Criminal Code of slandering the State and its leading bodies, of calling for anti-State activities and engaging in activities designed to cause unrest and rioting. According to his own calculations, the new charges could result in twenty one years in prison, in addition to the ten years he could receive if convicted under the charge mentioned by Jackowska the day before.

Denying the charges, Fr Popiełuszko exercised his right to decline to give testimony. At the same time, however, he stated that the materials and objects discovered in his flat had been placed there without his knowledge.

It must now have seemed that Fr Popiełuszko was in for a long stay either at the Mostowski Palace or the Rakowiecka remand prison. During the meeting with the Prosecutor, Edward Wende's wife, Ewa, was allowed to take him some food and two packets of cigarettes. As the lawyer was leaving, Fr Popiełuszko mentioned that he had been due to say a special Mass at St Stanisław's that evening at which workers were to take the pledge. He wondered if more of them would give up alcohol because of his absence.

Karol Małcużyński and I attended that Mass, and although many men did raise their hands in renunciation of alcohol — 1500 according to a later entry in Fr Popiełuszko 's diary — their thoughts were elsewhere. As Fr Bogucki called for special prayers for 'brave Fr Jerzy', one could hear and see women sobbing in the packed church. Mass ended with a particularly emotional rendering of 'Boże coś Polskę', the old hymn asking God to restore Poland's freedom.

At about 9 that evening, a uniformed policeman (the brother of a priest, the diary noted) told Fr Popiełuszko to gather his things together, as if he was being moved. He was taken first to a doctor and then to the room where he had been interrogated.

Shortly afterwards, he was joined by his two lawyers and the prosecutor who announced that the authorities had decided to release him, adding that further proceedings would depend on his behaviour.

At 9.45 pm, Fr Popiełuszko was free. Driven back to St Stanisław's he found burning candles laid out on the forecourt of the churchyard in the shape of a cross and the letter V and a crowd of people waiting outside the presbytery. 'Standing at a window, Fr Bogucki welcomed me back with tears in his eyes. My room was filled with flowers.' Before describing his return to St Stanisław's, Fr Popiełuszko noted in his diary that his release was so important it was reported in Polish radio and television news bulletins.

On the day after his release, however, he was angered by newspaper reports that neither Church authorities nor the police had known that he had a second, private flat. 'What diabolical malice,' he wrote. Fr Popiełuszko composed a brief statement in response, which was read out by fellow priests at St Stanisław's the following Sunday, 18 December. It said that his second flat had been bought for him by his aunt five years earlier, that the Church authorities had been informed of this, that he didn't know where the materials found in that flat had come from and that their presence there was a provocation.

It was a painful experience for the young priest to discover that he needed to explain himself in the face of charges thrown at him by the SB and never more painful than at his meeting with the Primate, Cardinal Glemp. It has always been difficult to be entirely objective about this encounter because the only details came from Fr Popiełuszko's diary written two weeks after the event, and in a letter he wrote immediately after the meeting on the day after his release, Wednesday, 14 December.

The only alternative version is based on the evidence of two 'close acquaintances' of Fr Popiełuszko at the Curia to whom he is said to have spoken. According to this version, Cardinal Glemp invited Fr Popiełuszko to see him on Wednesday, 14 December, at the Archbishops' House on

Miodowa Street to talk about the prosecutor's charges, and about anonymous complaints received by the Curia about his pastoral work.[5]

The Primate is said to have received a nervous Fr Popiełuszko with a pleasant smile before getting down to a candid conversation, in which the Cardinal spoke about the denunciations and the accusations of the Office for Denominational Affairs. Fr Popiełuszko, with tears in his eyes, according to this account, talked about his pastoral work, pointing out that he never did anything without the agreement of his parish priest. He described the accusations as a provocation not so much against himself as against the Church. The Primate, we are told, calmed Fr Jerzy down, recommended that he write an explanatory letter to his superiors in the Curia and said goodbye to him like a father'.

Fr Popiełuszko, however, emerged from the meeting very upset. He returned to St Stanisław's and immediately wrote a long letter to Bishop Miziołek and to Fr Król, the Chancellor of the Curia and National Chaplain of the Health Service.

Judging by the letter's opening paragraph, Fr Jerzy was offended not only by criticism of his work but also by a suggestion that he might be guilty of a kind of spiritual pride or vanity.[6]

> On the 14th day of December, His Eminence the Cardinal and Primate asserted in conversation with me that I have done nothing in the Medical Pastorate and that I should ask for a change of work. As for my work with the workers, he said that I am seeking only personal fame and glory. I present to you here that which my conscience and my heart dictate. The adoption of a decision I leave, humbly, in the hands of the Church authorities...

There followed sixteen paragraphs describing in detail his not inconsiderable achievements in his work with medical personnel, insisting that he did not attach people to himself but to God and the Church. He briefly outlined his duties at St Stanisław's, where the best judge of his work, he said, was Fr

Bogucki. As for the question of his relationship with the workers, his letter ended thus:

> I entered the workers' milieu at the personal request of the late Primate in August 1980. I served the workers as their chaplain in the days of triumph and I stayed with them in times of trial. I have done this work at the cost of my own free time and recreation, but not at the cost of my work as pastor of the medical profession.
>
> As for the effects of my work among the workers, only God Almighty knows that, as do the people I brought closer to God, strengthening their hope and cleansing them of hatred.

Fr Popiełuszko's letter is clearly a defence of his behaviour. It contains no suggestion of apology, nor any admission of fault. His own account of his meeting with the Primate, recorded in his diary, confirms that impression. According to that, he went to the Seminary (not to Miodowa Street) in response to a summons from Bishop Romaniuk. At the entrance he met the Primate.

> We went into a small room, and what I heard there surpassed my worst foreboding. It is true that the Primate could have been upset, for the letter written to Jaruzelski about my case cost him a great deal. But the accusations against me knocked me over. The SB during interrogation showed me greater respect. This is not an indictment. It is a pain which I see as an act of grace from God for my greater self-purification, something that will help make my work more fruitful. So I won't go into the details of that conversation.
>
> What hurt me most of all were the allegations that I had dropped my pastoral work in the health service, to which, after all, I had devoted myself heart and soul for five years. I wrote a letter about this to my superiors, Bishop Miziołek and Fr Król, who know all about my work in this sphere.
>
> Lord, what a great trial this is that you give me, but at the same time, you give me so much strength and human kindness.

These words were not written in the heat of the moment but two weeks later, when Fr Popiełuszko started his new diary.

The 'letter to Jaruzelski' referred to here was not a matter of public knowledge at the time. It was assumed later that it advised the General that his planned meeting with the Primate early in January — the first since the Pope's visit in June — could not take place if Fr Popiełuszko were to remain in prison. He was released, at any rate, after intervention by Cardinal Glemp and by Archbishop Bronislaw Dabrowski, who interceded personally with the Minister of Internal Affairs, General Kiszczak.

The Communist authorities were always delighted to see reports of dissension in the Church and went out of their way to encourage them. It was in this spirit, no doubt, that the government spokesman publicly welcomed the Primate's Christmas message to the nation, which said, among other things, that the Bishops, in accordance with the instructions of the Holy See, would be warning their priests against getting involved in politics. Mr Urban spoke as if the Church was about to crack down on the likes of Fr Popiełuszko. After the detention of Fr Popiełuszko, the Cardinal clearly felt the need to warn priests to watch their step but he also made a point of saying that the duties of a priest did not bar him from serving the nation. That was what Fr Popiełuszko believed he was doing.

Familiar themes reappeared in the young priest's diary as Christmas approached. Małgorzata Z. (one of his companions when he drove to Kielce in February) had been called in for questioning by the SB, who tried to blackmail her into collaborating with the police. Waldek Chrostowski had also been interrogated. And three days before Christmas, police searched the home of friends in Anin, the Warsaw suburb where he had once served as a curate. He knew there was more to come.

Christmas Day 1983 was the last Sunday of the month and his Mass for the Homeland was attended, according to his own estimate, by nearly 20,000 people in spite of rain. The theme of his sermon was peace on earth to men of goodwill and was made up largely of quotations from Popes John XXIII and John Paul II, and the late Cardinal Wyszyński. It should have been beyond reproach but some of the extracts, particularly from the Polish Pope, were pointed.

> There is no genuine freedom — the foundation of peace — when power is concentrated in the hands of one social class, one race or group, or when the common good becomes identified with the interests of one party which identifies itself with the State...

As Fr Popiełuszko noted in his diary, he didn't have to wait long for a reply and what he called 'revenge'. On 27 December, the Warsaw evening paper, *Express Wieczorny*, carried an article under an eye-catching headline: 'The Bachelor Flat of Citizen Popiełuszko'. The title itself was enough to suggest — no doubt intentionally — that the flat on Chłodna was some sort of love nest. It was a classic smear, made up of innuendo and lies. And it was reproduced the next day in other papers and on radio.

The article suggested, among other things, that Fr Popiełuszko's two defence lawyers behaved rather oddly when they declined to protect their client's interests by being present during the search of his flat, and that the police discovered not only illegal publications but 'other, even less religious accessories'.

The lies included the claim that neither the authorities nor the Church knew about the priest's 'conspiratorial flat'; that his friends had removed compromising political propaganda from his flat at the presbytery during his interrogation; and that the story of the 'kindly aunt' who gave him the flat was 'a fairy tale for simple-minded parishioners'.

The article, attributed to Michał Ostrowski, advised Western journalists and radio stations not to believe everything that Fr Popiełuszko said; he was slippery and evasive, it said, not just with state authorities but with his Church superiors. When going through the formalities of acquiring the flat on Chłodna, it alleged, he had concealed the fact that he was a priest and said that he was a teacher. This latter claim had an element of truth in it.

In a long letter sent to Archbishop Dąbrowski six days later, (replying to thirteen specific points in the article), Fr Popiełuszko explained that when he had applied to buy the flat, he had been told that it was part of a teachers' cooperative and one had to be a teacher to join. He had replied that it was part of his duties as a priest to teach religion, whereupon the official handling his application had said that it would make matters easier if he was registered as a teacher. Fr Popiełuszko said he had agreed to this in good faith but had not concealed his identity as a priest.

It did not seem likely that anyone who attended the Masses for the Homeland could be tempted to believe claims in the article, but after a month in which he had already spent a night in prison accused of storing ammunition and explosives and had then undergone a difficult interview with the Primate, Fr Jerzy could have been excused for feeling uncertain. His family was certainly worried. His brother, Józef, drove down from Okopy to see him, but as the diary records, he returned home reassured once he had seen how kind people were to his brother and how angry they were over the article. Other friends came to his aid.

In a letter to the Warsaw Curia on 29 December, Fr Bogucki described Fr Popiełuszko as an 'exemplary priest and a good Pole' who was 'ready and willing to help in any way, friendly, conscientious, hardworking and loved by youngsters and grown-ups alike'. Enumerating his various parish duties, his regular prayer meetings and retreats for medical personnel, Fr Bogucki confined his references to Fr Jerzy's association with workers to two points: that he had heard confessions and said Mass for striking steelworkers and students 'on the instructions of the late Stefan Cardinal Wyszyński' and that he had 'introduced lectures for workers on the Church's social teaching'.

On the last day of the month, more than fifty representatives of the medical profession wrote to Cardinal Glemp asking him to protest to the government over 'the crude and libellous attempts to compromise Fr Jerzy and the Catholic Church in Poland'. The signatories told the Primate that since Fr Popiełuszko had been looking after the spiritual needs of the health service, medical personnel had experienced a deepening of their faith, developing a greater love for one's neighbour, and participating more actively in the religious life. They said that their recent, well-attended meeting with His Eminence (organised by Fr Popiełuszko in the church of the Visitation Sisters just a few days earlier) for the traditional breaking of the Christmas wafer was clear evidence of this.

Fr Popiełuszko must have been reassured by these letters which were calculated to remove whatever doubts Cardinal Glemp may have had about his work. But that was hardly his main problem. While he had been released from custody, he was still under investigation, facing serious charges and the possibility of years in prison. The government spokesman had even said that, by rights, he should have remained in prison, under arrest.

If that wasn't bad enough, the article in *Express Wieczorny* had added slanderous suggestions, to which it was virtually impossible to reply in a land where the official censor could prevent publication. Fr Popiełuszko had decided from the start that it was beneath his dignity, as he put it, to enter into polemics with *Express Wieczorny*. The Warsaw Curia, however, sought an effective way to answer back. It saw the attack on the priest as an attack on the Church, part of a policy of sowing the seeds of division inside the Church.

Fr Popiełuszko would find further evidence of that early in the New Year.

# 7

# Torment by Interrogation

Fr Popiełuszko was supposed to go in for questioning on 5
January 1984, but the appointment was cancelled at the request
of Archbishop Dąbrowski because of the long awaited meeting
that day between General Jaruzelski and the Primate, Cardinal
Glemp. The interrogation was postponed until 12 January but
even then there were complications Lieutenant Mieczysław
Chylkiewicz, his regular interrogator, visited Fr Popiełuszko on
Tuesday, 10 January, and asked him to go in then for questioning. Fr Jerzy declined.

The next day he went with some friends to the flat on
Chłodna Street to see how they could make it secure. This, it
turned out, was a good idea, for in the shoe cupboard they
found two large envelopes containing 200 A4 size leaflets. Fr
Popiełuszko kept one copy from each envelope for his lawyer,
Edward Wende and the rest were burned by the concierge.
'Now I can understand', he wrote in his diary, 'why the investigating officer was so keen on my going along to be questioned
on Tuesday'. His fear, no doubt, was that the authorities could
have staged another search, 'discovered' the leaflets and taken
him into custody again.

When Fr Popiełuszko was questioned by Chylkiewicz in the
presence of Edward Wende on Thursday, 12 January, the day
after this discovery, he declined to answer any questions.

The next interrogation was fixed for Monday, 16 January. On the Saturday before that, Fr Popiełuszko and his friends went back to the Chłodna flat to install an alarm system and again found incriminating materials. In a top cupboard they discovered printing moulds, leaflets and a typewritten document entitled 'Report on the meeting of priests and the Primate. Notes supplied by Fr Jerzy Popiełuszko. Text authorised by Fr Kantorski.' The meeting referred to was the supposed encounter with Cardinal Glemp in December 1982 at which several priests were alleged to have accused the Primate of collaborating with the Communist authorities. (There is no mention of such a meeting in Fr Popiełuszko's diary at the time.)

His reaction to this latest discovery was one of shock. 'What satanic cunning,' he wrote in his diary on 15 January, 'in order to set the Primate at odds with me. Add to that the fact that today I found among my books a bundle of photographs depicting the Primate as an internee at Białołęka [the internment camp on the northern edge of Warsaw]. I don't even feel any malice towards them, just a strange pity. How is it possible?... Are they still Poles? How can they sell themselves in this way?'

For the underground editors of Fr Popiełuszko's diaries this discovery raised an interesting question. Fr Kantorski, they said, had been interrogated by police on 21 December and asked specifically about this same document. But how could the police have known of the existence of a document that had not been discovered when the flat on Chłodna had been searched? The only answer, the editors concluded, was that the SB had written it themselves. It seems possible, if not likely, that the SB were seeking to take Fr Popiełuszko into custody once more, thus reversing the decision of Generals Jaruzelski and Kiszczak to release the priest in December. But if that were the case, were they doing so with or without the knowledge of the Generals? Whatever the answer, Fr Popiełuszko did not report any further discoveries in the flat on Chłodna.

For the next six months and more the campaign against him was to be confined to frequent interrogation and abusive anonymous letters. As he wrote in his diary in the middle of January, his interrogator had told him he would be called in for questioning every week.

> This is simply a way of tormenting me. But Almighty God gives me strength of spirit. Mentally I feel fine. People are wonderful. All the time there are flowers. All the time letters speaking of solidarity. At the Mass which was said for me on 11 January, the church [that of the Visitation of the Blessed Virgin Mary in Warsaw's New Town] was packed. It was also surrounded by police cars and vans. The people chanted 'God Bless'. In the evening after an interrogation our church is full of people. For today's 10 am Mass [the one he said every Sunday] people couldn't get into the church. It's been like that for the last couple of Sundays.

Fr Popiełuszko may have been feeling fine but the Warsaw Curia remained concerned about how the Church should respond to the public attacks on him. The Secretariat of the Episcopate was used to receiving confidential complaints about him and other priests, but there had been nothing confidential about the publicity in December.

Writing on 6 February from the Secretariat of the Primate, Bishop Jerzy Dąbrowski (who was effectively Archbishop Bronisław Dąbrowski's deputy) said that in their treatment of the Fr Popiełuszko case, the official media had broken the law. It was a crime, for instance, to publish information about a person which might expose that person to loss of professional trust. It was also a crime, punishable by as much as one year in prison, to publish details without permission of a criminal investigation beyond the initials of the person being investigated. Not only had all of these rules been broken in the case of Fr Popiełuszko, the Bishop wrote, but the priest had been the subject of a slanderous article in *Express Wieczorny*, details of which had been repeated on television and at a news conference given by government spokesman Jerzy Urban.

There is no doubt that this was an organised campaign against Fr Popiełuszko, one that counted on his not having any chance to defend himself and was intended to intimidate him... Would the Minister be so kind as to instruct those departments which have an interest in writing about 'the activities' of Fr Popiełuszko that they should observe the law as guaranteed by the legislation of the Polish People's Republic.[1]

The official reply delivered more than six weeks later said it was 'astonishing' that the Bishop had complained about the frequent interrogations and supposed 'harassment' of Fr Popiełuszko. The charges against Fr Popiełuszko were such that he should be in custody under provisional arrest; it was solely at the request of the Secretary of the Episcopate (Archbishop Dąbrowski) that he was not in prison. Yet, 'the promised steps to prevent further criminal activity by Fr Popiełuszko' had not been forthcoming. The priest was 'still misusing the pulpit to make pronouncements of punishable content' and this could make it necessary to take 'preventive measures' under the law.[2]

There is no evidence that Archbishop Dąbrowski ever agreed that Fr Popiełuszko was involved in 'criminal activity', so it is difficult to imagine that he promised to stop it. The tone of the exchange between Bishop Dąbrowski and the Office for Denominational Affairs, however, was a telling indication of the depths to which relations between Church and State had descended. Only a couple of weeks earlier the Office had threatened that if the Church hierarchy did not take steps to prevent churches being used for political purposes, the government reserved the right to take action under its legal powers.

At this moment the Church was being frustrated by the authorities on several scores, but it was also prospering because of the authorities' actions. It was seen as the champion of the humane social ideals of Solidarity, the focus of an alternative culture, a haven for opposition thought and the source of assistance to those who had suffered for political reasons. More people were attending church and some of them were members of the Party.

Other members of the Party, of course, deeply resented the fact that the Church had become one of the most successful, if not the most successful, in Europe, let alone Communist Eastern Europe. It had more than 21,000 priests, more than 7000 young men training to be priests, nearly 15,000 churches and over 600 new ones under construction, a Catholic University in Lublin, a Catholic Theology Academy in Warsaw, and, of course, a Polish Pope in the Vatican.

To those in the Party and, in particular, in the Security Service who deplored the 'privileges' enjoyed by the Church in Poland, it must have been especially irksome to see that their target, Fr Jerzy Popieluszko, enjoyed immense and steadily growing popularity, despite their campaign against him. It is easy to imagine how soft and indecisive Generals Jaruzelski and Kiszczak might have seemed to those who really did believe in driving the priests into the catacombs.

By the end of January 1984, the public drama had gone out of the Popieluszko case and had been replaced by the wearing routine of interrogations. Did meetings take place at the flat? Did people go there to pick up leaflets or cassette recordings? Did he give anyone else the keys to the flat? Who edited his sermons? Were their contents agreed with anyone else? Who financed the performance of the actors at the Masses for the Homeland? Had he given interviews to the underground press? Or to foreign correspondents, and what did they offer in exchange? Who allowed the Masses for the Homeland to be recorded and how were the recordings distributed throughout the country?

To these and many other questions Fr Popieluszko exercised his right not to provide testimony. He did the same on 6 March when confronted with audio tapes confiscated from the Chłodna flat and asked why the people recorded on them addressed him as 'chief'.

By this time the interrogations were getting him down. On 15 March, Bishop Miziołek, as Vicar General of the Warsaw Curia, wrote to the authorities advising them that Fr

Popiełuszko could not answer a summons to appear at the Ministry of the Interior on Rakowiecka Street because of duties which could not be postponed. On 20 March, in a letter to Archbishop Dąbrowski, Fr Jerzy said that the interrogations, at which his lawyers were no longer allowed to be present, were getting in the way of his duties as a priest. He had just received his tenth summons to report for questioning and the SB were now trying to get him along to the Ministry for questioning as a witness in another investigation. It was, he said, 'absolute torment'.

There were, however, compensations. In February, he had lunch with Bishop Kraszewski who handed him a rosary, a present from the Pope. A few days later, Cardinal Glemp gave him a book inscribed with his blessing. And whenever he went to the Mostowski Palace to be interrogated, parishioners, friends and supporters would be there to see him go in, and they would wait, with flowers, to see him come out.

As already stated, Fr Popiełuszko did not go out of his way to enlist the interest of Western correspondents. At the time, in fact, Western journalists were well occupied with news stories of more immediate interest, although some involved issues and causes that had featured in his sermons.

In the second week of January, a well known and highly respected defence lawyer, Maciej Bednarkiewicz, was arrested in Warsaw on the morning he was preparing to make a speech at a lawyers' meeting with the Primate, Cardinal Glemp. He was accused, according to the initial announcement, of aiding a police deserter, offering inducements to give false evidence and incitement to betray state secrets. The news was of particular interest to the BBC office in Warsaw because it had consulted Bednarkiewicz in May the previous year when a suspect, supposedly disaffected young policeman had contacted us following the raid on the Primate's charity at St Martin's and just before the death of Grzegorz Przemyk.

The lawyer now detained had investigated the St Martin's raid and was the legal representative of Przemyk's mother, Barbara Sadowska. The trial of six men — two policemen, two ambulance men and two doctors — charged with responsibility for the boy's death was expected to start within weeks.

The general reaction to the arrest was that it was prompted by the approaching trial and that the authorities were intent on thwarting justice. The government spokesman, Jerzy Urban, vigorously denied this connection but the details of the charges against Bednarkiewicz contradicted him. He was accused (among other things) of inciting a deserter from the ZOMO riot police to reveal secrets about that organisation and the operations of the SB, and of using the deserter to try to find witnesses who would be prepared to testify for money that policemen were responsible for the death of Grzegorz Przemyk. Mr Urban also announced that investigations into the Przemyk case were being reopened because of new evidence. State television reported later that one of the accused ambulance men had admitted causing the boy an injury which could have proved fatal.

It seemed obvious that the authorities were determined to ensure that the policemen were not found guilty of causing the boy's death. This sentiment was reinforced a month later by one of Poland's leading defence lawyers in an open letter to General Jaruzelski. Władysław Siła-Nowicki, at the age of seventy, was a tall, bald-headed, somewhat daunting man and a legendary figure, having fought in the underground Home Army against the Germans in the Second World War and having been sentenced to death more than once by the Communists after the war. Now he told the General that Maciej Bednarkiewicz had been cynically 'framed' in order to protect those responsible for the death of Grzegorz Przemyk. Bednarkiewicz, he wrote, had indeed been in contact with a man claiming to be a ZOMO deserter in March of the previous year. But this man had made the approach. Bednarkiewicz had told Siła-Nowicki in August that he had not taken up the case because he considered him suspect. Bednarkiewicz's arrest, Siła-Nowicki wrote, indicated a profound corruption on the part of certain representatives of state power.

The case of Maciej Bednarkiewicz had two features in

common with that of Fr Popiełuszko. Both men were intimately associated with the Przemyk case and both were targets of criminal proceedings based on fabricated evidence and false charges. In both cases there was also a strong suspicion that although Generals Jaruzelski and Kiszczak may not have sanctioned or known about everything that SB officers did on their behalf, they would stand by them whenever possible.

As it happened, a series of mysterious and unexplained incidents which had a direct, almost prophetic bearing on the fate of Fr Popiełuszko were taking place at this time a considerable distance from Warsaw.

Regrettably, word failed to get through to the Western press corps which suddenly found itself preoccupied for several weeks with two 'causes célèbres'. The first concerned Fr Mieczysław Nowak, a curate in the parish of St Joseph the Worker in the industrial suburb of Ursus on the southwestern edge of Warsaw. He visited the offices of Western news agencies to tell them that he had been interrogated for hours by the SB and that Cardinal Glemp was giving in to pressure from the authorities and having him transferred to a country parish.

The Primate confirmed that Fr Nowak was, indeed, being transferred, but said that he was actually being promoted to parish priest. This was not good enough for some parishioners, one of whom told me that Cardinal Glemp was 'dancing to the Communists' tune'. When a local Dean called from the altar for acceptance of the transfer, he was laughed at and heckled. A small group of parishioners began a hunger strike, but by then Fr Nowak had changed his story, saying it was his duty to obey his Bishop. Fr Nowak departed, leaving behind a sizeable number of parishioners believing that the Primate was a collaborator.

Cardinal Glemp was much happier with the second of the news stories, the so-called 'war of the crosses'. Early in March, some four hundred students at an agricultural college southeast of Warsaw began a sit-in strike in protest against the removal of crucifixes from their classrooms — a development the Bishops had noted in one of their statements some months earlier. The authorities closed the college, used riot police to block a protest march and demanded that parents sign a pledge that their children would recognise the secular nature of their college. The parents refused. Thus it was that Garwolin, a quiet town on the road from Warsaw to Lublin, came to be visited almost every day by car loads of Western journalists, prompting one local priest to proclaim from the pulpit that 'Christ is now speaking from Garwolin to the whole world'.

The crisis lasted roughly one month, with the government spokesman blaming the trouble on 'expansionist clericalism', the Bishops promising to hold fast and Cardinal Glemp wondering what statesmen now found so upsetting about the crucifixes they used to see on their schoolroom walls when they were boys. Early in April a compromise was announced: crucifixes would not be allowed on schoolroom walls but they could be displayed in dormitories, worn by pupils or placed on pupils' desks.

These two affairs were perhaps, inflated out of all proportion, certainly given the fact far more sinister events elsewhere were deserving of greater attention.

Early in February, a 33-year-old farmer and former Rural Solidarity activist, Piotr Bartoszcze, failed to return to his home near the town of Inowrocław south of Bydgoszcz after visiting his brother. The next morning, his car was found in a roadside ditch with a scratch along one side of it. The engine was switched on, all doors were closed, but the rear window had been smashed in from the outside.

Piotr's brother and his father, one of the men beaten up in the Bydgoszcz incident of 1981, began a search. In a ploughed field they found four sets of footprints which were far enough apart between strides to suggest that they had been made by people who were running. The footprints led to Piotr's body lying next to a drainage well, around which the soil was all churned up. It suggested a fight. On the basis of the visual evidence it was possible to surmise that Piotr had died after a struggle with three other persons who had chased him across the field. People living nearby remembered hearing a cry of sorts around 11 pm.

The official explanation of Piotr Bartoszcze's death was that he had suffocated when soil blocked his respiratory passages while he was under the influence of alcohol. Blood tests were said to have indicated an intake of 300 gms of vodka, but the female doctor who carried out the analysis admitted that she had not been present when the blood sample was taken. A second postmortem, carried out at the family's request, confirmed the presence of alcohol, but it was in the lungs and not in the blood — a fact that argued persuasively that vodka had been poured into his throat by force. In addition, Piotr Bartoszcze was a well known teetotaller. The official version also failed to explain four deep weals on Piotr's back or why his fingers were broken. His father wrote to General Jaruzelski asking for help. His son, he said, had been murdered by the police.[3] Nothing was done. The official version prevailed.

Disturbing events elsewhere in that same Kujawy region of Poland, west of Warsaw, indicated that it was a dangerous place for anyone known to be associated with Solidarity. Four people were kidnapped on the streets of Toruń, northeast of Inowrocław, in the space of three weeks in February and March by men who identified themselves as police or SB. All four were released after forty eight hours. The tale told later by Antoni Mężydło, an engineer in a local radio and television plant and formerly a free trade union activist in Gdańsk, whose fiancée was abducted on the same day, contained features common to all four cases.[4]

Mężydło was walking home from the bus stop after work on Friday, 2 March, when an orange van pulled up sharply next to him. Three men jumped out shouting 'police'. They grabbed hold of him and shoved him onto the floor of the vehicle, which sped away before the doors had even closed. His hands were cuffed at the front, a scarf was tied over his eyes and a bag placed over his head. After two stops on the way (one of them, he thought, at a police station), Mężydło was eventually taken out of the van in woodland. For the next forty minutes or so, he was secured with handcuffs to one tree after another. At each one, his captors bombarded him with the same questions about the Solidarity underground — its leaders, its organisations, its printing presses — and every time he said he didn't know, he was struck over the head or kicked. Finally, he was told he was going to be shot. Behind him, he heard weapons being loaded. However, he was put back in the van and driven to a single-storey barrack building where they sat him down on the floor of an unheated room, securing his feet and hands to pieces of furniture. There he stayed until Sunday afternoon, interrogated for most of the time about the underground by five or six men. At one point he was stood up on his feet and punched in the stomach. When he fell he was stood up again and struck about the head, face, chest and ribs. During the first night, his blindfold was removed and the handcuffs removed for a time. His captors wore stocking masks.

Mężydło was not allowed to sleep; whenever his eyes closed, water was poured down the back of his neck. Nor was he allowed to use the lavatory. On Saturday, he remembered, they tried to get him to work for them: he could leave for the West, they said, and inform on Solidarity agencies there. On Saturday evening they said they could kill him by simulating an accident. On Sunday morning they played him a recording of his fiancée pleading with him to answer all questions. That afternoon, they took him to another room, laid him down on his back, and tied his outstretched arms to the legs of two chairs. Then they began forcing his lips apart and pouring vodka into his mouth. He spat it out.

During the final interrogation, about the whereabouts of an underground duplicator, Mężydło's shoes were taken off and the soles of his feet were beaten with a stick. There was talk of finishing him off. Eventually he was carried back to the van which was driven off amidst talk of a simulated road accident. Once again his captors poured vodka into his mouth and when he kept spitting it out they poured it all over his clothes. Shortly afterwards, the van pulled up. He was led out by one of the men who removed the scarf blindfolding him and told him to lie face

down on the ground. Mężydło looked up as the van departed
and found himself lying beside a rubbish tip. In a nearby house,
where he was able to clean up, he learned that he was in the
town of Brodnica, northeast of Toruń. He got home by train at
about one o'clock in the morning. In his bag, which one of his
captors had looped over his head, he discovered a leaflet:

> And they worshipped the dragon
> who gave power to the beast;
> and they worshipped the beast, saying
> 'Who is like the beast? Who is able to fight him?'
>
>                                  (Apocalypse 13,4)

Communiqué Number 1

We announce the formation of the Anti-Solidarity
Organisation. Jaruzelski's inept team and the bureaucratised
security service will not succeed in overcoming the cancer
consuming our society, the conspiracy or the vogue for opposition. Solidarity is that cancer. We will try to answer the
question posed in the Apocalypse — we will fight the beast.
The contest has begun. We will strike wherever we are not
expected. We will operate under the banner of various institu-
tions, maybe even of the Solidarity TKK. So beware. We have
given a sample of what we are capable of.

    The Leadership Group of the OAS
    Kujawy and Pomerania Region

These disturbing details of the Bartoszcze case and the Toruń
abductions did not become publicly known until months later.
At his Mass for the Homeland at the end of March, Fr
Popiełuszko gave no indication that he knew about them. In his
sermon, he mentioned all the key issues of the moment — the
Solidarity leaders still imprisoned without trial, the young people
of Garwolin standing up for the cross, the Przemyk case and the
arrest of Maciej Bednarkiewicz — but said nothing about Piotr
Bartoszcze or the abductions.

    The emergence of this violent group of vigilantes, apparently determined to make up for the failings of the government by taking the law into their own hands, confirmed that within the ranks of supposed government supporters there were some who were disenchanted with Jaruzelski's handling of Solidarity. Judging by Antoni Mężydło's account, they were closely associated with the police and could count on their traces being covered up.

# 8

# Indictment and Amnesty

As spring came to Warsaw in 1984, Fr Popiełuszko seems to have been bearing up quite well under the pressure of regular interrogations at the Mostowski Palace, in spite of some upsetting surprises. During his questioning on 11 April, for instance, the police abused and even threatened a number of middle-aged and elderly women who were waiting for him outside with flowers.

There were nevertheless some memorable high points. On Fr Jerzy's name day — the feast of St George, which happened that year to be the day after Easter Sunday — St Stanisław's parish church was overflowing for a midday Mass said for his intentions. Afterwards, at a gathering in the crypt, he received gifts from workers at Huta Warszawa and the car factory as well as from the parish's volunteer guards, the 'Solidarity gorillas', as one volunteer named them. And according to the diary, the 'gorillas' counted as many as eleven hundred people bringing flowers. It was a remarkably successful week for Fr Popiełuszko. He missed his next appointed interrogation by producing a doctor's certificate but two days later, on the last Sunday of the month, he officiated as usual at the Mass for the Homeland. This was a special occasion, the third anniversary of the blessing of the Solidarity banner of Huta Warszawa, attended by Bishop Kraszewski, Andrzej Wajda, the film director, and by two

Solidarity stalwarts from Gdańsk, Alina Pienkowska and Anna Walentynowicz. Fr Jerzy said Mass on the balcony over the front entrance to the church, looking down on a congregation estimated by the Bishop to number 30,000. 'For us', the diary recorded, 'it was a kind of victory.'

On the morning of May Day, Fr Popiełuszko's Mass for the workers was attended by a congregation only slightly smaller, but they soon discovered that the police were also there in force. In a letter to the Episcopate the next day, Fr Jerzy said that the police closed off all streets around the church and stopped all buses and trams so that members of the congregation could not make their way home in peace but were forced together in one place. 'These people were then attacked with water cannons. Jets of water actually reached the grounds of the church. This was not a matter of breaking up a demonstration, for no demonstration took place; it was an attack on the faithful leaving church after Mass...'[1]

At Warsaw's St John's Cathedral, where pro-Solidarity demonstrations normally began after Mass, no real demonstration was possible because the police presence was so great. The only other dramatic incident on what was a very quiet May Day took place in Gdańsk, where Lech Wałęsa and supporters forced their way into the official demonstration and stayed in it long enough to march past the reviewing stand flashing victory signs to puzzled dignitaries.

Later that day, government spokesman Jerzy Urban alleged that in Gdańsk, Warsaw and Częstochowa, churches had been used in attempts to create disturbances. The main television news program reported that 'some people' were asking whether the time had not come 'to drive the political traders from the temples'.

Both statements foreshadowed a development the following day that did not become public knowledge until 1985: the Minister in charge of the Office for Denominational Affairs, Adam Łopatka, despatched a lengthy letter to the Primate himself, complaining that at church services on 1 May, a number of priests had 'created a climate conducive to political excesses'.

He made specific mention, among others, of Fr Popiełuszko, whose May Day sermon he alleged had provoked a demonstration when his congregation left the church, causing a disturbance of public order. The Minister warned Cardinal Glemp that if Fr Popiełuszko and Fr Jankowski were to continue making statements that stirred people up, the authorities would be obliged to speed up criminal proceedings against them and take them to court.

On the evening of Constitution Day, the overflow crowd outside St John's Cathedral during Mass was hemmed in by police lines and water cannons more tightly than ever. The last bars of the final hymn at the end of Mass had scarcely died away before police loudspeakers began warning the crowd that they could not depart in the direction of the city centre. With all other exits closed, the people moved into Old Town Market Square, where they remained for about half an hour chanting the names of Lech Wałęsa and Solidarity, calling for the release of political prisoners, waving Polish flags and shouting 'Tu Jest Polska', (Here is Poland, This is Poland). Riot police then attacked. In the ensuing chase through narrow streets normally the haunt of tourists, Karol Małcużyński and I found ourselves invited with others to take refuge in a private home with no questions asked, as if this was a perfectly normal occurrence. Emerging shortly afterwards, we found that the crowds had been expertly driven down from the Old Town onto the riverside meadows below, where they were quickly dispersed or taken into custody by riot control units assisted by mounted police.

When General Jaruzelski flew to Moscow the next day for his first formal meeting with Konstantin Chernenko, newly installed as Soviet leader following the death of Yury Andropov, it seemed obvious what had prompted the events of the previous days. The General wanted to take with him fresh examples of his firm handling of the political opposition. Curiously, though, the authorities were being less than firm in a matter which Soviet comrades, no doubt, considered supremely important.

For some two weeks, the country's top political prisoners — 'the Eleven' accused of trying to overthrow the State system by force — had not been allowed to receive visitors or see their lawyers. Asked why, the government spokesman, Jerzy Urban, said he didn't know. After prison visits were resumed some days later, Solidarity sources revealed that a United Nations representative had met some of the prisoners at the beginning of the month and told them that they could be set free without trial if they agreed to go abroad for six months and gave a pledge not to engage in political activity when they returned. Asked about this, Mr Urban had nothing to say. Almost immediately, however, word came that the authorities had dropped their demand that the prisoners should go abroad; they could be released in Poland as long as they gave a satisfactory pledge. Moreover, if the Eleven were released, all other political prisoners would be freed as well.

At a news conference on 3 May, the government spokesman, Jerzy Urban, was unable to say why the 'Eleven' accused of trying to overthrow the state by force-had not been allowed to see visitors or their lawyers for two weeks. In a matter of days, however, it emerged that the authorities were engaged in delicate, secret talks in which the Eleven were being offered their freedom without trial if they agreed to refrain from political activity for a number of years.

The negotiations were conducted with the active encouragement of the Church through intermediaries whom the Eleven knew and respected. But the form the talks took and the secrecy surrounding them could not disguise the fact that the authorities themselves were negotiating with men supposedly guilty of seeking the overthrow of the Communist state.

Within days of the government offer becoming known, Adam Michnik made his attitude known in a message smuggled out of the Rakowiecka prison. He was not taking part in the talks, he said, because a prisoner was not in a position to negotiate. After being imprisoned for two and a half years without cause, he demanded either to be tried or released unconditionally.

On Sunday 13 May, Janusz Onyszkiewicz, the most reliable of Solidarity sources, informed me that the government offer, which required a pledge of no involvement in politics for three years, had been finally rejected by the Eleven.

Acceptance, could have been interpreted as an admission of guilt by innocent men and a renunciation of Solidarity. It would also have discredited the intermediaries and the Church which had been caught, according to Adam Michnik, in the government's 'negotiations trap'. Writing a year later, in yet another spell in prison, he would describe the authorities' use of the Church and of friends of the prisoners, people of supreme honesty, to promote their scheme as an act of 'satanic cunning' — a term once used by Fr Popiełuszko.

After negotiations had failed, a joint statement — with no mention of failure — announced that government and Church representatives were engaged in confidential talks on solving the 'problem' of the Eleven and others imprisoned for political offences.

The authorities may have hoped that this statement would help cover up their loss in a battle of wills to the men behind bars. But it could hardly have done so for those in government service who knew what had happened and who may have believed — as did the OAS kidnappers in Toruń — that Jaruzelski and his colleagues were too soft. For some, no doubt, the negotiations with the Eleven, which were seen by Adam Michnik as a devilish trick, were not clever at all but proof that the Party and state leadership did not have the courage to bring to a conclusion what it had set in motion with the arrests.

While the government's performance in the weeks and months ahead would confirm them in this view, there were cases in which the authorities did not hesitate to use their powers decisively. When Professor Klemens Szaniawski was elected Rector of Warsaw University by democratic vote, the Minister of Higher Education simply vetoed his appointment because of his association with Solidarity. A Warsaw historian and Solidarity activist, Jacek Szymanderski, was arrested after petitioning the Sejm calling for a special status for political prisoners. In

Wrocław, Józef Pinior, one of the Solidarity underground's
national leaders until his capture in 1983, was sent to prison for
two years.

All this happened in May 1984. But Fr Popiełuszko demonstrated how little he had changed under pressure from the
authorities when he spoke at his Mass for the Homeland in May.
In a sermon on the virtues of truth and courage, Fr Jerzy
touched on an event of supreme importance to Jaruzelski, the
local elections due in the middle of June. The leaders of the
Solidarity underground had already issued an appeal for a
boycott stating that the only way to express disapproval of the
government was by not voting at all.

Armed with quotations from Pope John Paul II and the late
Cardinal Wyszyński, Fr Popiełuszko reached a similar conclusion in carefully measured moral terms.

> To a large extent we ourselves are to blame for our loss of
> freedom if, out of fear or by taking the easy way out, we
> consent to evil and even vote for the mechanism by which it
> functions. If, out of fear or by taking the easy way out, we
> support the mechanism through which evil works, then we
> have no right to condemn that evil since we ourselves become
> its creators and help to make it legal...[2]

Nobody, including foreign observers such as myself and least of
all the SB observers in attendance that evening, could have been
in any doubt about the meaning of Fr Popiełuszko's words.
Earlier in the Mass, he had read from a proclamation issued by
the Polish Bishops before the crucial national elections of
January 1947 spelling out, among other things, the right of
Catholic voters not to vote for candidates whose programs and
methods were 'inimical... to the good of the nation, Christian
morality and the Catholic view of the world'. (Under the allied
agreements at Yalta and Potsdam, the 1947 elections were
supposed to be free and unfettered but were neither. The British
and American governments protested but the Communists had
consolidated their hold on Poland.)

Fr Popiełuszko knew very well what he was doing and to judge from his diary entry on 8 June, he rather enjoyed the official response. 'This must have hurt them, for a piece appeared this week in all the papers throughout the country and it was reported in radio news bulletins for a whole day that the views of Fr Popiełuszko are his own private views.'

The article in question, supposedly based on comments by unnamed representatives of the Episcopate, tried to give the impression that Fr Popiełuszko's views on the elections were being disowned by the Episcopate. But when the government spokesman, Jerzy Urban, announced after the elections that some 75 per cent of the electorate had voted (as opposed to the 57 per cent claimed by the Solidarity underground) he remarked, rather peevishly, that the government saw no need to share the credit for its achievement with any 'spiritual authorities' since it had received no help from them.

By the time the elections took place in June, however, they were no longer of such burning interest. Other developments seemed to quicken the pace of political development. Not only had the authorities announced the arrest of Bogdan Lis from Gdańsk, one of the original leaders of the Solidarity underground; they had also announced that four of the Eleven, those previously associated with KOR — Jacek Kuroń, Adam Michnik, Henryk Wujec and Zbigniew Romaszewski — would go on trial before the Warsaw Military District Court on 13 July.

No one could quite believe that the government which had tried so hard in May to avoid the embarrassment of trying these men was ready to take them to court now, knowing that the accused were looking forward to the opportunity to speak in court. But a more absorbing trial had already begun in Warsaw on the last day of May, that of the six men accused in connection with the death of the teenage schoolboy, Grzegorz Przemyk.

As I hurried along the corridors of the huge court house on the opening day, I practically bumped into Fr Popiełuszko and Władysław Siła-Nowicki going in the opposite direction. They told me where to find the court room but said the police had refused to let either of them enter. 'Gentlemen,' they were told, 'you have no right to go in.'

As an accredited correspondent, I had a special pass for that day and I was able to get past the barriers placed across the corridor and past the policemen, but I was not allowed to take a tape recorder into the court. The right to record and to film appeared to be granted exclusively to technicians from the SB. Moreover, it soon became obvious that the SB was exercising some control over proceedings. One man in particular caught my attention. Dark haired and with a very pale and unusually smooth facial complexion, he always sat towards the back of the court room on the public benches. Whenever he left the room, this was invariably followed by the announcement of a recess. Whenever the room filled up after a recess, his re-entry was followed almost immediately by the return of the judge.

Fr Popiełuszko's diary contained an interesting entry on the same topic: 'The control and direction of the trial', he wrote, 'is being exercised from the room belonging to the basic Party organisation.' According to the underground editors and publishers of the diaries, this was room 218a. On the basis of information gathered with the help of bugging devices, among other things, the editors said that a conference took place in this room at 8.15 am every day the court was in session. A Colonel Bieniasz and a Colonel Pawlowski, who were permanently stationed in the room, would talk over specially installed telecommunication lines to a General, determining the course of the trial. Monitors were unable to catch the name of the General, but they were able to establish that room 218a was the source of instructions passed to the judges, the prosecutor, the police in charge of security and agents planted among members of the public.

The trial was a disgrace, not least for the way in which the Chief Prosecutor, a Mrs Bardonowa, behaved as if she was defending the two policemen in the dock and not prosecuting them. When a key prosecution witness took the stand — one of Przemyk's friends who had followed him to the police station after his detention and stood outside listening to his cries of pain — she set out to show him up as an unreliable witness by means of aggressive questioning and jumping on any sign of hesitation. This performance prompted an exchange of satisfied smiles between the men and women among whom, as a latecomer, I had found an empty seat. It was then that I realised I was sharing a bench with the SB.

The evidence against the police, however, was very strong. Cezary Filozof, the school pal who was taken to the police station with Przemyk, said that he saw the policemen beating his friend. The family doctor, a woman, who sent Przemyk to hospital, said that he had told her that the police had beaten him. The hospital doctor who had operated on the boy, said his internal injuries were like those caused by car accidents and could not have been caused by a single blow unless something with a surface of 20 to 25 centimetres had been applied with great force. Michal Wysocki, the ambulance man who had supposedly confessed to causing Przemyk a possibly fatal injury by treading on his stomach, withdrew all his previous statements and said his confession had been forced out of him by a police colonel.

Finally, a team of forensic medical experts told the court that they had concluded, after considering all the evidence, that Przemyk's fatal injuries had been inflicted in a series of blows by something hard and blunt such as a boot, a fist, an elbow or a knee. The injuries were such, they said, that even if the two doctors who had examined Przemyk at the first aid clinic had made a correct diagnosis, they would have had little chance of saving the young man's life. And even if one of the ambulance men had trodden on Przemyk this would not have been fatal, it would only have aggravated injuries sustained previously. They confirmed that the eyewitness evidence of Cezary Filozof, who said that Przemyk had been beaten inside the police station, agreed with their own medical findings.

At the time, this evidence seemed to be crucial, even decisive, but another five weeks were to pass before the judges would hand down their verdicts.

It came as no surprise when Fr Popiełuszko spoke of justice

and uses of the law at the June Mass for the Homeland. Calling openly — as had the Primate and the Bishops a week earlier — for the release of political prisoners, he seemed also to be speaking directly to members of the legal profession.

> ... the paragraphs and regulations of the law are frequently used not only to seek out the truth but also to torment man. We should examine our conscience and consider to what extent each of us has the courage to stand up for justice...[3]

The reference to torment may well have had something to do with his own ordeal of regular and wearing interrogations. At the same time, Fr Jerzy was finding it irksome to be a celebrity. 'It's difficult for me to appear in public because people start cheering and I have to autograph pictures and books. I would like to be on my own and able to concentrate on my work. But as it is, it's a treadmill from morning till night.'

It was not long after that diary entry, towards the end of June, that I had my only private conversation with Fr Popiełuszko, in very public circumstances. It was at a reception at the residence of the Australian Ambassador, an occasion attended by many notable guests including writers and independent members of parliament. But while they all went out onto the terrace or down into the garden, for it was a fine evening, he remained, as though rooted to the spot, half in and half out of the doors opening onto the terrace. He was smoking a cigarette, somewhat nervously I thought, and holding it in the old-fashioned way between forefinger and second finger, leading me to conclude mistakenly that he was not a regular smoker. But there was no mistaking that here, first and foremost, was a priest whose shyness and apparent vulnerability at the edge of this social gathering belied his reputation as the admired, even beloved champion of the outlawed Solidarity movement. This priest, who could speak directly and personally, even through microphone and loudspeaker, to each of the thousands who made up his congregation at St Stanisław's and elsewhere, was not so at ease at a diplomatic party.

During our conversation, which lasted five to ten minutes, Fr Popiełuszko described one of his sessions under interrogation at the Mostowski Palace. The interrogator, he said, had floated some of the leaflets 'discovered' in the Chłodna Street flat across the table to him. The intention was that he should pick them up and maybe provide the police with incriminating fingerprints. Instead he simply lifted the skirts of his cassock and let the leaflets land there.

He said nothing about some nasty anonymous letters he had been receiving. In fact, he must have just received one of the worst. It was dated 16 June.

> you dirty fascist!
> Your mates should not be surprised to find you shortly with your throat slit. you whore. Say a prayer, it might help you a bit. You degenerate creature.[4]

In his diary entry of 26 June, Fr Popiełuszko said he had told his congregation at the end of the Mass for the Homeland about the many anonymous letters he had been receiving. 'I could see tears in people's eyes. For a long time after the Mass, the crowd chanted "God Bless You". On the 25th at 9 am, I left for Gdańsk with Fr Jancarz.'

These were Fr Popiełuszko's last words in his black exercise book.

There was, in the meantime, a barely perceptible change taking place politically. In a sermon in the town of Radom south of Warsaw in the middle of June, the Primate, Cardinal Glemp, had made a well argued call for the release of all political prisoners. Some days later, the Bishops, meeting in conference under his chairmanship, had called for 'a new political climate' in Poland. There were no grounds for expecting the authorities to respond. But the first days of July did bring rumours of the release of political prisoners under an amnesty to mark the fortieth anniversary of 'People's Poland' on the 22nd of the month. Jerzy Urban did not deny this possibility but said that the question of an amnesty had not been considered by the authorities.

On 2 July, Fr Popiełuszko was informed at the Prosecutor's Office that the charges against him had been extended to cover the period ending on the last day of June. He was also told that it had been decided that his alleged offences could be termed 'continuous' and 'persistent', which meant that sentence upon conviction could be increased by half. On 6 July, Bogdan Bujak, elder brother of Zbigniew, the underground leader, went on trial in Warsaw for alleged participation in a demonstration. On 10 July, Maciej Bednarkiewicz, the lawyer whose arrest in January prevented his participation in the Przemyk trial, was freed on bail awaiting his own trial. On 11 July, an indictment was lodged against the writer, Marek Nowakowski, accusing him of cooperating with foreign centres of subversion to get his works published abroad. On 12 July, the final act of indictment against Fr Popiełuszko was signed and delivered by Deputy Prosecutor Anna Jackowska, who had delivered her closing speech at the Przemyk trial only the day before.

On Friday, 13 July, the most sensitive political trial for many years began in the Warsaw Military District Court. Jacek Kuroń, Adam Michnik, Zbigniew Romaszewski and Henryk Wujec — all prominent figures in Solidarity and before that in KOR, the Committee for the Defence of the Workers — were ready to answer the charge of trying to overthrow the State system by force.

It came as no surprise to anyone familiar with the trials of Soviet dissidents in the 1970s to be told that the court room was too small to accommodate anyone other than close relatives of the accused and a few official Polish journalists. Friends and colleagues of the accused, among them Lech Wałęsa and elderly founding members of KOR, crowded the steps leading up to the court entrance, but eventually left on learning that the accused had been taken in by another door. Journalists and diplomats who remained throughout the day were repeatedly moved on by policemen, one of whom was heard to mutter:

'Can't think why you bother. Don't you know there's going to be an amnesty?'

This remark coincided with yet another unconfirmed report that a parliamentary commission would be discussing an amnesty the following week. When the KOR trial was adjourned until the Wednesday of the coming week, we were left to wonder how it was possible for the government to pursue its political enemies with such apparent vigour in the courts while preparing to set them all free.

The following Monday, 16 July, brought two examples of how the law could be subordinated to the Polish *racja stanu*. The court in the Przemyk case reassembled that morning to hear the verdict of the three judges. No one expected justice to be done. Indeed, at the very beginning of the trial, the dead boy's mother, Barbara Sadowska, had withdrawn from her own suit as a private plaintiff because she did not want to lend her name or legitimacy to a trial in which there was no chance of a just verdict. Her prediction was confirmed when Judge Jankowski and his two colleagues swept into court and began reading their decision.

The two policemen were acquitted and the two doctors were let off under an amnesty. But the two ambulance men were sentenced to two and a half years in prison, having been found guilty on charges quite different from those for which they had been tried. As Judge Jankowski explained, he and his colleagues had been unable to establish that one of the ambulance men had beaten or kicked Grzegorz Przemyk. Instead, they had found both of them guilty of treating him roughly and so worsening his condition. This, the judges said, dispensed with the need to reopen proceedings and hold a new trial.

As for the cause of young Przemyk's injuries, the judges made the remarkable statement that nobody had been identified as having taken part in beating him. This in spite of the evidence of Cezary Filozof that he saw the police beating Przemyk and in spite of the corroborative evidence of the forensic experts who said their findings agreed with Filozof's testimony. It was difficult to understand how General Jaruzelski and General

Kiszczak (the Minister responsible for the police) could have allowed the system of justice to be compromised so blatantly, so clumsily and so publicly. But they did so, just as a measure designed to appease the opposition at home was set in motion.

In the evening of that same Monday, it was announced that an appeal for an amnesty for political prisoners had been sent to the Sejm by PRON, the pro-government front organisation that Jaruzelski had created as the mouthpiece of 'public' opinion. This confirmed that an amnesty was on the way.

On Wednesday, the presiding judge adjourned the KOR trial indefinitely and made it clear that he did not expect the court to meet again. The next day, the Party daily, *Trybuna Ludu*, clarified that there would be no forgiving or forgetting for the accused because 'the odium attaching to political subversives and agents will stay with these men forever'. When the amnesty was announced in the Sejm on Saturday, 21 July — in the presence, incidentally, of the Soviet Prime Minister, Nikolai Tikhonov — it was more extensive than anyone had expected.

All political prisoners, some 650 of whom only fifty one had been sentenced, would be set free over a period of thirty days. Anyone under investigation or indictment but still at liberty awaiting trial would also benefit from the amnesty. None of those set free, including many thousands of common criminals, would be required to sign a pledge of any sort.

On the face of it this was a dramatic and welcome announcement. Not only did it mean freedom for the Eleven, four of whom had been in the dock only days earlier; it also looked as though Fr Popieluszko would be a beneficiary.

Solidarity activists in the underground or abroad were told that no proceedings would be taken against them if they gave themselves up by the end of the year. That seemed an unlikely prospect but General Jaruzelski, in the presence of the Soviet Prime Minister, had to sound humane but tough. The amnesty, he said, was an act of goodwill, but it did not signify a change in the government's attitude to anti-State activity. For that, he threatened, there would be no leniency. And the offer was not unconditional. Anyone committing the same or a similar alleged offence before the end of 1986 would forfeit the benefits. This amounted to a demand that those amnestied should abstain for more than two years from the sort of activity which the authorities dubbed politically subversive and criminal.

In effect, the government was trying to achieve by means of the amnesty what it had failed to achieve in negotiations with the Eleven in May. Instead of offering freedom in exchange for a pledge of 'good behaviour' from eleven political prisoners, General Jaruzelski was letting them go with the warning that one false step could put them behind bars again.

Lech Wałęsa was quick to point out that unless the amnesty was followed by political reforms the prisons could be filling up again within months. Nonetheless, he and six other Solidarity leaders, including Zbigniew Bujak of the Warsaw underground, issued a statement welcoming the releases with joy and restating Solidarity's aspirations. The mood of the country was lifted. People gathered as close to prison gates as the police would allow to wait for their husbands, fathers, brothers, friends or simply heroes to come out, and it was clear that their freedom far outweighed any fears for the future.

What was less clear to any of us at the time was the serious concern for Fr Popiełuszko among those close to him. Within days of the amnesty being announced, five men from the steel works wrote to Archbishop Dąbrowski asking him to support with the Primate their suggestion that Fr Jerzy should be sent abroad to study the Church's social teaching. Continued work in Poland, they said, would 'inevitably expose him to acts of repression at the hands of the state authorities' Noting that Fr Popiełuszko had been the target of 'provocation, slander, blackmail and even attempts to threaten his life', the steelworkers said they felt a moral responsibility for the priest because of the amnesty and the possibility that he would benefit from it 'under the declared conditions'.[5]

The letter did not elaborate on this point but it was at the heart of the workers' anxiety. Solidarity leaders and activists released from prison could and probably would resume their former activities and, given the experience gained by the under-

ground in the previous two and a half years, they had a reasonable chance of not being caught. This could not be said of Fr
Popiełuszko, who had been indicted primarily because of his
monthly sermons. As a priest, he could not desist from giving
sermons, nor could he stop saying in his sermons what his principles and faith dictated.

Hence the unusually moving and defiant sermon by Fr
Bogucki at the Mass for the Homeland on 29 July. Fr
Popiełuszko was saying the Mass and made a brief statement at
the start thanking God for answering prayers for the release of
those imprisoned unjustly and voicing hopes for the future. For
his parish priest, however, even his opening words suggested a
certain urgency. 'Dear Fr Jerzy, we are happy that you are with
us and will remain with us to offer up the most holy sacrifice for
our beloved homeland.'

All of us — priests and faithful — respect public order under
the law... None of us priests operates to the detriment of the
homeland. We neither betray it, nor sell it, nor demoralise it.
Every priest, like another Christ, is marked out to offer
sacrifice and to preach the word of God... A priest cannot
abandon this mission...

Just as no one can stop the sun from shining, so no one can
forbid a priest to speak the truth. Preaching the word of God
is not politics, though the Church has the right to enter the field
of politics when politics goes against the rights of God and
man. It has the right to speak out for respect for man, for social
justice, to teach love of one's homeland and to step forward in
defence of the oppressed. These are the duties of a priest. An
attack on priests is an attack on the Church they serve, an
attack on the nation of which they are the light. 'You are the
light of the world' — Christ told the Apostles...

Dearly beloved, I had intended today to speak of
something else, but the Holy Spirit pushes me the way he wants
and has directed my thoughts... onto something that fills and
pains my heart. I consider it my pastoral duty, against the background of false courts and unjust verdicts, to speak of the

noble figure of Fr Jerzy, whom I number among the best of priests, zealous and filled with the spirit of God, and among the finest Poles, noble and dedicated wholeheartedly to their country.

Everyone can bear witness that Fr Jerzy has not incited hatred or revenge. On the contrary, he has encouraged people to love and to forgive. He has not stirred people up; he has calmed their turbulent hearts... Fr Jerzy is not an anarchist. He urges all to be peaceful, considerate and patient...

We place our hope in God that no one in Poland will do him harm...[6]

Fr Bogucki spoke for a few minutes more, but these were the words best remembered that night.

# 9
# The Final Weeks

On 24 August 1984, Fr Popiełuszko was informed officially that the case against him had been dropped on the strength of the July amnesty. Two days later, on the last Sunday of the month, the Mass for the Homeland at St Stanisław's began as ever at 7 in the evening and Fr Jerzy delivered a sermon in keeping with everything he had said since the beginning of 1982.

He spoke of the traditional devotion in Poland to the Virgin Mary and in particular about the legendary role played at various points in the nation's turbulent history by the image of the Black Madonna of Jasna Góra. During the years of the partitions, he said, when Poland was divided up for more than a century between Prussia, Austria and Russia, patriotic demonstrations were dominated by 'the religious and Marian theme', especially on territory occupied by the Russians.

Tsarist officials fought against the hymns to Mary that rang out inside the churches. The Cossack 'hundreds' saw Our Lady of Częstochowa as their enemy. Homes were searched for her image. Her pictures were torn down from the doors of houses and from the walls of buildings where they had been stuck like leaflets without words. It was with some apprehension that the Tsar's men on the investigating commissions heard about the so-called 'military feats' of the Lady of Jasna Góra and during the December Uprising they did not hesitate to describe her sometimes as the chief revolutionary.[1]

The image of the Madonna, Fr Popiełuszko said, had also been present at the birth of Solidarity in the shipyards of Gdańsk and Szczecin in August 1980. Solidarity, he went on, was not only a trade union; it was 'the Solidarity of the Polish nation', representing 'the entire nation's desire for truth, justice and freedom'. The word Solidarity could not be held in contempt or consigned to some allegedly inglorious past.

The hopes of August 1980 are still alive, and we have a moral duty to cherish them... We have to rid ourselves of fear... We have a duty to demand that the hopes of the nation should begin, at last, to be realised. We have to do this with courage and with discretion. We have to take account of the geopolitical situation in which we find ourselves but, at the same time, that situation must not serve as a convenient excuse for surrendering the rights of the nation.

There is a need then for sitting down at the table and starting a sincere dialogue... with authentic representatives of the nation... instead of creating the fiction of talks with organisations called into existence artificially. The Bishops once wrote that the parties to a social accord are the governing authorities and credible representatives of social groups, including Solidarity which has wide support.

The barriers in the way of dialogue between the nation and the authorities have to be removed completely. In the first place, the amnesty for all those imprisoned for political offences has to be carried through honestly to its conclusion. The hurt, and in particular the moral hurt done to those who loved their country in their own, disinterested way has to be repaired. Those who are in hiding must be able to return to normal life unconditionally... The Polish nation carries no hatred within itself and is therefore capable of forgiving a great deal, but only if there is a return to truth, for truth and only truth is the first condition of trust...

Fr Popieluszko's call for genuine negotiations 'between the nation and the authorities' would receive a positive answer only four years later when General Kiszczak invited Solidarity in 1988 to join in round-table talks which were to mark the beginning of the end of Communist rule in the Soviet Bloc.

In August 1984, however, the priest's appeal and the form in which it was made was a repetition of alleged criminal activity for which he had been indicted in July. The indictment had accused Fr Jerzy of giving sermons in which 'he made use of a tendentious selection of facts and referred to various historical events as well as the current social and political situation in Poland to glorify the former Solidarity and its activists while trying to demonstrate that the activities of the State authorities aim at the maximum curtailment of civil rights and freedom and the destruction of truth and justice'. One can disagree with the charge, but the sermon clearly fitted the formula.

Were the authorities, however, preparing to take Fr Popieluszko to court on the grounds that he had forfeited the benefits of the amnesty? There were no signs that they were. In fact, when the Office for Denominational Affairs had complained to the Episcopate at the beginning of August about the special welcome given in some churches to former political prisoners released under amnesty, it gave details and names of those involved in such occasions in Wrocław and Poznań but devoted little more than a line to saying that 'similar ceremonies' had been organised at St Stanisław Kostka's in Żoliborz. Fr Popieluszko was not mentioned. And yet St Stanisław's, with St Brigid's in Gdańsk was certainly one of the parish churches most visited by returning political prisoners, Catholic and non-Catholic alike. It seemed that the government was reluctant even to mention Fr Popieluszko, let alone enforce the conditions of the amnesty.

At a press conference early in September, government spokesman Jerzy Urban made the astonishing announcement that some legal experts were proposing that people guilty of serious crimes against the State arising — as he put it — from a stubborn refusal to respect the constitutional principles of the country's system, should be banished from Poland for a period fixed by the sentence of a court. This was one of several proposals, he said, in a study looking for ways to make the law more effective in the fight against crime. He would not say anything about the government's view, but he did say that certain countries outside Europe were willing to take people who might be expelled.

My own reaction as I sat through that press conference was one of disbelief. Having failed to destroy opposition by imprisonment followed by amnesty, could the authorities really be thinking of resolving their problem by getting rid of the people? Or was the spokesman highlighting a proposal which had little chance of being accepted simply in order to shock and provoke? It was one of the things we had come to expect from Minister Urban.

Fr Popiełuszko certainly took it seriously and in a sermon the following Sunday morning his response was forthright and measured. 'Maybe someone will accuse me of playing at politics, but in a country where politics tries to enter each and every sphere of social life with impunity, the more need there is to look at some things from the moral point of view.'

Having quoted the key passages from Urban's statement word for word, Fr Jerzy declared that the fact that such an idea could enter the head of a Pole was 'a crime against the nation'. He continued:

> The spokesman did not have common criminals in mind, he was talking about the country's finest sons who oppose the destruction of the spirit of the nation... Maybe it would be worthwhile for the people who think up these ideas to examine their own ties with the homeland, their own patriotism. And maybe the nation would have no objections if it was they who took themselves off into banishment...[2]

For a change, Fr Popiełuszko was not alone in his public criticism. The official newspaper, *Zycie Warszawy*, said it would be a retrograde step to less civilised days. The Catholic weekly, *Tygodnik Powszechny*, in an article censored in two places, said that banishment, like burning at the stake, was one of those 'flagrantly uncivilised forms of punishment' rightly abandoned by modern legislators. Three members of the Sejm asked the Minister of Justice to tell them who had authorised the government spokesman to raise this question with the world's press, thus lowering Poland's international prestige.

Nonetheless, Fr Popiełuszko was by now attracting the attention of Soviet observers. He came under direct attack from Moscow. On 12 September, the newspaper *Izvestiya* carried a 'Letter from Warsaw' by its correspondent there, Leonid Toporkov. It was a good example of that mixture of distortion, half-truths and lies that had been the familiar diet of readers and foreign journalists alike in the long years of Soviet government control.

Toporkov deplored the fact that opponents of the Polish government had treated the July amnesty not as evidence of great humanity but as a sign of weakness. These people, he said, were refusing to accept defeat and even using churches to demand a revision of Poland's post-war frontiers. One such church, he said, was that of St Stanisław Kostka. At one service there, attended by three of the Eleven — Jacek Kuroń, Adam Michnik and Seweryn Jaworski — Toporkov claimed that the church had reverberated to impudent, shouted demands for the return of Lvov and Vilnius, both part of pre-war Poland.

'Only recently, in the same church,' Toporkov reported, 'the militant Fr Popiełuszko addressed to those amnestied an appeal which amounted to this: you've had a rest, it's time now to get down to work, but with more energy and greater cunning than before. The most important thing is not to be afraid. Everything suggests that the priest himself is not afraid. He turned his flat into a storage place for illegal literature and cooperates closely with implacable counter-revolutionaries.'

Fr Popiełuszko's sermons, Toporkov said, sounded more like leaflets written by Zbigniew Bujak, the Warsaw underground leader. The question being asked more often in the mass media, he said, was whether this priest and others like him could engage in such activity against the wishes of the Church hierarchy. Toporkov found it difficult to imagine that an ordinary priest could do it on his own initiative.

Toporkov was obviously referring to Fr Popiełuszko's sermon at the August Mass for the Homeland and he was probably there, observing the scene from a discreet distance at the edge of the outdoor congregation, where I had seen Soviet journalists standing on previous occasions. Up to a point, he was reacting to Fr Jerzy's remarks about the war waged in the past by Tsarist officials against the image of the Black Madonna; his words would certainly have been interpreted as an allegory for modern, Soviet oppression. But there was more to it than that. Moscow was saying obliquely what the OAS in Toruń had stated plainly in its leaflet: Jaruzelski was being weak in the face of counter-revolution.

This message was not lost on the authorities in Warsaw. Five days after the article had appeared in *Izvestiya*, the Office for Denominational Affairs delivered to the offices of the Episcopate its fiercest protest so far. Following *Izvestiya*'s lead, it spoke for the first time of counter-revolution and even appended as evidence copies of Fr Popiełuszko's sermon at his Mass for the Homeland on 26 August. Declaring with regret that some Roman Catholic clergymen belonged to a 'small but active group of people' who were trying to destroy the achievements of the nation 'in the name of alien interests', the message hastened to report that 'this activity has recently taken on a new quality'.[3]

An illegal, counter-revolutionary organisation of clergy and layfolk has come into existence on a national scale. It is contrary to the law of the Polish People's Republic and to Canon Law. The aims and structure of this organisation, its scope and its methods of operation, were revealed on 26

August by Fr Jerzy Popiełuszko in the church of St Stanisław
Kostka in Warsaw...

The message complained of the subject matter of sermons, the
distribution of illegal publications inside churches, and of
journeys made all over the country by the organisation's most
active members. These activities, it said, took place in close
coordination with Radio Free Europe, through which the
organisation was said to maintain contact with anti-Polish
centres of subversion and espionage.

> The Church of St Stanisław Kostka has for some time been the
> main bastion of this organisation... In spite of the soothing
> reassurances and declarations of representatives of the
> Episcopate, the Hierarchy invariably tolerates and even shelters
> the organisation's activity. This helps it to grow and undertake
> new activity. The state authorities expect the Episcopate to take
> determined steps without delay to liquidate the organisation
> under discussion.

In keeping with established practice, which treated such communications between Church and State as confidential, this
remarkable document was not published at the time. If it had
been, it would have caused a sensation and been met with widespread incredulity as well as mirth in Poland.

Counter-revolution, of course, was no minor offence. When
perceived on a national scale it could provoke Soviet intervention as in Hungary in 1956 and Czechoslovakia in 1968. In this
instance, however, the allegation of counter-revolution was
difficult to believe. Having dropped the case against Fr
Popiełuszko on a lesser charge a few weeks earlier, the Jaruzelski
government was now claiming to have uncovered a previously
unnoticed counter-revolution without providing any credible
explanation of how or why. The only reasonable explanation
was that the authorities felt the need, for reasons of state, to
repeat and place on record in their own name the Soviet allegations of counter-revolution made by *Izvestiya*. On paper, at

least, but not in public, the government had raised the stakes in the struggle against Solidarity and its supporters. But the fact that it had not mentioned Solidarity in its protest to the Episcopate must have disappointed Moscow and those in the party and the SB who saw Solidarity as the source of counter-revolution.

On 19 September, two days after the Episcopate received the government's confidential missive, the public had the opportunity to read in the weekly *Tu i Teraz* (Here and Now) what the government spokesman Jerzy Urban, writing under the well-known pen name of Jan Rem, thought of Fr Popiełuszko. In an article headlined 'Sessions of Hatred', recalling George Orwell's *1984*, he poured scorn on the priest he described as 'a political fanatic' and as 'the Savonarola of anti-Communism'.

> Clad in liturgical vestments, he says nothing that could be described as new or of interest to anyone... It is sessions of hatred that are staged in Fr Popiełuszko's church... All he does is manipulate collective emotions.
>
> A feeling of political hatred for Communists, for the authorities and for everything that is post-war Poland is brought into the auditorium by its habitués, but it is under the direction of Fr Popiełuszko that this feeling ceases to be something eating away inside. Political feelings find public release in the midst of people who feel the same. The disciples of the fanaticised Fr Popiełuszko have no need for arguments, enquiry or discussion; they don't want to learn, to take issue, to reflect or reach any conclusions.

Urban, as always, tried to be witty and optimistic, claiming that moderation and rationalism would outlive 'the phantoms released by the political magician of Żoliborz from beneath his chasuble'.

At the same time, though, he regretted the dearth of similarly 'inspired' speakers capable of holding the attention of large crowds among the professional lecturers of the Communist Central Committee.

If Polish television were able to employ the services of some
sort of Rasputin, that, unfortunately, would be an offer worth
considering. This is very sad but true as long as Fr Popiełuszko
has his clientele and his black masses enjoy popularity...[4]

Not many weeks would pass before people would look back at
this article. I would mention it myself when I reported the first
news of Fr Jerzy's disappearance. Eventually, though, Urban's
article came to be seen by some in a more sinister light and
blamed, in effect, for contributing to a climate conducive to the
murder of Fr Popiełuszko. I found this judgement too harsh.

More important, no doubt, were those in 'the forces of law
and order' who had access not only to the article in *Izvestiya* —
which was read by very few people in Poland — but also to the
government's protest to the Episcopate. Though it had agreed
with *Izvestiya*, the Office's letter merely turned up the volume
of threats made in the past. The government did not act in any
way to deal with the impatience expressed in different ways in
*Izvestiya* and by the OAS in Toruń.

In the weeks that followed the publication of Urban's article
no one said they saw it as a threat to Fr Popiełuszko. Nor was
there any obvious reaction from the Bishops to the government's message about Fr Popiełuszko and counter-revolution.
When they met in Warsaw towards the end of September under
the chairmanship of Cardinal Glemp, they called once again for
a return to the agreements which brought Solidarity into
existence and repeated the Pope's phrase about the 'great initiative' of August 1980 which sought solutions through talks
rather than force.

Only on the last day of September was it possible to detect a
hint of change. On Sunday, 30 September, thousands of
workers converged on the hill-top monastery of Jasna Góra and
the shrine of the Black Madonna in Częstochowa, south of
Warsaw. It was the second annual pilgrimage of 'the world of
work', an occasion organised by Fr Popiełuszko with the help of
like-minded priests from all over the country.

More than twenty priests, including Fr Popiełuszko, concele-brated Mass on the open-air altar high above the monastery's battlement walls. With them close to the sanctuary, were Lech Wałęsa and three Solidarity leaders released only recently from prison: Marian Jurczyk from Szczecin; Andrzej Słowik from Łódź; and Seweryn Jaworski from Warsaw. Below the altar, on the path that runs along the top of the walls were more of the big names of Solidarity: Gwiazda, Rulewski, Palka, Rozpłochowski, Romaszewski, Wujec, Celiński, Mazowiecki, Onyszkiewicz, Kropiwnicki, Walentynowicz and Switon. Solidarity banners were hanging on the walls beneath us and many more were held high among the crowd on the sloping meadow below.

It was a striking occasion but it was tinged with a sort of pathos and even sadness. There were no Bishops present and the sermon was given not by one of the priests associated with the workers' movement but by the Prior of the monastery. He told the assembled pilgrims, who included recent political prisoners, gaoled only for their beliefs, that what they needed was religious strength and moral solidarity. 'Our strength, par-ticularly in this place,' he said, 'lies in prayer and not in slogans, banners or victory signs.'

It is possible that the Prior did not intend to cause offence but I think he did in dismissing the symbols of Solidarity so insensitively. It also looked as though the young priests, such as Fr Popiełuszko, who had always identified Solidarity as the embodiment of the Church's social teaching, were not being allowed to speak.

I was given a lift back to Warsaw by Chris Bobiński of the *Financial Times* along with Andrzej Celiński, a former Solidarity spokesman, and Tadeusz Mazowiecki, the future Prime Minister, who was to remind me years later that that was the last time we saw Fr Popiełuszko.

There were two things we did not know at the time. One was that a series of meetings had begun in Department Four of the Ministry of Internal Affairs to discuss what more could be done about Fr Popiełuszko. The other was that Fr Jerzy had just accepted an invitation from one of the priests he met at Jasna Góra to go and preach in his parish church. Towards the end of October he would be going to Bydgoszcz.

# 10

# Department Four

Department Four of the Ministry of Internal Affairs was a remarkable institution, devoted exclusively to keeping an eye on the Church. Until the events of October 1984 few people knew of its existence. When it did become public knowledge, the authorities would claim that it did a good job, providing security, for example, during visits by the Pope and helping maintain good Church-State relations through its liaison with the Bishops. But as the Church knew and as subsequent revelations were to confirm, the prime task of Department Four was not to help the Church but to ensure the security of the Communist State by spying on the Church, trying to counteract its influence and, where possible, undermining it. Its role was not unlike that of Soviet policy towards the West during the era of détente — a matter of coexisting peacefully with the chief ideological enemy whose elimination, however desirable, was too risky to contemplate.

The Department's methods were basically those of any secret police force. For example, whenever a young man entered a seminary to begin studying for the priesthood, the local representative of Department Four would open a file on him and that would be kept up to date after the young man's ordination wherever he went thereafter. Priests were not necessarily unaware of the close attentions of the SB. In one of his final entries in his diary, Fr Popiełuszko described how, while waiting in a corridor of the Mostowski Palace before a routine interrogation, he had been approached by a Lieutenant Larek, 'my minder for many years, ever since my first parish'. Larek had suggested a private chat, 'without witnesses', but Fr Jerzy declined: 'We wouldn't find anything to talk about.'

Department Four was actively involved in the search of Fr Popiełuszko's flat on Chłodna Street in December 1983, when Solidarity leaflets, ammunition and explosives were discovered. As Fr Jerzy said at the time, these incriminating materials had been planted by the SB. Now, in the wake of the *Izvestiya* article and the government protest to the Church about counter-revolution, the priest from Żoliborz stood at the centre of attention of Department Four.

On 19 September 1984, at the end of his summer holidays, Lieutenant Colonel Leszek Wolski of the SB returned to his desk at the Mostowski Palace, only to be instructed to report to Department Four the next day because of what was described, in his typically bureaucratic words, as 'the need to prepare a concept in the area of Fr Popiełuszko's extra-religious activities'. As Head of Section Four at the Warsaw City Office of Internal Affairs, Wolski was the officer chiefly responsible for reporting on Fr Jerzy's activities.

Wolski, who was fifty, went first to the office of a man who was a couple of ranks his junior and seventeen years younger but was, nonetheless, his supervisor, thirty-three-year-old Captain Grzegorz Piotrowski. This, doubtless, was an anomaly but Piotrowski, it seems, was a rising star with a background considered to be highly desirable. The son of an SB Colonel in Łódź, where he was born, he was married to the daughter of an SB man. After only nine years in the SB — six in Łódź and three in Warsaw — he was already head of a Department Four section with more than one officer of higher rank under his command.

It was not Piotrowski, however, who had summoned Wolski to the Ministry. The summons had come from the Captain's immediate superior, Lieutenant Colonel Adam Pietruszka, the senior of three Deputy Directors of Department Four. A rather grey man who looked older than his forty six years, Pietruszka had spent twenty three years in the SB. By now, after nine years in Warsaw, he was in a position of considerable authority, though not, perhaps, as much as he would have liked. Having been appointed Deputy Director of Department Four in 1981, Pietruszka was about to be promoted to full Colonel following a recent spell as Acting Director during the absence on unspecified detached duty of his boss, General Zenon Płatek.

Płatek, fifty seven, had been appointed Director of Department Four in December 1981, the month martial law was imposed. As Director, he was a key figure in the hierarchy of the Ministry of Internal Affairs. His immediate superior was a Deputy Minister, General Władysław Ciastoń, the Head of the SB, who, in turn, was responsible directly to the Minister, General Czesław Kiszczak.

One can only assume that Płatek was promoted to Director because he was considered good enough to fill the shoes of his predecessor who went on to become a Deputy Minister. And yet, when it comes to the case of Fr Popiełuszko, the sketchy picture of Zenon Płatek which the authorities allowed to take shape was of a man who seemed to notice little, if anything, of what was going on under his nose. It may well be that this image was encouraged because the chain of command stretching from Kiszczak to Piotrowski was quite short, and because General Płatek took part in one of the fateful meetings about Fr Popiełuszko of which the world outside the Ministry would know nothing until the Popiełuszko murder trial.

There were three such meetings: on 20 September, on 25 September and the third in the first ten days of October, most probably on 9 October. Pietruszka, Piotrowski and Wolski took part in all three, while Płatek attended just one, on 25 September.

All information about these discussions was to come from these four men and from a small number of close associates who heard something about them. Since Pietruszka and Piotrowski and two junior officers ended up in the dock —

while Wolski and Płatek, in the opinion of the general public, should have joined them there — their evidence, whether given at trial or under interrogation before the trial,[1] can hardly be treated as the whole truth.

In the event, the testimony of three of the four men can be summed up briefly. Colonel Pietruszka and Lieutenant Colonel Wolski both denied discussing the use of illegal methods or physical violence against Fr Popiełuszko. General Płatek would tell interrogators, in language suggesting shock, that he couldn't imagine the possibility of anyone going to him with a suggestion that the priest should be kidnapped; there was no such discussion 'in the leadership of the department'. The odd man out was thirty-three-year-old Captain Piotrowski. His testimony had a touch of verisimilitude; it sounded more like the truth if only because the words and attitudes he attributed to the others and himself seemed to be in character.

Piotrowski said that at the first of the three meetings, his superior Adam Pietruszka had got all worked up when he heard Wolski's account of what Fr Popiełuszko and another Warsaw priest, Fr Stanisław Małkowski, had been up to since the July amnesty. The Colonel said he had had enough of playing around with those two; they should both be given a good going-over even if it took them to within an inch of having a heart attack. According to Piotrowski, Pietruszka thought that Małkowski should be their first target. It would be perfect, he said, if someone were to attack him and rough him up and if the uniformed police were to turn up minutes later and collar some villain for it.

Piotrowski disagreed, suggesting that Fr Popiełuszko should be the prime target. He said that Małkowski was just 'an ordinary little windbag', who was to all intents and purposes 'on his own', whereas Popiełuszko was 'someone far more important' and usually enjoyed 'protection'. Piotrowski argued that if Małkowski were to be hit first, Popiełuszko would intensify the protection and become virtually untouchable. It was agreed that Fr Popiełuszko should come first.

Piotrowski testified that he had also suggested that if they were to 'harass' Fr Popiełuszko, 'then we must have him at our disposal'. To this, he said, Pietruszka had commented: 'Fine, Comrades, you go and think about it'.

It was also agreed, according to Piotrowski, that although the Department knew a great deal about Fr Popiełuszko's activities, it did not have detailed knowledge of his life 'hour by hour'. Pietruszka asked the other two to draw up a plan of action to put this right. Piotrowski quoted him as saying: 'There's nothing to add, Comrades, apart from telling you that this is a top level decision'.

Back in his office downstairs, Piotrowski said, he had promised to help Wolski in his surveillance of Fr Popiełuszko by lending him a car and communications equipment.

Wolski would agree that he was instructed to intensify his surveillance of Fr Popiełuszko but he thought that it happened on another date. Pietruszka would agree that he had changed his mind about which priest should be their first target, but he denied ever suggesting physical violence. What exactly Pietruszka wanted to be done, apart from watching the priest's every move 'hour by hour', would become a matter of some mystery, but there was good reason to believe that he was, indeed, under pressure from those at the 'top level' to get something done.

Piotrowski's testimony about the second meeting had Colonel Pietruszka reacting with disgust to Wolski's latest report and accusing him of dragging his feet. When Wolski protested that he was making plans but encountering difficulties, Pietruszka retorted: Don't just plan, do something. Wolski complained that he was short of staff and equipment and repeatedly referred to problems with his superiors at the Mostowski Palace (Warsaw City Police Headquarters). 'Don't bother them,' Pietruszka said. 'What they don't know won't hurt them.' Piotrowski said he could not remember for sure whether Pietruszka had said this on 25 September or some other time.

That second meeting was the one supposedly presided over by the Director of Department Four, General Płatek. Yet Piotrowski, who remembered such vivid quotations from the mouth of Adam Pietruszka, did not quote the General as saying anything at all. This was odd, since it was this meeting, according to Wolski, that adopted a plan of action in the Popiełuszko case.

But what was this plan of action? General Płatek never stated what it was, though nobody appears to have asked him. Nor did the hapless Wolski, but he at least admitted that Pietruszka wanted him to do something and do it quickly. Pietruszka himself would claim, unconvincingly, that all he wanted was a more efficient application of the old strategy. This consisted of collecting evidence against Fr Popiełuszko and passing it on so that the Office for Denominational Affairs could put pressure on the Bishops in the form of protest memoranda.

According to Piotrowski, immediately after the 25 September meeting he took Wolski to his own office downstairs and told him that the only possibility he could see, was for them to 'get their hands on Popiełuszko — which presumably meant kidnap him — and torment him' (*mu dokuczyc*). Wolski, he thought, was 'inclined to agree', but kept going on and on about the problems he faced. To judge from this, it seems that there was no fixed plan of action, just a demand from above that Fr Popiełuszko be silenced, and that it was left to Piotrowski and Wolski to decide how best this could be achieved.

Piotrowski portrayed himself increasingly in testimony as being frustrated on the one hand by Wolski's inaction and driven by Pietruszka's impatience on the other into thinking of abandoning his role as Wolski's supervisor and taking action himself. Pietruszka kept summoning him to ask if there had been any progress. But however much he tried to explain the difficulties of Wolski's position, Piotrowski never had anything to report.

When it became known that Fr Popiełuszko was about to visit Katowice with Professor Szaniawski, Pietruszka had asked how long were they going to allow him to go on such trips. Moreover, Piotrowski testified that when he had said that Fr Popiełuszko and the Professor were going by train and not by car, Pietruszka had replied that the priest could be thrown off the train. At the time, Piotrowski said, he did not believe that

Pietruszka was being serious. Pietruszka had complained again when it was discovered that Fr Popiełuszko would be going to Gdańsk as well. 'Right,' said Piotrowski, 'we'll do it ourselves.'

Captain Piotrowski had nothing specific to say about the third meeting, in Pietruszka's office, but by the time it took place, he had done something which made the meeting virtually academic. He had recruited and sworn to secrecy two members of his staff to join him in an operation to kidnap Fr Jerzy Popiełuszko.

As he would explain later, Captain Piotrowski was looking for men who got things done, men he could trust and men who were big enough and strong enough to use physical force if necessary. His choice fell on Lieutenant Leszek Pękala, a thirty-two-year-old bachelor, and Lieutenant Waldemar Chmielewski, a married man of twenty nine. Since Piotrowski himself was only thirty three, there was little age difference between them.

Piotrowski and Chmielewski, however, had much more in common. Chmielewski, who came from Wrocław, was also the son of an SB officer and was married to the daughter of an SB officer. Chmielewski had one child of around eighteen months old and Piotrowski had two children, aged eight and six. In a way, Chmielewski had the better 'professional' background. Piotrowski was a mathematics graduate of Łódź University and had done some teaching before joining the SB. Chmielewski, on the other hand, had done his military service in the ranks of the ZOMO riot police, then graduated from the Higher Police Officers' School at Szczytno, north of Warsaw, and had finally taken a correspondence course of the Academy of Internal Affairs. He had then been taken on in Department Four on the specific recommendation of Adam Pietruszka, a friend of his father, a Colonel working in the same department.

By comparison, Leszek Pękala's connections were obscure. He went to school and technical college in Rzeszow in south-eastern Poland and completed his education with an electronics course in Wrocław in Silesia. He joined the uniformed police, the MO, and served in Wrocław and Tarnów before being transferred to the SB at the Ministry in Warsaw in 1981. Pękala may have lacked the family connections of his colleagues, but he was chosen, it seems, because he was a good operator with first-hand knowledge of the target of the proposed operation. After all, he helped 'discover' the Solidarity publications, the ammunition and explosives during the search of Fr Popiełuszko's private flat on Chłodna Street in Warsaw in December 1983.

Piotrowski's plan, as explained to Chmielewski and Pękala, seems to have been straightforward. Fr Popiełuszko had to 'disappear' for two to three days. This would cause confusion and alarm among those close to the priest and in the ranks of 'the former Solidarity'. Piotrowski and his two accomplices would kidnap Fr Popiełuszko when he was on one of his trips outside Warsaw, take him to a remote spot where they could safely keep him incommunicado and terrorise him into changing his ways and divulging secrets of the Solidarity underground. The trio discussed a variety of ways this could be achieved, including tying the victim to a tree in the forest and burying him up to his neck in sand. Finally, if all went well, they would get the priest drunk and release him in a public place. This, they imagined, would compromise him in the eyes of Solidarity.

Any similarity with the methods employed by the OAS in Toruń was not, apparently, accidental. It emerged later that Captain Piotrowski had spent six months working in Toruń earlier that year.

Piotrowski never said exactly when he approached the two men and asked them (as he put it) whether they were prepared to take part in a special mission which could be dangerous. Chmielewski said it was round about the end of September or the beginning of October. Pękala was more precise: 'a week before 13 October'. In that week, he said, he and Chmielewski were under instructions to choose suitable places for their operation and also to buy or acquire whatever gear they thought they would need for it. Piotrowski gave them both the week off to do this; Chmielewski was reported sick, while Pękala was said to be on leave owed to him because of working overtime.

Clearly, Captain Piotrowski was in a hurry to satisfy Pietruszka's demand for results and he probably had his eye on the calendar. On Saturday, 13 October, Fr Popiełuszko would be driving to Gdańsk for a ceremony at St Brigid's, Fr Jankowski's parish church. The following Friday, 19 October, he would be going to preach in Bydgoszcz, and there were plans for a trip soon after that to Stalowa Wola southeast of Warsaw. The preparations of the two young lieutenants, however, suggested that they and their boss were concentrating on the trips to Gdańsk and Bydgoszcz.

Two places were quickly picked out as ideal for the planned operation. Both were on or close to the E77, the main road north used by most if not all of the traffic to and from Warsaw and Gdańsk on the Baltic Coast and Bydgoszcz and Toruń to the northwest.

One was in the Kampinos Forest, the large area of woodland, marsh and sand dunes stretching westwards from the northern perimeter of Warsaw. This was the choice of Chmielewski, who was familiar with parts of the forest because he had organised summer camps there for scouts. He suggested that Fr Popiełuszko could easily be held incommunicado for a few days in one of a number of disused wartime bunkers near a place called Cybulice. This could be done, he said, by forcing the priest into a shallow niche and blocking the exit with heavy stones.

The route to Cybulice involved driving north from the capital, and turning off to the left just as the highway bore right a mile or so short of the bridge over the Vistula at Modlin.

This bridge was the second place chosen. Piotrowski suggested taking a look at it when he was being driven out of the Kampinos Forest after inspecting the bunkers at Cybulice. Pękala thought it would be a good place to frighten the priest by threatening to throw him off the bridge into the water. Piotrowski's thoughts were more drastic. According to Pękala, Piotrowski said that if, as he expected, Fr Popiełuszko did not weaken and crack, it would be necessary to throw him into the water. Chmielewski, for his part, claimed to have protested that this would hardly be possible on such a busy bridge with people fishing on the banks of the river below. To this Piotrowski had said something like: 'People fishing? At that time?'

One might have thought that Chmielewski and Pękala would have protested at what seems to have been a clear statement by Piotrowski of murderous intent. But neither of them knew at first hand what was said by Pietruszka, Piotrowski, Wolski or General Płatek at their meetings about Fr Popieluszko. They could only testify to what Piotrowski told them and what they understood him to mean by his words. But that was enough, it seems, to make them sure that their operation had been given the go-ahead 'upstairs'.

According to Chmielewski, Piotrowski told them repeatedly that the operation had the approval of his superiors. Pękala went further, declaring that in the two weeks that preceded Fr Popieluszko's visit to Bydgoszcz he had become confirmed 'in a profound and fanatical conviction that what we were planning to do was necessary, right and in the interests of the State, bearing in mind internal and maybe also international affairs'. He had become convinced, he said, that the abduction of the priest was 'merely part of some bigger operation' which Piotrowski had organised 'not on his own but with someone we didn't know about'.[2]

Chmielewski was less dramatic about it. Piotrowski had shown confidence in him by asking him to take part, so he could hardly refuse because he was 'directly involved in matters affecting Fr Popieluszko'. Undoubtedly, he and Pękala also believed that the operation would advance their careers. This, presumably, helped them — if they needed help — to confront the possibility that kidnapping the priest could end not in compromising him but in taking his life. Piotrowski led them to believe that it was understood 'upstairs' that there was a chance that the priest would die and that, if so, they should dispose of his body.

Pękala said he was convinced that their plan of action had been approved 'very high up, even if it entailed the accidental death of the kidnapped priest'.[3] Chmielewski said that the pos-

August 1984, Jerzy Popiełuszko two months before his murder.

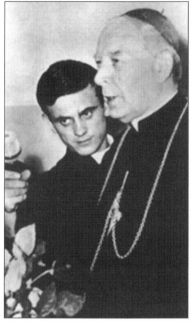

Jerzy Popiełuszko and Cardinal Wyszyński.

The adolescent Jerzy in the army.

Young Jerzy's first Communion day, with his parents, probably 1954.

27 October 1984, one week after the abduction: the priest's parents in the yard of their Okopy home.

PHOTO BY R. DUTKIEWICZ

September 1981, Archbishops's House, Warsaw (*left to right*): Fr Kalwarczyk, Seweryn Jaworski (later one of 'The Eleven' political prisoners), Zbigniew Bujak (the popular leader of Solidarity Warsaw), Krzysztof Śliwiński, Fr Popiełuszko, Janusz Onyszkiewicz (Solidarity spokesman), Fr Łucyk, Lech Wałęsa (Solidarity leader) and Fr Zach-Chrobołowski (*kneeling*).

PHOTO BY E. CIOŁEK

1983, St Stanisław's presbytery: Fr Jerzy's guests include Seweryn Jaworski, a worker and Solidarity leader from the Warsaw Steel Works, and (*left*) Prof. Szaniawski of Warsaw University.

*Above and below*: inside St Stanisław Kostka's during a Mass for the Homeland, celebrated at seven on the last Sunday of the month.

General Jaruzelksi, Party Leader and Prime Minister of Communist Poland.

State leaders: General Kiszczak, Minister of Internal Affairs (*right*), next to his reputed foe, Mirosław Milewski, former Minister and Politburo member for Internal Affairs.

General Kiszczak addresses the Sejm. In the background General Jaruzelski (*on the left, wearing dark glasses*).

May 1983, Fr Popiełuszko next to the grave of Grzegorz Przemyk.

June 1984, mass celebrated by Fr Jerzy on the balcony of St Stanisław Kostka's as Fr Bogucki watches (*middle right, white hair*).

13 August 1984, Fr Popiełuszko and Lech Wałęsa at St Brigid's Gdańsk.

Colonel Adam Pietruszka.

Captain Grzegorz Piotrowski.

Lieutenant Leszek Pękala.

Lieutenant Waldemar (Waldek) Chmielewski.

Trial evidence: remnants of hair and tissue.

Fr Jerzy's soutane after the murder.

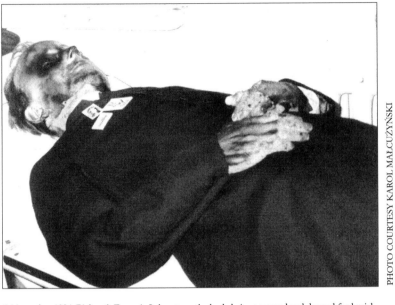

2 November 1984, Białystok Forensic Laboratory: the body being prepared and dressed for burial (*above and below right*).

October 1984 (*above*): 'Give us back Fr. Popiełuszko'. St Stanisław being draped with banners after news of the abduction.

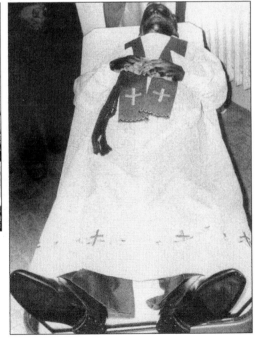

2 November 1984, Friday evening: Waldek Chrostowski (*front right*) helps carry the priest's coffin into St Stanisław Kostka's.

Bronisław Geremek (later Foreign Minister), Lech Wałęsa (recipient of the Nobel Peace Prize in 1983 and later President), Tadeusz Mazowiecki (later Prime Minister), arriving for the funeral.

3 November 1984, Saturday: crowds of people cram the main street on which the church stands and the Paris Commune Square in the background.

3 November 1984, Saturday morning: the funeral congregation outside St Stanisław's and on the roofs, seen from the presbytery.

During the interment, Jerzy's mother (*front*), father and Waldemar Chrostowski (*stretched arm*) holding up their hands in a victory sign.

3 November 1984: the interment. Cardinal Glemp (*middle, book in hand*) officiates at the graveside.

Victory signs in the crowd.

The moment of burial, with silhouettes of men standing on roof tops near and far.

Night time: the area next to St Stanisław's lit up by crosses made of lanterns after the funeral.

Crowds gather in the evening near the church.

The dock in Toruń: Piotrowski speaks, Pietruszka is to his right.

The four accused during the Toruń trial of 27 December 1984 to 7 February 1985.

June 1992, Warsaw. General Władysław Ciastoń (*left*) and General Zenon Płatek on trial.

June 1987, Pope John Paul II kisses the gravestone in the church yard of St Stanisław's.

sibility of Fr Popiełuszko dying as a result of their operation had been taken into consideration by them before the trip to Gdańsk on 13 October. Captain Piotrowski himself would testify in court that he had asked Adam Pietruszka what would happen if Fr Popiełuszko died of a heart attack because of what they were doing. To this, he said, Colonel Pietruszka had replied: 'It's his bad luck if he has a weak heart.'

Piotrowski and his two accomplices knew what they wanted to do and had a rough idea of how to do it, but they could not predict or dictate the precise circumstances. This meant that their tactics would have to be decided virtually at the last minute, and made some of their testimony confusing, if not contradictory. Chmielewski, for instance, testified that if Fr Popiełuszko were to be accompanied by more than one person 'we had no intention of undertaking any action against Fr Popiełuszko in the sense of detaining or kidnapping him'. Pękala, on the other hand, would testify that if there were three people in the car, their plan was to cause an accident.

The conspirators, to judge from the testimony of Chmielewski and Pękala, had two basic plans: the first for when Fr Popiełuszko had two companions, the second for when he had one. And the articles and tools that Chmielewski and Pękala assembled for the operation say more about their actual intentions.

The list included a padlock, two small spades or shovels, a bedspread or coverlet, one litre of vodka, a sports bag, two tourist bags, three torches, three pairs of gloves, three ski hats (which could be pulled down over the face), adhesive tape, cotton wool, various lengths of cord, rope or string, an undervest torn into rectangular pieces or strips, a towel, a pair of scissors, and four sacks, two made of jute, two of artificial fibre.

It is easy enough to guess what some of these articles were intended for. Two of the sacks were filled with heavy stones collected on one of the visits to the Kampinos Forest. They were stowed away with the rest of the gear in a cupboard in Pękala's room at the Ministry. In a chillingly matter-of-fact piece of testimony under interrogation on 29 October, Pękala explained what these props were for.

> … We were to stun Fr Popiełuszko and his driver with a wooden stake wrapped round with rags… Placed in a large sack, as well as being bound and gagged, Fr Popiełuszko was to be put into the boot of the car. We had a large sack… Chmielewski and I had sewn together two artificial fibre sacks with strong thread, joining the top of one to the bottom of the other which we had unstitched. We did this in my room at the office before we left for Gdańsk… The driver was to be stunned, bound and gagged, wrapped in the bedspread and placed in the back of the car behind the front seats.
>
> Later, further along the road, we were to stop, tie on the stones — we had two sacks filled with stones for this purpose — and throw them from a bridge into the water.

Under interrogation on the same day, Waldemar Chmielewski said that they 'took into consideration the possibility that Popiełuszko would die as a result of our operation and that it would be necessary to do something with his remains such as throwing him into the water. That was the purpose of the stones and the bags. It was a question of weighing down the body'. Chmielewski was referring to the trio's discussions as they drove to Bydgoszcz on 19 October (as was Pękala in the testimony above), but explained that this was not the first time they had thought of this. 'I would like to add that the possibility that Popiełuszko would die as a result of our operation had been taken into consideration by us in conversation earlier, before the trip to Gdańsk.'

Later, in the same interview, he continued: 'We also took into consideration the possibility that something could happen to the person accompanying Popiełuszko, i.e, to put it simply, that that person could die, and then it would be necessary to dispose of the body by submerging it in water. That was why we had prepared two sacks of stones.'

By the evening of Friday, 12 October, the eve of Fr

Popiełuszko's departure for Gdansk, his would-be assailants were ready. Their equipment had been augmented by two walkie-talkies and some socks which Piotrowski contributed, suggesting that they would make handy weapons when filled with sand.

From a car parked in the Muranow district of Warsaw, where the Mostowski Palace was situated, Chmielewski and Pękala had stolen a set of number plates with movable letters and digits. They had switched these around to make a false registration plate: KZC 0423.

The most important acquisition, however, came from Adam Pietruszka. This was a special pass, the W pass, so called because it declared its holder's free (Wolne) from traffic police checks while on the road on special missions. There were two such passes in Department Four, one held by the Director, General Płatek, the other by Adam Pietruszka.

The Colonel was already at home that Friday evening when Piotrowski phoned him about the pass and learned that it was in Pietruszka's official car parked at the Ministry. It was agreed that Pękala should go to the Colonel's house, pick up the car keys and leave them with the duty officer after picking up the pass. Pękala drove to Pinkowski Street with Chmielewski. When Pietruszka handed over the keys to the car, he said, he wished them success. Pękala took this to mean that Pietruszka knew what they were up to.

# 11

# On the Gdańsk Road

Captain Piotrowski and his two lieutenants were up early on Saturday, 13 October. They met at the Ministry at about 6 am and loaded their gear into a government Fiat 125, registration number WAB 6031—a small but pivotal fact for what followed. Before 7 am, they were parked near the parish church of St Stanisław Kostka.

Three hours went by before Fr Popiełuszko left the presbytery and got into the light green Volkswagen Golf he was borrowing from his friend, Fr Bogdan Liniewski. As the car moved off, with Waldemar Chrostowski behind the wheel, it passed the SB Fiat. Chmielewski lay down, on Piotrowski's instructions, so as not to be seen. But Pękala noticed a third man in the Golf. It was Seweryn Jaworski, the Solidarity leader from the Huta Warszawa steel mill who only a few months earlier had been among the country's top political prisoners, one of the Eleven. He, more than most, would need to be present at St Brigid's in Gdańsk that evening when Fr Popiełuszko and the parish priest, Fr Henryk Jankowski, were each to receive the honorary title of Chaplain of the Workers (or as Piotrowski would have it, 'Chaplain of the Underground').

Jaworski's presence would presumably have removed any doubt that Fr Popiełuszko was on his way to Gdańsk. However, Piotrowski claimed at the trial to be still uncertain. He had, in the run up to 13 October, asked 'a certain person' to phone the Ministry's Duty Officer or his own office that morning and confirm the trip with an agreed code word or phrase. But no such message had been received. Piotrowski would testify to calling his secretary on the car's radio telephone to ask if there was any news for him. Chmielewski, in contrast, would testify that when Piotrowski was making a call, the voice he heard at the other end was that of General Płatek. According to Chmielewski, the voice said: 'You are talking to the wrong person and there is no news for you.'

Chmielewski's evidence was as suspect as anyone else's, but this sentence, the first directly attributed to the General, may have contained the signal Piotrowski was waiting for.

Another odd incident that supposedly took place that morning only adds to the uncertainty about who knew of Piotrowski's mission. When Major Janusz Dróżdż, Piotrowski's deputy, got to work that Saturday morning, he found a note from his boss under his ashtray. It said that the Captain and Chmielewski had had to leave town on urgent business, that Adam Pietruszka knew about their departure and that Pękala was off sick.

Some time later, according to Dróżdż, he received information that Fr Popiełuszko was going to Gdańsk that day. He asked one of his staff, Józef Żybura, to check with Gdańsk whether this was true but nobody answered the phone. Dróżdż himself tried to contact Colonel Pietruszka or General Płatek but they were out. Eventually, General Płatek phoned Dróżdż and asked him to go up to his office. Dróżdż had hardly begun his story before Płatek interrupted him so that Pietruszka could come in and hear it too. When Dróżdż resumed his report he was interrupted again, this time by an angry Pietruszka who accused him of bypassing him by going straight to Płatek with information which was, in any case, rubbish. He, Pietruszka, knew for a fact that Fr Popiełuszko was in Warsaw.

Surprised and shaken by Pietruszka's outburst, Dróżdż said he returned to his office and got in touch with his informant who confirmed that the priest was indeed on the road to

Gdańsk. When Pietruszka phoned him again to give him another telling off, Dróżdż claimed, he replied that he had confirmed for certain that the priest had left and that the Colonel had lied.

There's a sense of authentic personal animosity and maybe rivalry between Pietruszka, forty six, and Dróżdż, forty three, in this encounter. But one thing can be said for certain: it incriminated Pietruszka and tended to exonerate Płatek from any suggestion of complicity. Any suspicion that it was tailored to do just that might be justified by the fact that the story Dróżdż told in court — as above — was fuller and more rounded than in his pre-trial testimony.

Fr Popiełuszko and his companions made good time on the road and arrived at St Brigid's in Gdańsk at about 2 pm. The SB men adopted a more leisurely pace giving themselves plenty of time to work out how they were going to make their move against the priest now that he had two friends with him, not one. Their best plan, they decided, was to cause his car to crash on the return journey that night. They would do this by casting a heavy stone against the windscreen of the oncoming Golf on a difficult section of road.

According to Piotrowski, this was Pękala's idea. It was Pękala, too, who chose what he thought was the ideal spot on the twenty-nine kilometre stretch between Olsztynek, little more than a village, in the south and the small town of Ostróda in the north. It was a place I remember well, on the edge of one of the lake districts, where the road winds its way up and down relatively gentle but demanding gradients between tall, densely packed trees and undergrowth through which one can occasionally catch a glimpse of sunlight on water.

Pękala stopped the car near a sign for the village of Rychnowo. At this point drivers heading south from Gdańsk via Ostróda are suddenly faced with a left turn downhill followed quickly by a right turn at the bottom of the hill as the road bridges a narrow stream, the river Drwęca, close to its source. The hill is not too steep and the turn at the bottom is not too sharp, but a fast driver, even one who knew the road well, could be in serious difficulties if his windscreen were shattered by a heavy stone.

On reaching Gdańsk, the SB men drove straight to St Brigid's, where Piotrowski had a look inside the church. With a long time to wait before the evening service was to begin, they drove on to nearby Sopot and had lunch in the splendid Grand Hotel looking out over a broad sandy beach. This must have been a bit of a treat for the two lieutenants. The lunch was good, apparently, and Pękala was surprised at the cost, nearly 4000 zloties. Piotrowski, who paid the bill, said that since they were on a special assignment, money was no object. Earlier, he had given Pękala and Chmielewski 5000 zloties each to cover expenses, a lot of money in those days. For these two young men, lunch at the Grand and the 'expenses' may have been the first taste of the sort of job satisfaction they were hoping for in the SB.

After their sumptuous lunch the three men made their way to Oliwa, the district of Gdańsk where Solidarity staged its first congress in 1981, and changed their number plates from WAB 6031 to KZC 0423 in preparation for their intended crime.

A little later, the men arrived at St Brigid's at about six in the evening. Piotrowski and Chmielewski went into the church on two occasions, the second time after Mass had begun. Like other SB colleagues, Piotrowski's testimony referred to the Mass as a 'show'. He reported after the Mass that Lech Wałęsa 'did a turn' and that Fr Popiełuszko was given a 'big hand'. Afterwards, the congregation emerged for a procession around the perimeter of the church. At least another hour went by before the Golf in which Fr Popiełuszko had arrived came out of the presbytery yard, turned right and began winding its way through the streets towards the road leading south to Warsaw. It was 9 pm or later when Leszek Pękala moved off in its tracks.

With a couple of hours driving before they would reach the ambush location, Piotrowski and his accomplices had plenty of time to establish for sure that Fr Popiełuszko still had two companions with him. They did this by overtaking the Golf on a clear stretch of the highway and pulling in to the side of the road further ahead. They took a good look at the priest's car as it passed them. Waldek Chrostowski was driving. Seweryn Jaworski was in the front passenger seat. Fr Popiełuszko was in the back.

Pękala then overtook the Golf again and stayed well ahead, travelling at some points at nearly 140 km/h to be sure of reaching the hill at Rychnowo in good time. Once there, Pękala concealed the car in the trees at the top of the hill and took up his position as look-out at the side of the road. Piotrowski and Chmielewski positioned themselves as planned in the under-growth further down the hill. In the palm of Piotrowski's hand was a stone he had selected from one of the sacks in the car's boot. It weighed about half a kilogram.

A few minutes after confirming that their walkie-talkies were in good working order, Chmielewski received the signal from Pękala that someone was coming — 'and it's them'. Piotrowski went out onto the road.

Fr Popiełuszko and Jaworski were both dozing as the Golf reached the turn at the top of the hill and Chrostowski saw a man run out onto the road in front of him.

I thought he had a stocking mask over his head. I was travelling at about 90 km/h... and he was 50 to 70 metres away... I saw him raise his arm and bend it backwards. As I aimed the car to the right, the man seemed to hesitate, his arm movement changed. I then swung the car to the left and passed him on a big curve. If I had driven straight I would have run him over. When I swung to the left he was 10 to 15 metres away. I saw him throw something but it missed the car. It was a sideways throw, not from above the head. I missed him by about three metres, crossing to the other side of the road. If anything had been coming the other way I wouldn't have been able to do this and it's hard to say what would have happened. The next turning was close and it was dark.

My passengers woke up and I told them there'd been a bandit attack... I slowed down. It was midnight. I said I was going back to teach him a lesson but my passengers advised against it. They said it could have been some kind of ambush and that I should leave well alone. We thought the man must have been some sort of idiot, a hooligan or a drunk. We didn't attach much importance to it...[1]

Seweryn Jaworski was jerked into wakefulness as the car swung from side to side and actually saw the man with his arm raised in front of them. He thought he must be drunk.

When he and Chmielewski rejoined Pękala at the top of the hill, Piotrowski merely said that he had missed because the driver of the Golf had handled the situation well by driving straight at him and then turning sharply, maintaining control throughout. Piotrowski was to claim later that, pretending to be drunk by entering the roadway with 'zigzag steps', he had deliberately thrown the stone high, over the top of the car, having decided at the last moment not to go through with the attack. Few would believe that. According to Chmielewski's account, Pękala reacted angrily, openly criticising his superior officer for making a mess of it.

The three men retired briefly to a parking area at the village of Wola Rychnowska and changed the number plates of their car before driving back to Warsaw. When they reached the Ministry, they carried in all their gear, including two sacks of stones, returned them to the cupboard in Pękala's room and went home.

The next day, Piotrowski said, he reported to Adam Pietruszka on the failure of the mission, explaining that Jaworski as well as Chrostowski had been in the car with Fr Popiełuszko. In response, he alleged, Pietruszka had said: 'What a pity. With them on board, it would have made a nice little traffic accident.'[2] Colonel Pietruszka would deny hearing any such report or saying anything of the sort.

Fr Popiełuszko and his friends told few people about this incident. If more people had known, perhaps more might have gone to Bydgoszcz with him six days later.

# 12
# Bydgoszcz

Fr Popiełuszko had been invited to preach at an evening Mass for workers at the parish church of the Polish Martyrs in the Wyżyny district of Bydgoszcz on Friday, 19 October. Fr Osiński, a curate of the parish who had extended the invitation during the workers' pilgrimage at Jasna Góra, had since written to Fr Jerzy, enquiring, among other things, about his arrangements for getting to Bydgoszcz and back to Warsaw.

There were some doubts, as the date of the trip approached, about whether Waldek Chrostowski would be able to accompany his friend. He had been feeling unwell (not too surprising, since his flat had been gutted by an unexplained fire). So Fr Osiński sent a driver. Marek Wilk arrived at St Stanisław's in Warsaw at about 8.30 am. He parked his red Fiat Sports some distance away because he felt uneasy about another car parked nearby, a Fiat 125 with some men in it, apparently waiting. At 9 am, he went into the presbytery and met Fr Popiełuszko for the first time. They talked for fifteen minutes or so before being joined by Chrostowski who had decided to go after all. It was then that Marek Wilk learned for the first time about the attempted attack on the previous Saturday. His impression was that it made no particular impression on them.

When they left the presbytery some time before 10 am, Fr Popiełuszko was dressed in civilian clothes. Wilk drove off in his own car and headed into town to check if anyone was following, having agreed to link up with the other two at Modlin. This they did, continuing their journey together until just before reaching Toruń, when Fr Popiełuszko transferred to Wilk's car for the final stretch. They reached the parish of the Polish Martyrs a little after 2 pm.[1]

Marek Wilk had been right to be suspicious of the Fiat parked near St Stanisław's. On Piotrowski's instructions, Pękala and Chmielewski had been watching the church and the presbytery since 8 am. Strangely, though, they did not see Fr Popiełuszko leave — perhaps they expected him to be wearing a soutane. But they did see Chrostowski leaving and even followed him for a while before pulling away in the belief that Fr Popiełuszko was not with him.

Piotrowski, it seems, was untroubled by the news that they had failed to confirm the priest's departure. He simply told them to report back to the Ministry; they were going to Bydgoszcz all the same.

In the hours before their own departure, the three conspirators completed their collection of documents, gear and weaponry. Piotrowski picked up the 'W' pass, apparently from Colonel Pietruszka, and a document authorising the trip and the use of the same 125 Fiat of the earlier attempt, also signed and stamped by Pietruszka. Chmielewski, on Piotrowski's instructions, borrowed a police sergeant's jacket and a cap with a white cover, the sort worn by traffic police. He had already borrowed a pair of handcuffs. None of these items were obtained through official channels. Pękala had laid his hands on a torch with a red filter, as used by traffic police. After loading their gear into the car, they filled up the fuel tank and their 20-litre canister at the Ministry's petrol station and picked up coupons for 50 litres, which were valid at ordinary civilian stations.

They also drove to Piotrowski's flat to pick up his service pistol and two magazines of ammunition. Earlier, the Captain had ordered Chmielewski to take his pistol as well, but the Lieutenant would claim that he took no ammunition. Piotrowski collected something else from his flat — a 5-litre canister of petrol to be used, he said, to set fire to the priest's car 'after seizing its occupants'. The trio left Warsaw for Bydgoszcz at about 1:30 pm.

Piotrowski's secretary, Barbara Story, would testify that her boss had told her that morning that Colonel Pietruszka knew the reason for his absence and where he was going. Later, she said, General Płatek had phoned, asking for Piotrowski or his deputy, Janusz Dróżdż. She had told the General that Dróżdż had been sent to Gdańsk by Pietruszka, and that the Colonel knew why Piotrowski was absent. The General had phoned again later that afternoon only to be told that Piotrowski was still absent.

The rule in the Ministry was that either the head of a section or his deputy had to be on hand, in his office, at all times; they could not be out of town at the same time. The above testimony, therefore, was very bad for Pietruszka and, at the same time, wonderfully good for General Płatek. If true, it meant that Colonel Pietruszka had not only deliberately broken the operational rules of the Ministry but knew where the absent Piotrowski had gone and why. The General, in contrast, would seem to be in the clear: frustrated by the absence of Piotrowski and Dróżdż and unaware of what might be going on in Bydgoszcz.

Captain Piotrowski and his two lieutenants followed the same route to Bydgoszcz as Fr Popiełuszko and his companions. They made a number of stops on the way.

At a small place called Jeżewo, Pękala suddenly stopped. He, stepped down into a field and returned with a wooden stake broken in two. Pękala suggested that the two pieces — 55 cm long and 4 cm thick — would make better weapons than socks filled with sand as suggested by Piotrowski.

The trio paused again at Studzieniec, to the west of Sierpc, where there was a sharp turn at the foot of a hill and the road ran along a ridge. This, they thought, was a suitable setting for an 'accident' such as the one they had attempted on the road from Gdańsk. There was a third stop near Lipno when the fan belt broke.

Between Toruń and Bydgoszcz, the three men chose a deserted spot for a possible abduction. They later stopped for a while at a simple roadside restaurant called Lesniczanka, and arrived in Bydgoszcz shortly after 5 pm. They went straight to the local Police Headquarters and both Piotrowski and Pękala entered the building. While Pękala visited the lavatory, Piotrowski asked where he could find the Ministry's filling station and claimed to have phoned Warsaw and spoken to the Deputy Duty Officer of Department Four. The latter, unnamed, was to deny this. According to Pękala, Piotrowski also asked the way to the Wyżyny district — a surprising question from an officer supposedly on a secret, undercover operation. Leaving the police station, they visited the petrol station and drove on in search of the church. When they reached the church of the Polish Martyrs, it must have been, at the latest, not long after Mass began at 6 pm.

Leaving Chmielewski to keep watch outside, Piotrowski and Pękala went into the church, to confirm that Fr Popiełuszko was there. There was no evidence of his presence on the street, for Waldek Chrostowski had put the light green Golf in the presbytery garage. After Fr Popiełuszko's presence was confirmed, Pękala and Chmielewski drove to the outskirts of the district and replaced their Warsaw plates, WAB 6031, with KZC 0423. They also wrapped strips of an old vest around the ends of the two wooden stakes picked up by Pękala on the way to Bydgoszcz, tying them on with string. Blows struck with such weapons were supposed to leave no mark.

Two local plain-clothes policemen were on duty near the church that night and had already noted the arrival of a Fiat 125 with three male passengers and very grubby Warsaw number plates. After Pękala and Chmielewski had returned and parked again near the church, one of the plain-clothes men noticed that the car's number plates were not only cleaner but different. It was as they sat in the car during one of Piotrowski's periodic absences that his two accomplices heard one of the men draw his colleague's attention to the fact in a loud voice. When Piotrowski returned, Chmielewski told him that they had noted down the change of number plates. 'Let them,' the Captain said, as if it didn't matter.

By that time Fr Popiełuszko was feeling distinctly unwell. He had been ill all day with a feverish cold. As soon as he had arrived that afternoon, he had asked if he could lie down. He had rested in the presbytery before saying Mass. As soon as Mass was over he returned to the presbytery to take his temperature, but went back to lead the congregation in saying the rosary, giving a short meditation before each of its mysteries.

While the three SB men were waiting for him outside, he spoke some particularly pertinent words:

> In order to defeat evil with good, in order to preserve the dignity of man, one must not use violence… It is the person who has failed to win on the strength of his heart and his reason who tries to win by force… The idea that requires a weapon to support itself will die away of itself. The idea which maintains itself exclusively by the use of violence is flawed… Solidarity astonished the world so quickly because it did not use violence in its struggle but knelt, rosary in hand, at open-air altars and spoke out in defence of the dignity of work, of dignity and respect for man… Solidarity… proved that for social and economic reconstruction there is no need at all to break away from God.
>
> Let us pray that we may be free from fear and intimidation, but above all from lust for revenge and violence.[2]

They were the last words Fr Popiełuszko uttered in public.

After the rosary, Fr Popiełuszko had joined a small group of workers for supper in one of the presbytery's upstairs rooms. Marek Wilk was among them. He could tell that the priest was unwell, and saw him taking tablets.

Eventually the Volkswagen Golf was driven to the front of the church by Waldek Chrostowski. Fr Popiełuszko prepared to leave, still wearing his soutane, and it was almost 9.30 pm when he said goodbye to Marek Wilk, who was to lead the Golf out of town onto the road to Warsaw. He told him: 'I'm not important to them now that I've given my sermon.'

As he went to his red Fiat Sports, Wilk noticed a grey Fiat parked near the church. It was similar, he thought, to the one he had seen parked near St Stanisław's that morning. As he drove away, with the Golf behind him, he could see that the Fiat was following. It stayed with them through the town and out onto the straight stretch of dual carriage-way leading to Fordon, where those driving to Warsaw turn right.

At Fordon, Marek Wilk waved goodbye to the Golf, and headed back towards Bydgoszcz. As he did so, he noticed that another Fiat, which he had earlier observed following them, turned left behind him. The car, which he thought was brown, followed him all the way back to town but lost him, according to Wilk, when he turned into heavy traffic.

The green Golf, meanwhile, with Chrostowski at the wheel and the ailing Fr Popiełuszko in the front passenger seat, had left the well-lit highway, crossed to the right bank of the Vistula and entered the dark country road leading to Toruń.

In the Fiat behind them, Piotrowski told Chmielewski to change into the uniform. The captain and his two lieutenants began the chase.

# 13

# Kidnapped

Waldek Chrostowski was a professional driver with the fire service and didn't think much of the Golf. It was old and he would describe it later, in court, as a bit of a corpse. He was making good time, travelling at about 120 km/h, and was roughly a dozen kilometres short of Toruń, when he noticed in his rear view mirror a car coming up behind with its headlights on full beam. Remarking to Fr Popiełuszko that they had been joined by 'some sort of nut', Chrostowski tried accelerating to get out of range of the blinding lights and then slowing to let the car pass. The car behind began flashing its lights and eventually began to overtake. It was a light-coloured Fiat.

As it drew level, Chrostowski saw a policeman in the front passenger seat signalling them to stop, waving a torch with a red light. The Fiat pulled up on the roadside ahead of them, but Chrostowski carried on past it. He was reluctant to stop at night in deserted countryside next to a wood, but did so when Fr Jerzy insisted, 'otherwise there could be trouble'. They stopped a couple of kilometres past the farming village of Górsk.

With the Golf parked four or five metres in front of the Fiat, Chrostowski got his documents out — identity card, driver's licence and car registration — and lowered his window halfway. The policeman approached, saluted, remarked on the speed with which Chrostowski had been driving and asked for the documents. All this was perfectly normal. But as Chrostowski handed his documents over, he saw another man, in civilian clothing, standing behind the policeman. This one demanded the car keys. Chrostowski switched off the engine and was about to hand them over when he hesitated, realising that this was not normal procedure. The keys were snatched from his hand.

Chrostowski was then invited to go to the other car for a breath test. He was put into the front passenger seat and as the door slammed behind him the driver said, 'Give me your hand.' He consented, thinking this was part of the test, but was instantly handcuffed. Someone behind him seized him by the neck and gagged him by stuffing a piece of towelling into his mouth. The man in the back then passed a pistol to the driver and told him to keep an eye on Chrostowski while he went for the priest.

Chrostowski could only watch as the two men talked Fr Popiełuszko into getting out of the Golf. They led the reluctant priest back towards the Fiat, crossing to the driver's side. Halfway across, Chrostowski saw the priest hesitate, whereupon the two men grabbed the sleeves of his soutane and jerked him forward. Through the driver's open window, Chrostowski could hear Fr Jerzy complaining. He expected the men to put him into the back seat but they carried on. He wanted to look back to see what was happening but the driver warned him not to move. This was when the violence began, as Chrostowski would testify.

> They couldn't have got further than one or one and a half metres from the car, when there was a dull thud as if someone had hit a sack of flour with a big stick. I noticed how the driver reacted. There was a sort of revulsion, he sort of flinched or winced. I realised that Fr Popiełuszko had been struck and that this was the driver's reaction to the blow... he winced, he clenched his teeth... I realised that something awful had happened to the priest.[1]

It was an account Waldemar Chrostowski was to repeat consistently. What he had not noticed was the hefty wooden stake which the man in civilian clothes, Captain Grzegorz Piotrowski of the SB, took with him as he went back to the Golf to get Fr Popiełuszko, whose window was partially lowered. According to Piotrowski, the priest was reluctant to get out of the car 'for purposes of identification', but did so after the Captain had inserted the end of the stake into the gap between the door frame and the glass.

At this point, Chmielewski testified, Popiełuszko was ordered to switch off the Golf's lights but failed to do so. Getting into the seat just vacated by Fr Popiełuszko, Chmielewski couldn't find the light switch and when he tried to get out he couldn't find the door catch. He lowered the window and opened the door from the outside. As he did so, he said, he was summoned by Piotrowski who said the priest was refusing to get into the Fiat. When he asked Fr Popiełuszko why he wouldn't get in, Chmielewski testified, the priest replied, 'Because this man is dragging me somewhere.'

They were standing, Chmielewski continued, at the rear of the car 'on the road side' (on the left hand or driver's side), and Piotrowski was holding the priest's soutane with his left hand near the shoulder blade.

> Fr Popiełuszko was given a tug by Piotrowski and propelled forward behind the boot of the car. I saw Piotrowski strike the priest with the stake. He hit him in the upper part of the body, in the area of the head... He certainly hit him more than once... and largely from behind... The priest was already reeling from that tug... the first blow was struck as he fell. Further blows were struck when he could already have been lying on the ground...[2]

Piotrowski's testimony, in contrast to that of both Chrostowski and Chmielewski, was that he led Fr Popiełuszko along the other side of the Fiat, where the ground fell away sharply at the edge of the road. He would claim that it was the priest's attempt to get away, after refusing to get into the car, that led to the violence.

> When we were level with the boot... Jerzy Popiełuszko gave a determined pull. I caught hold of him with my finger tips but he broke free, slightly losing his balance, and tried to escape. I then hit him with the stake...
>
> I cannot say how many times I hit him. At least twice, most probably three times, though I can't exclude the possibility that I struck him a fourth time... It was after the last blow that Jerzy Popiełuszko fell down, sinking to the ground about two metres from the boot. It all happened very quickly. I don't remember whether it was a blow to the head. I think it was in the area of the head... the top of his back, the neck, the head... That was the beginning of the entire catastrophe...[3]

According to Chmielewski, they dragged the priest off the road into the bushes. On Piotrowski's instructions, he had then transferred some things from the boot to the back seat of the car and got some cord or string with which Piotrowski tied the priest's hands. Neither of them could remember whether or not the priest was gagged, but they agreed that his body was limp as they crammed it into the boot. Chmielewski saw the lights of a car coming up behind. Slamming down the lid of the boot, they jumped into the car, Chmielewski behind Pękala, Piotrowski behind Chrostowski. Piotrowski shouted, 'Put your foot down — let's go,' and the car sped away, leaving behind the Golf with its lights on.

Chrostowski had felt the car give as Fr Popiełuszko was loaded into the boot. But as he explained later in court, he could not be sure from what he had heard and felt whether or not the bandits, as he called them, had actually abandoned the priest in the woods or on the road while only pretending to put him in the boot by pressing down on the rear bumper of the car.

After the car had gone some 300 metres, Chrostowski said, one of the men behind him (it was Piotrowski) tied a cord over his gag, knotting it at the back of his head. 'This is to keep your mouth shut on your last journey,' a voice said. Chrostowski also noticed the driver pass the pistol to someone in the back of the car. 'I felt something touching me from behind,' he said, 'and heard the words: "Sit there quietly, don't move."' He then heard the same voice urging the driver to 'turn into the first track in the woods'.

Chrostowski agonised over what he could do, but he had little choice. He thought of seizing the wheel and causing an accident. He was handcuffed with his hands in front, not behind his back. But if Fr Popieluszko was in the boot, a crash would surely kill him. And since he did not have his seat belt fastened, his own chances of survival would be very small. At the same time, the voice in the back kept telling the driver to turn off into the woods. This persuaded Chrostowski that his own life, as well as that of the priest, was in serious danger.

He decided to try to jump out of the car, somewhere where there would be witnesses so as to leave some trace of the crime. 'I realised,' he said, 'that a stain on the road might be all that remained of me.'

> I leaned forward and felt for the door catch with my little finger… No one ordered me to sit back in my seat. I kept leaning forward and waited for witnesses to appear, people or other vehicles on the road… After we had gone some four or five kilometres from the spot where the Golf had been abandoned, I saw a 'maluch', a Fiat 126p, ahead of us… I also saw two men standing by a motorcycle… I decided to do the jump with the small Fiat's headlights on us, so that they could see what was happening. When we had overtaken the small Fiat and I could see a glimmer of its lights, I opened the door with my shoulder and threw myself out onto the road head first.[4]

Chrostowski estimated that when he jumped, the car was travelling at between 90 and 110 km/h. On hitting the road, he had slid forward and then wrapped himself into a ball so that he could roll. When he came out of the roll and got to his feet, he found that the handcuffs had come off one of his hands.

Without pausing to examine his injuries, Chrostowski stepped out onto the road and tried to stop the small Fiat. When the car drove round him — which he found shocking — he ran back to the motorcyclists and tried to persuade one of them to take him as a passenger and either chase after the kidnap car or go back with him to see if they could find the priest near the abandoned Golf. Once again he was disappointed. The bike's engine wouldn't fire. Then Chrostowski noticed a large, well-lit building some 180 to 200 metres further ahead. 'I ran towards it across the fields... not knowing what it was.' It was the farm workers' hostel at Przysiek.

As Waldek Chrostowski ran for help, the kidnap car drove on, presumably because there were witnesses. Pękala had slowed down automatically when Chrostowski jumped, but Piotrowski told him to drive on as quickly as possible. Looking back, he had seen Chrostowski hit the roadway raising a spark, from his handcuffs no doubt, and then rising to a kneeling position. Chrostowski was not badly hurt, Piotrowski said, and anyway his escape had saved them the bother of finding a tree to tie him to.

Chrostowski was in a state when he staggered into the hostel. He couldn't see anybody downstairs but upstairs he found a group of young men drinking. Seventeen-year-old Mirosław Malanowski said later that Chrostowski 'fell into the room'. He was shaking, excited and unsteady, and was bleeding from abrasions to one of his hands and the area of his ribs. His jacket was in tatters, his jeans were torn and he was wearing only one shoe. He said he must use the telephone.

Chrostowski was led downstairs to the receptionist, Ewa Affelt, in the basement. He told her that Fr Popiełuszko had been kidnapped and that he wanted to phone the Curia and the Episcopate in Warsaw. She phoned the police and ambulance service in Toruń, but failed to get through to the Church authorities in Warsaw. According to the official record, Police Headquarters in Toruń received the call from the hostel at Przysiek at 10.05 pm. The Duty Officer there responded by phoning the police post in the village of Zlawieś Wielka, nearest the scene of the abduction (in fact Toruń was just as close), and instructed the local constable to investigate and report back.

An ambulance arrived very quickly, according to Chrostowski, and by the time the police turned up, he had gone. The doctor had agreed to take him by ambulance to the nearest church, where Chrostowski could tell his story to someone he trusted. At that moment he could not trust men in police uniform.

He was taken to the parish church of the Virgin Mary in the centre of Toruń. The parish priest, Fr Józef Nowakowski, answered the door bell between 10:20 and 10:30 pm. Chrostowski, he said, looked like a scarecrow. 'He told me that I must rescue Fr Popiełuszko, who had been kidnapped.' Fr Nowakowski listened to Chrostowski's story and got him to go through it a second time. When he asked him to repeat it yet again, one of the ambulance men protested and Chrostowski left the priest's house for the Toruń first aid clinic to be X-rayed and treated. He did so reluctantly. As the only witness to the crime, he thought he could be attacked again.

Not long after hearing Chrostowski's account of the abduction — 10 minutes later at the most — Fr Nowakowski got through to the police by phone. 'I underlined that one of the assailants was wearing a uniform, that they were pretending to be police and were, for that reason, virtually untouchable. The officer who took the call said they already had that information…'[5]

As Fr Nowakowski made clear at the trial, his conversation with the police officer over the phone went on for some time. He told the officer that this was not the first abduction in the Toruń area. There had been several kidnapping cases earlier in the year, he said, all of them with a very similar modus operandi involving cars and handcuffs. On Fr Nowakowski's insistence, an SB officer was called to the phone. The priest told the same story and advised that if the police were short of manpower, he could call on people to start searching for Fr Popiełuszko. This, the parish priest was told, would not be necessary.

Fr Nowakowski's testimony included one other curious

feature. He said that he had not phoned Church authorities at the Warsaw Curia because the police officer he had talked to first had advised against it. 'He said that the people who had kidnapped the priest might be listening in, so it was better not to ring.' He did phone a Warsaw presbytery but got no reply.

After talking to the police, Fr Nowakowski and another priest drove out to Górsk, where they found the abandoned Golf. It was being guarded by two uniformed policemen with a radio car. Told not to start searching in the woods — 'as someone might be lurking in there' — the two priests walked along the edge of the woods, flashing a torch and calling on Fr Popiełuszko to come out. 'There's nothing to be afraid of,' they shouted.

Later, on the way home, Fr Nowakowski and his colleague met two armoured cars and felt pleased to see that a search was under way. They reached home at about a quarter past midnight, by which time Fr Popiełuszko was dead.

# 14

# The Murder

There are no independent witnesses to the murder of Fr Popiełuszko. All evidence of what happened to him after Waldek Chrostowski's escape has been provided exclusively by the murderers. Inevitably, their testimony was suspect, not only because they were defending themselves, and indeed their lives, but also because the organisation that investigated the crime was the Ministry of Internal Affairs, for which they were working when they killed the priest. The evidence is confusing and frequently contradictory, but a picture, however incomplete, does take shape, and the words of the accused are sometimes as dramatic as any imagination could devise.

As they drove into Toruń at around 10 pm that Friday night, the kidnappers heard a loud bang coming, apparently, from the front of the car. It happened, according to Pękala, as they were crossing some tramlines. Chmielewski remembered hearing it when they were not far from a building with a police car outside — a police station, in fact. Piotrowski said that he did not know the street although he had worked in Toruń for six months.

It was while they were on that street, according to Chmielewski, that he noticed from the back seat a commotion inside the boot; the priest was forcing up the lid. And it was after this that he and Piotrowski started screaming at Pękala to turn off as soon as he could.

Pękala turned right by the Kosmos Hotel and then followed his chief's instructions. 'Piotrowski guided me, saying, "Now right, now left" and we entered a kind of plaza or open area on the River Vistula near a bridge. The bridge over the Vistula was to the left of this open space.'[1]

Some reports have suggested that the violence which now ensued took place in the car park behind the hotel. But if you follow Piotrowski's instructions to Pękala, as I did on the second anniversary of the crime and at roughly the same time of day, after 10 pm, you end up not in the car park immediately behind the hotel, but in a large open space below the hotel, on the other side of a fence and some small trees, and on the river bank with the bridge visible to the left, a place deserted at that time of night and well out of sight and earshot of the hotel. Captain Piotrowski claimed not to know Toruń very well but this 'open space without any buildings', as he described it, could not have been better suited to dealing with the problem, in his words, of having 'a car that wouldn't go and Popiełuszko in the boot'. On reaching this spot, he said, there had been a second loud bang, to which Pękala had responded 'Now we're really finished'. Piotrowski continued:

We jumped out of the car to check the wheels and the engine. We opened the bonnet. I think now that possibly Pękala opened the boot instead of the bonnet. I saw Popiełuszko dashing across this open space. I shouted and ran after him. I caught up with him and stunned him with several blows from behind... hitting him in the area of the head — the shoulders, the neck, the head. Jerzy Popiełuszko fell down inert. I think he was unconscious when he fell. Then I completely, sort of... it doesn't matter.[2]

At this point in his testimony, Piotrowski said that Fr Popiełuszko was the first person he had struck since primary school. As he stood over the priest's inert body, he had told Pękala that he couldn't touch him again. There was 'a fear of his body'. He remembered only being helped to put Fr Popiełuszko back into the boot.

Chmielewski would tell the court that what happened in Toruń was 'incomprehensible' and that it 'went beyond what had been agreed'. And in one important respect, he failed to corroborate Piotrowski's account. In testimony before the trial, he indicated that on getting out of the car, Piotrowski went straight to the boot to see about Fr Popiełuszko and not to the bonnet to see what was wrong with the car.

He was able to see what happened because he went to the rear of the car having been told to change the false number plates back to normal. Six days after the crime, with events presumably still fresh in his memory, he told interrogators that he saw the priest 'tear himself away from Piotrowski'. A week later, he filled in the picture.

> From the boot came the sound of Fr Popiełuszko crying out. Then I saw that Piotrowski was standing over Popiełuszko who was already getting out of the boot. Popiełuszko tore himself away and with a shout began to run away. I noticed that a length of rope was dangling from one of his arms... I can't explain why Piotrowski allowed Popiełuszko to get away at that moment... Piotrowski and Pękala brought him back. It looked as though they were holding him up, supporting him under the arms. They laid him down on the grass next to the car...

Chmielewski's account was supported in part by Pękala when he told the court that Piotrowski had ordered him to open the boot (not the bonnet). Pękala, however, was a very poor witness when it came to describing what he saw when he and Piotrowski recaptured the escaping priest. His testimony was a confusing mixture of firm statements followed rapidly by others casting doubt on them.

> Piotrowski shouted to me to open the boot. I think I heard the sounds of beating with a stake. The priest ran away shouting

'save me'. Piotrowski caught up with him and I saw him hit him
with the stake… The priest covered his head with his hands.
He keeled over…

Twice in this same passage Pękala said he could not say whether
Piotrowski had had a stake in his hand but he insisted that the
Captain had struck the priest several times. In spite of the
confusion and the doubts, Pękala's testimony — like that of
Piotrowski and Chmielewski — suggested that this bout of
violence had been more than he could stand.

Pękala was far more at ease when discussing practical details.
He was quite clear, for instance, when describing the priest's gag;
it was part of a torn towel bearing the inscription of Orbis, the
State tourism and hotel agency. He had secured it, he said, with
a length of nylon thread tied round the head. He was less sure,
however, when it came to describing the priest's condition as he
was being bound and gagged. According to Piotrowski, Fr
Popiełuszko was unconscious. According to Chmielewski, the
priest did not say anything and did not stir. Pękala simply didn't
know whether the priest was unconscious or just stunned. He
'behaved calmly', he said.

It was only after locking Fr Popiełuszko back in the boot that
the trio checked the car's engine and discovered that the loud
bang had been caused by the oil cap blowing off. After replacing
the cap with a glove stuffed into the hole, they drove off.
Chmielewski,however, had changed only the rear number plate.
For the rest of the journey they travelled with odd plates at back
and front.

For a reason never conclusively explained, Piotrowski, who
was now in the front passenger seat, directed the car not onto
the road to Lipno and the northern route by which they had
arrived, but across the bridge over the Vistula. One can only
speculate why Piotrowski did this. He may, for instance, have
been afraid that if they drove through the city, Fr Popiełuszko
might stage another noticeable commotion inside the boot if
and when they were brought to a halt at one of the several tram
stops on the route out. It is a fact, however, that this road led

past the dam over the Vistula at Włocławek, on the south side of the river.

None of them remembered much about their exit from Toruń. Chmielewski, in the back seat, was keeping an eye on the boot in case the captive priest caused more trouble. Pękala, behind the wheel, was concentrating on Piotrowski's directions because he did not know the way. And Piotrowski recalled only a vague memory of passing three cars being checked by traffic police. He also said he saw some stationary police radio cars and wondered about road blocks. His main concern, though, was the condition of the car; it was making slow, stuttering progress, he said, and the oil warning light was on. Then they saw a filling station on the left. They didn't drive into the station, afraid that Fr Popiełuszko might attract attention by banging against the boot lid. Instead they pulled up a short distance past the station.

While Piotrowski ran back to buy some oil, Pękala executed a U-turn leaving the car boot facing away from the filling station. On getting out of the car with Pękala, Chmielewski said they found a pronounced bulge or swelling on the boot's lid. Having failed to press it down with their hands, they sat on the lid until Piotrowski came back. When they did this, Pękala said, the priest, who had been moving again, fell silent. Piotrowski returned with two bottles of oil, one of which he poured into the engine, and they set off again in the direction of Włocławek.

At this point in the trial, Captain Piotrowski announced that he would exercise his right to silence; he would say no more for now and answer no questions. He said that he could remember only two occasions on which he had struck Fr Popiełuszko; the first was at Górsk, where the priest was kidnapped, and the second was in Toruń. The testimony of his two assistants, however, was clear. Chmielewski said that when he noticed that Fr Popiełuszko was knocking inside the boot and forcing up the lid, they pulled up and all three got out of the car.

> Then I saw Piotrowski with the pistol in his hands saying: 'You just move and I'll shoot you.' He handed the pistol to Pękala and told him: 'Shoot if he moves.'

I just stood on the roadway like an idiot. I couldn't take my eyes off the priest. Piotrowski was doing something with the gag. Leszek said he should squeeze the priest's nose... to make him open his mouth. Piotrowski did so and managed to fix the gag. The priest did not move. We slammed the boot shut and Piotrowski told Pękala: 'Drive on and turn off straight away.' Piotrowski and I didn't get back into the car but walked behind it keeping the lid of the boot down with our hands...

Eventually we turned off the road into a side lane... We went in some 20 to 30 metres... and entered an area of bushes and tall grass... the car stopped and the boot was opened. Piotrowski said something to the priest. I think the priest moved violently. Piotrowski said something like 'Keep still' or 'Keep quiet'.

Chmielewski said he couldn't remember how or when the priest was taken from the boot and put back in it but he did remember him lying on the grass.

I saw Piotrowski hit the priest with the stake. He hit him on the head and maybe on the shoulders. The priest, I think was lying on his side. I can't really explain this but I then got hold of the car and started to rock it. I couldn't go near the priest. Piotrowski called me to go nearer... He flashed the torch and I said: Put it out.

Leszek Pękala was by the priest's head. Give me a hand, he said. I then held the thread securing the gag while he tied it behind the head... After leaving that place, I remembered, from the touch of it, that the gag was made of gauze...[3]

Pękala's testimony differed in one crucial respect from that of Chmielewski. He said that after he had stopped the car in the thickets and opened the boot 'Fr Popiełuszko was beaten with the stake' while 'still lying in the boot'. He went on: 'At least once I heard the distinctive sound of the stake hitting against the car's bodywork. Piotrowski could have hit him several times.'

Chmielewski said nothing about this. But if, as he and Pękala testified, he and Piotrowski entered the thickets on foot, holding the boot lid down with their hands, he should have been able to see what happened when the lid of the boot was raised. All he said was that he couldn't remember whether they all lifted the priest out of the boot.

Pękala next testified how he re-tied the bonds on Fr Popiełuszko's hands and legs as he lay on the coverlet spread out on the grass. He could not say whether the priest was conscious; 'his body was inert'. Piotrowski, he thought, had hit him again but he could not say whether he did so with his fist or with the stake.

Pękala's testimony, as already noted, was never entirely definite. At this point he said that Piotrowski had shouted out loud at least once: 'I'll throttle him with my own, bare hands'. Under questioning he said that he never saw Piotrowski beat the priest or throttle him in the boot — 'I didn't want to look' — but that the priest was 'unconscious' and 'offered no resistance' when taken out of the boot. He thought that Piotrowski, as it were, 'pacified' him. Pressed further, Pękala said he was unable to explain how it happened that Fr Popiełuszko was conscious before the car entered the thickets and found to be unconscious when taken from the boot.

Given the conflicting evidence, it is difficult to say what exactly happened in the thickets. But given also the reactions of Chmielewski, who admitted that he started rocking the car, and of Pękala, who said he didn't want to look, we have to guess that it was extremely unpleasant. The fact that Piotrowski chose to say nothing at this point is also significant.

Having again loaded Fr Popiełuszko back into the boot, the three set off towards Włocławek. How far they went before they stopped again is impossible to determine on the evidence provided by Chmielewski and Pękala. But Chmielewski provided the better clues.

> After some time I proposed that we should abandon the priest somewhere... We drove into a sloping entry point but... Pękala said the car was sinking, getting stuck. Piotrowski told

him to back out and find another track... Once again, the priest started beating violently against the underside of the boot lid, denting it badly... After five to ten minutes we turned into a wide track in the woods... It was near Toruń, straight after the fly-over, I think... not a typical fly-over, just a kind of archway. We stopped after several dozen metres...

The statement that they turned into the woods 'after several minutes' is less helpful than it sounds in piecing together the events of that night. Was it several minutes after leaving the thickets or several minutes after Piotrowski told him to turn into the woods?

We all got out of the car. Piotrowski was in front of me, by the boot... I saw Piotrowski hit Popiełuszko as he lay in the boot. I could hear him hitting even the bodywork. I'm not in a position to say where exactly he hit him. I didn't want to look, and besides, the boot lid concealed the upper part of the priest's body. He certainly hit him more than once. He struck the car bodywork once...

We all lifted Fr Popiełuszko out and laid him down near birch trees. I remember that we all stood there. I didn't know what I was supposed to do. For a moment we all stood there, next to each other, next to the priest as he lay there... He made no noticeable movement.

Then the boss said: 'What's this? Do I have to do everything myself?' I bent down over the priest's face and noticed that his gag was sticking out. I thought about adjusting it but couldn't. The priest's mouth was tightly closed. At that moment, I heard a hoarse noise coming from his nose. I was terrified that if I adjusted the gag I could make him suffocate. I stood up and went back to the car. I touched the gag but couldn't adjust it.

I saw Piotrowski standing close to the car. Then he moved. He had a stake in his hand. 'Stones on the feet,' he said. Since I was standing by the car, I reached for the sack of stones. I thought to myself it could not be possible that such a thing was happening. I crouched with the sack of stones at the priest's feet and fumbled around with the cords. I think I threaded the cords over those tying his feet together. At that moment I had the impression that one of the priest's legs moved. At that same moment a train passed nearby. I seized this opportunity to leave the sack untied and escape back to the car. Piotrowski continued standing there. Pękala was doing something next to the priest. I don't know what.[4]

Leszek Pękala explained that he helped Chmielewski tie the sack of stones to the priest's feet while Piotrowski stood over them, supervising their work. Then he described his own distinctive contribution.

I looped a noose around Fr Popiełuszko's neck. The rope ran down the length of his spine. I tied the ends to his feet and then to his hands. The priest's legs were bent backwards. The noose was tied in such a way that it would tighten on the priest's throat if he were to straighten his legs. I tied it this way so that the priest would not try to lift the lid of the boot with his body. I did this because the priest had been unconscious several times before but had then recovered consciousness and tried to lift the lid.[5]

Pękala then held up Fr Popiełuszko's head as Chmielewski wound sticking plaster over the gag and round the head and face two or three times. The nose was not covered, Pękala said.

Then, according to Chmielewski, Piotrowski gave the order 'Pakujemy' — 'Let's pack him away' — and all three lifted the priest, trussed and weighed down by a sack of stones, and placed him for the last time in the boot of the car.

As Fr Popiełuszko was driven towards Włocławek it seemed certain that if he were to recover even the minimum of consciousness and respond to his instinct for survival, the rope would tighten round his neck. And with the gag, covered by sticking plaster, now immovable, the priest from Żoliborz had been silenced.

Each of the priest's three captors now knew what was happening and the likely result. Pękala told the court that when he attached the sack of stones to Fr Popiełuszko's feet, he understood that the priest 'could die, could be thrown into the water', but still hoped it would end otherwise.

On the drive into Włocławek, he and Chmielewski said they tried to convince Piotrowski that there was no need to kill Fr Popiełuszko. Chmielewski pointed out that if the priest should die, Pękala could be identified by Waldemar Chrostowski who had sat next to him in the kidnap car before escaping. Both of them argued that after everything Fr Popiełuszko had been through that night, he would certainly give up his previous activity; he could safely be abandoned in the woods. Piotrowski's reply came in two words: 'Tylko woda', 'Only the water', which meant — as Pękala later explained — 'regardless of whether he was dead or alive'.

'At that moment,' Pękala said, 'I felt powerless, trapped. I ceased to think critically. I asked myself how it could have come to this. I told myself, "I must be obedient." Now I know I was wrong. Chmielewski maintained to the end that the priest should be set free. But then, like me, he fell silent. He said no more...'[6]

Chmielewski said the arguments went on for quite a long time but Piotrowski told him to keep his eye on the boot. 'The priest kept quiet all the time... There was no movement. I was terrified. I thought that the priest had not survived the beating and died... I said nothing more...'[7]

Asked by one of the medical experts how long this final drive lasted, Pękala replied 'Up to an hour'.

Captain Piotrowski, resuming his testimony from the moment they left the woods, said that they made slow progress, unable to go any faster than 50 to 60 km/h. He said he wanted to get Popiełuszko to Warsaw but described what changed his mind.

Waldek [Chmielewski] said that Popiełuszko was not showing any signs of life... I turned towards the back... leaned

backwards as best I could and saw the face of Popiełuszko...
It seemed to me that this was the face of a dead man... One
of my colleagues said we should leave him there. They judged
that he was alive... But do you leave someone presumed dead
in a ditch?[8]

... We drove on and came to a road junction. According to
the map we had reached the road to Łódź. In the distance I
could see a police patrol... A policeman got out of the radio
car and signalled us to stop. Leszek slowed down and I showed
the pass through the window. The policeman waved us on. We
drove on for another 50 metres and I had another look... and
I saw the face of a dead man; through the crack... the light was
on. That was the face of a dead man. I told Pękala: 'Leszek,
turn round. We'll go across the dam.' I was convinced that I
had killed Popiełuszko. We drove past the policeman and onto
the dam.[9]

According to Piotrowski, the gap between the boot lid and the
car body below the rear window through which he said he saw
the priest's face now measured nearly 5 cm.

As instructed by Piotrowski, Pękala did a U-turn and drove
north, past the stark silhouettes of industrial buildings on the
left and up onto the dam. It looks not unlike an ordinary
bridge (and is used as such) except for tall metal structures
that dominate its eastern side. They passed these on their
right and stopped in a small parking area on the north side of
the river.

Piotrowski looked down into the water. 'There's no sense in
taking him further,' he said. 'We have to get rid of him here.' But
Pękala said they couldn't do it there because of concrete pylons
sticking out. They drove back to the middle of the dam. They
the three men lifted Fr Popiełuszko out of the boot, hoisted
him over the rail and dropped him. The body fell some 16 to 17
metres before hitting the water.

Piotrowski's account was terse, but he recalled that it proved
difficult to get the body out of the boot because it had become

wedged and the priest's soutane had caught on something. Pękala said more:

> I was the last to reach the open boot. It was my impression that Fr Popiełuszko was dead. His brow was covered by large beads of sweat. My impression was that it was cold sweat. By accident I touched one of the priest's hands and that was definitely cold. No one checked whether he was alive or dead... As we lifted the body out of the boot, the priet's soutane got caught on the lock...[10]

Chmielewski remembered hearing 'a loud splash'. The priest's body, he said, was horizontal when dropped. 'We simply lifted it across the rail and let go of it at the same time. I was holding the sack of stones separately.'[11]

Chmielewski had already provided a more detailed picture during interrogation in Toruń on 25 October, the Thursday after the crime.

> Pękala opened the boot. I took hold of the sack on the priest's legs. I remember that Fr Popiełuszko was wearing unusual shoes. Pękala got hold of the middle of his body. Piotrowski held him near the head. We lifted the body across the rail and dropped it into the water on the river side, not the reservoir side of the dam. To put it another way, we were facing in the direction of Włocławek.

The three SB officers wasted no time in getting away from the dam as the clocks ticked towards midnight on Friday, 19 October 1984 — the fifty-ninth birthday, as it happened, of their most senior commander, General Czesław Kiszczak, Minister of Internal Affairs.

Leszek Pękala executed another U-turn and headed north to Lipno, and then east to Warsaw.

# 15

# Removing the Traces[1]

By all three accounts, it was a grim journey through the dark and silent countryside back to Warsaw. According to Piotrowski, the atmosphere inside the car was one of shock and fear. He felt obliged to comfort his accomplices, assuring them that they would be 'rescued' and might even be posted abroad.

But Captain Piotrowski, it seems, was in two minds about what the future might hold. He said that everything would be fine as long as the body was not found. But he went on, according to Pękala, to say that if the body were to be found, 'then it's the gallows for us'. Chmielewski remembered how Piotrowski assured them that Fr Popiełuszko's body would not be found as long as they said they knew nothing, if questioned. And anyway, he continued, 'nobody will allow us to be interrogated, to have our prints taken or to be confronted by anyone'.

Pękala was not so easily reassured. He was afraid of being identified by Chrostowski, the priest's driver, who must have seen him closely. Furthermore, he admitted, his finger prints were already on police files. Piotrowski had insisted that there was nothing to worry about — 'The criminal investigations department is ours'.

Pękala said he needed a drink, and the three quickly finished off about half a litre of vodka. As Piotrowski was to explain, this was drinking not for celebration but for its deadening effect.

The three young and ambitious SB officers must have been very conscious of the danger to which they had exposed themselves. There were two obvious leads for any investigation to follow. The first was the story to be told by Waldek Chrostowski, who by then found himself, rather unhappily, in the safekeeping of the Toruń SB. The second was the fact that the two policemen outside the church in Bydgoszcz had noted the arrival of the kidnap car with Warsaw number plates (WAB 6031) and its later reappearance with different plates (KZC 0423). If normal police procedures were followed, Piotrowski, Pękala and Chmielewski were in danger of being arrested sooner rather than later. The best hope Piotrowski could offer as they drove back to Warsaw was that they would be protected against such investigation.

On the northern approaches to Warsaw, the car stopped briefly on the bridge over the Vistula at Modlin, the one they had inspected for the purposes of their operation some ten days earlier. Piotrowski threw the keys to the priest's Golf into the water. Chmielewski got rid of some other things in the same way but admitted later that he had been throwing out anything he could lay his hands on throughout the journey — bits of rag, rope, stones and the empty vodka bottle among them.

As they drove into Warsaw along the Vistula embankment road, they were stopped twice by traffic police patrols, first near the Gdańsk Bridge, then at the foot of the street called Tamka. They got through, as usual, when Piotrowski produced the 'W' pass, but it wasn't as easy as that. The police on patrol near the Gdańsk Bridge were not content, apparently, with having the pass merely flashed at them. They chased after the kidnap car, brought it to a halt and let it proceed only after the pass had been handed over and examined closely.

The trio carried on to the Ministry of Internal Affairs on Rakowiecka Street. According to all three, Pękala transferred to his private car — the smaller Fiat 'maluch' — and Chmielewski took the wheel of the kidnap car. Both then drove off to Bernardyńska, a street of several tall blocks, where Piotrowski and a number of his SB colleagues had apartments.

With both cars parked at the foot of the building where Piotrowski lived with his wife and two children, the SB trio set about removing evidence. They checked the car for blood stains but found none. Then they began filling a sack with various articles they had taken with them or worn during the Bydgoszcz operation. These included lengths of cord and rope, two socks filled with sand, and pieces of rag that had been wrapped round the wooden stakes, one of which was simply thrown into some nearby bushes. Also packed into the sack were three knitted ski hats, three gloves (the missing fourth had been stuffed into the mouth of the car's oil filler), a shopping bag, the bedspread on which Fr Popiełuszko had lain, a roll of sticking plaster, a piece of towelling bearing the mark of an Orbis hotel, a pair of black moccasin shoes worn by Chmielewski (instead of his usual brown shoes) when he donned the police uniform, a navy-blue jerkin which had been worn by Piotrowski, and the two false KZC number plates. It was only then that Chmielewski realised that he had replaced only one of the plates on the car. The remaining one was torn off by Pękala.

Having loaded the sack with stones to make it sink, the trio drove to a small bridge over Lake Czerniaków less than a minute away and dropped it into the water. They then drove to another spot close to the lake and burned Chrostowski's documents and Fr Popiełuszko's identity card after dousing them with petrol. It was between three and four in the morning and time to go home.

Piotrowski was dropped off at his apartment block nearby and Pękala and Chmielewski headed back to the Ministry in separate cars. Chmielewski said he used the 'W' pass to enter the grounds and park the light grey Fiat. Pękala, in his smaller Fiat, took Chmielewski to his flat on Iwicka Street before driving to his own flat on Grójecka across town.

At first glance, the trio's account of their return to Warsaw may sound quite plausible. On closer examination, however, it raises questions.

Why, for instance, did they go straight to the Ministry? Could picking up Pękala's car have been the sole reason? On the evidence available Pękala's car was not needed at Bernardyńska, where the trio had removed evidence outside Piotrowski's apartment block. It was needed only to take Chmielewski home after they had covered up their tracks and returned the Fiat 125. Pękala's 'maluch' could surely have stayed at the Ministry until then.

The Vistula embankment road, on which the trio re-entered the capital, was probably the quickest route through Warsaw from north to south and certainly the most direct route to Bernardyńska. If they had stayed on it instead of going to the Ministry, they could have gone straight to Bernardyńska and got rid of the incriminating materials far more quickly. But Piotrowski chose to go to the Ministry first.

Presumably there must have been a compelling reason for doing this, a reason more pressing even than the need to remove all traces of the crime, the urgent need, perhaps, for Piotrowski to talk to someone about what had happened.

This, without doubt, is speculation. It was prompted, however, by something Chmielewski told the court. Having testified that they drove to the Ministry where Pękala got into his own car, he also said 'I don't remember our carrying any things into the building. No, we didn't go in'. But no one had asked whether or not they had gone in. So why draw attention to what they did not do? If they did go into the Ministry building, did they conceal that fact in order to protect someone not with themselves and Colonel Pietruszka in the dock? This question would re-emerge in another trial several years later.

General Płatek's testimony about the start of the investigation which he was to supervise was not the first or last piece of evidence offered in court that would prompt doubt — or plain disbelief.

# 16
# First Announcement, First Arrest

The first public announcement of Fr Popiełuszko's abduction was broadcast towards the end of the main television news bulletin shortly before 8 pm on the evening of Saturday, 20 October, about 22 hours after the event.

I remember it clearly. After spending most of the day in court where the Association of Defence Lawyers had been contesting attempts by the Minister of Justice to curtail its independence, I had just returned to my twelfth-floor flat on Starościńska, a side street across the road from the Ministry of Internal Affairs. With the volume on my TV turned up high, I was opening kitchen cupboards in search of something to eat when the fateful words came through from the other room.

> At about 10 pm on the 19th of this month, Fr Jerzy Popiełuszko... a resident of Warsaw, was kidnapped by unknown assailants in the vicinity of Przysiek near Toruń...

The announcement said that one of the assailants had been dressed as a traffic policeman, that there had been a sham drink-driving test and that Waldek Chrostowski, who had been driving the priest's car, had escaped. Preliminary investigations, it went on, had established that Fr Popiełuszko's car was followed out of Bydgoszcz by a car with false number plates, KZC 0423. A police cap badge had also been found on the road next to the abandoned Volkswagen Golf.

As I drove back to the office, past the long line of tall iron railings guarding the Ministry of Internal Affairs's front courtyard, it did not occur to me that the car with the false number plates just mentioned on television could be parked inside. There would be similar moments in the days to come when I would be physically close to the truth, so to speak, without knowing it.

After filing my report to the BBC, I had a brief, chance meeting with Janusz Onyszkiewicz, the Solidarity spokesman, who recalled the spate of kidnappings in the Toruń area earlier in the year.

At St Stanisław's, meanwhile, crowds had started to gather soon after the announcement. A special Mass was said at 10 pm for Fr Popiełuszko's safe return. Another was said at midnight, after which some members of the congregation stayed on in the church throughout the night.

On Sunday morning, Seweryn Jaworski, who had accompanied Fr Popiełuszko to Gdańsk the previous weekend, announced a round-the-clock vigil at St Stanisław's until the priest returned. The 10 am Mass normally said by Fr Popiełuszko was attended by Lech Wałęsa, his wife and four of their children, who had been on the road to attend a christening elsewhere. Speaking from the altar at the end of the Mass, Wałęsa said that if even one hair should fall from Fr Jerzy's head, someone would be assuming a terrible responsibility.

Karol Małcużyński and I missed that occasion, although we were in the Żoliborz neighbourhood that morning, searching for more details of the kidnappings in the Toruń area earlier in the year. This took us to the flat of Anna Szymańska, a Solidarity supporter and veteran journalist, who gave us the whole story, much as it would appear later in an underground publication. It was the first time we had heard anything about the shadowy Toruń organisation known as the OAS.

In the absence of further information from the authorities, this was more than enough for another despatch to the BBC, one which required no artifice to emphasise the danger to the missing priest as well as the possibility that he, like the previous kidnap victims, would be released after forty eight hours.

On Sunday evening, almost 48 hours after the the event, a second communiqué from the Ministry of the Interior offered no such hope and made no mention of the Toruń abductions. It also showed little sign of progress in the investigation, although it contained descriptions of the three kidnappers, provided by Waldek Chrostowski, and of the kidnap car — a light-coloured Fiat 125 with a distinctive red light on its dashboard. The announcement added that the search was continuing for the three passengers of an ash grey Fiat 125 seen in Bydgoszcz on Friday wearing the false number plates KZC 0423.

On hearing this, the public could have imagined that the police were looking for two vehicles: the light-coloured Fiat described by Chrostowski and the ash grey one with the false plates reported by a witness or witnesses yet to be identified. For the first time, the authorities were saying that the car with false plates had three passengers, as did the kidnap car. But they were giving the impression that they had yet to identify the real number plates of the ash grey car.

In an appeal for help from the public, the communiqué also asked for information not only about people who answered the description of the kidnappers but also about 'persons who either produce or make use of car number plates illegally, and also persons who possess or use police uniforms or police equipment, such as handcuffs, illegally'.

This suggested, at the very least, that the authorities were seriously investigating the possibility that the kidnappers were not legitimate police officers but were impersonating police. People who heard the announcement on TV and radio on Sunday evening or read it in the newspapers on Monday morning were clearly being prepared for such an explanation of the crime, but few if any seemed to find it credible. The commonly held belief seemed to be that since the SB had been keeping Fr Popiełuszko under close surveillance day and night, he could not have been abducted without the SB's knowledge; the culprits had to be SB officers.

Marek Wilk, who had driven Fr Popiełuszko into Bydgoszcz on Friday afternoon and escorted him out of the city that night, told the police as much when they took him in for questioning on Sunday morning. He readily agreed to make a statement about his movements on Friday evening and told the two plain-clothes men interrogating him that he thought the SB was responsible for the priest's abduction. The plain-clothes men blamed the Solidarity underground. The evening announcement from the Ministry of Internal Affairs was less specific but was open to that interpretation.

On Monday, it became clear that any faint hope that Fr Popiełuszko would be freed after two days — as had happened in the other Toruń kidnappings — was misplaced. A candid statement from the press office of the Catholic Episcopate went straight to the point. There was fear for the priest's life, it said, and there was fear, too, that kidnapping could become an instrument of political competition in Poland. What information there was about the abduction, it said, indicated that the priest's assailants had acted from political motives.

That afternoon, the government spokesman, Jerzy Urban, put a political slant on the crime. In response to enquiries from Western news agencies, he described the abduction as a carefully timed 'provocation' against the authorities. He did not suggest who might be responsible, but passed on a report by the official Polish News Agency which said that a woman had phoned the police claiming to have seen Fr Popiełuszko getting out of a car, in the company of two men, in the Saska Kępa district of Warsaw at lunchtime on Saturday.

I was surprised to see this report on the telex machines of a Western news agency; I found it unbelievable, and told London so. If the two men supposedly with the priest were his captors, surely they would not have brought him back to Warsaw where he was so well known. If they were his friends, why wasn't Fr Popiełuszko back at St Stanisław's, where people were main-taining a twenty-four-hour vigil praying for his safe return? Why give credence to an unconfirmed report which almost suggested that the story of the priest's abduction was suspect? A phone call to Urban's office confirmed that the alleged sighting of the missing priest was just one of many public responses to the police appeals for help and was thought no more credible than any other. The report, nonetheless, featured on the main television news bulletin on Monday evening; the authorities, it seemed, had nothing of greater substance to report.

Karol and I had been at St Stanisław's that Monday afternoon and were startled, when leaving, by the sound of a small explosion coming from the kitchen garden next to the priests' house. It appeared that someone had thrown a fire-cracker or even a percussion grenade into the garden from the narrow street on the other side of the presbytery. Whoever it was, it was no friend.

This was as much as we could learn on the third day, Monday, 22 October. As night fell, the public had little reason to believe that the authorities had made any progress in their search for Fr Popiełuszko or his kidnappers. The suggestion that he might have been seen in Warsaw was rejected widely as bogus, particularly at St Stanisław's, where the crowds praying for his safe return were also anxiously awaiting the release from SB 'protection' in Toruń of Waldek Chrostowski. His eyewitness account of the crime would be the first they could believe with certainty. But on Monday night, Chrostowski still had reason to be afraid.[1]

After intensive questioning throughout Saturday, he had insisted on being allowed to stay with Fr Nowakowski only to be told bluntly that he couldn't. He spent the ensuing night in conditions of excessive security with four uniformed policemen in his bedroom, two in the connecting room next door, and more in the corridor outside. When he went to the lavatory, two policemen went with him and he had to leave the door open.

On Sunday, Chrostowski underwent further repeated questioning, not knowing for some time that he had visitors from Warsaw — his son Krzysztof, his lawyer Edward Wende, and Dr Zofia Kuratowska, a medical specialist and prominent

Solidarity supporter. He eventually saw them, separately, but always in the presence of a police officer.

On Monday, Chrostowski helped a police artist from Warsaw compose an identikit portrait of Leszek Pękala, the only kidnapper he had seen clearly. (Talking almost a year later, Chrostowski said the picture had apparently been so good that it had frightened the life out of Piotrowski when it landed on his desk at the Ministry.)[2] By this time Chrostowski had reason to believe that he had done as much as he could for the investigation and would soon be on his way back to Warsaw. Late on Monday morning, though, he was told that he would be required to take part in a reconstruction of the kidnapping at the scene, and at the time it had taken place. He had already shown the police the spot where he had jumped from the kidnap car and the police had found his lost shoe. They had also recovered from Fr Nowakowski's the cord which had been used to keep Chrostowski's gag in place. But now, they wanted to reconstruct the kidnapping in detail and in darkness.

Naturally, Chrostowski refused to take part without his lawyer present. On Monday afternoon, Edward Wende was called out of a Supreme Court hearing and told that he was needed urgently in Toruń. He left immediately by car and reached Toruń before 6 pm. He asked to see his client immediately but was kept waiting for an hour and a half, before a police colonel took him to a small room where he was eventually joined by Chrostowski accompanied by a *komandos*, an armed anti-terrorist police officer. According to Wende, the officer looked distinctly embarrassed when Chrostowski asked him how Tajniak was getting on. *Tajniak*, meaning secret policeman, was the name Fr Popiełuszko had bestowed on his pet dog. The officer stayed with them throughout the two hours it took Chrostowski to relate everything that had happened to him on Friday night.

At 10 pm Chrostowski and Wende were driven out to Górsk for the re-enactment. It was dark, raining and cold. The road had been closed to normal traffic and both sides were lined with police. According to Chrostowski, a television crew from

Gdańsk shot some footage before being told to leave by the prosecutor, who was accompanied by his entire investigating team. Wende felt that he and Chrostowski were very much alone, and protested in vain when they were placed in separate cars for the experiment, Chrostowski in a black Volga and Wende in a Fiat.

The police were particularly interested in determining the speed of the kidnap car or Chrostowski's estimate of it at the moment he had jumped. They covered the speedometer with a towel and asked him to say when they reached the right speed. When he said 'That's it', they snatched the towel away to reveal a reading of 100 km/h. Why the police used the bigger, heavier Volga rather than a Fiat like the kidnap car remains unclear.

The exercise ended at 1.30 am. Chrostowski was taken back to the SB clinic and Wende spent the night as Fr Nowakowski's guest in the presbytery of the parish church. Both were looking forward to making an early start for Warsaw in the morning, but again there were complications. On Tuesday morning, the fourth day, Chrostowski was interrogated yet again from 9 am till about midday, after which Wende, who had been present throughout, was told that he and his client could not leave for Warsaw before talking to the local police commandant, Colonel Lukasiak. It wasn't until early afternoon that Lukasiak summoned Wende to his office, where two men from the prosecutor's department, two police officers and a lieutenant from the anti-terrorist squad were already seated at a long table. A lengthy argument ensued.

The Colonel told Wende firmly that his instructions from Warsaw were that Chrostowski should be taken home under commando escort and not in the same car as his lawyer. When Wende suggested that Chrostowski's son, who had been waiting for this moment, should travel with him, he was told that this too was out of the question. At the Colonel's suggestion, Wende went to the clinic next door and fetched Chrostowski, who said he wanted to go back to Warsaw with either Wende or his son Krzysztof.

Colonel Lukasiak responded by saying that protecting

Chrostowski was as important as protecting the Prime Minister or Communist Party leader.

At this point, Edward Wende suggested a compromise: let Chrostowski go with the commandos under escort, while he and Krzysztof followed immediately behind. Colonel Lukasiak accepted this proposal and it was agreed that the route they would take to Warsaw would be north of the Vistula, via Lipno and Sierpc.

Three vehicles were waiting in the yard of the Police Headquarters — a Polonez, a Mercedes and a Nysa van. Wende had parked his borrowed turbo Golf on the other side of the building, some 150 to 200 metres away. The commando lieutenant agreed to wait while Wende and Krzysztof ran to the front to get the car. The diesel engine started first time and took just a moment to warm up, so there was no delay. But when they drove round to join the others, the yard was empty. A policeman with a walkie-talkie said the convoy had just left, taking the road to the right. That was not the agreed route, so Wende, suspecting a trick, turned left instead, heading for the road to Lipno. In fact, the policeman had pointed them in the right direction, but Wende's suspicions were also right. He had been double-crossed.

The Chrostowski escort, consisting of only two cars — the Polonez in front and the Mercedes behind — had taken the road to Włocławek south of the river, the same road on which the kidnappers had driven Fr Popiełuszko. Chrostowski, who was seated in the back of the Mercedes between two commandos, reported later that he had been astonished at the high speed at which they had travelled especially on the narrow river road from Włocławek to Płock. This route, however, was marginally longer and certainly more difficult than the one through Lipno, with which it joined up just north of Warsaw.

This probably explains why measures were taken to ensure that the lawyer, in his nippy Golf turbo, did not get too far too quickly. Edward Wende had put his foot down in spite of heavy rain. But as he and his companions — Krzysztof Chrostowski and Jacek Lipiński from Huta Warszawa — reached the outskirts of Toruń, they were stopped by a police officer whom Wende remembered seeing back at Police Headquarters. Responding with a smile to the lawyer's suggestion that he was playing a dirty trick, the officer examined the passengers' documents carefully before carrying out a meticulous inspection of the car. He looked at the engine, the contents of the boot and demanded to be shown the engine number. Since Wende had borrowed the car from a friend and didn't know where the number was, the officer suggested that maybe this was a stolen car and maybe it would have to be towed back to headquarters.

After something like three quarters of an hour, Wende and his companions were allowed to continue. But 20 kilometres later they were stopped again for similar treatment, and for a third time as they approached Nowy Dwór and Modlin just north of Warsaw. This time, anti-terrorist *komandosy* took their documents to a radio car in which they spent a long time on the telephone, observed with increasing anger during Wende's hour-long wait. When allowed to continue, Wende drove straight to St Stanisław's, where Chrostowski was supposed to be taken, arriving there some time after 6 pm, Chrostowski was not there, as he feared all along.

On reaching Warsaw, Chrostowski's commando escort drove not to St Stanisław's but to the Bemowo district. They parked in a dark lane next to some allotments and a large, empty space that was once an airfield. The senior officer in the Mercedes switched off the car's radio communications channel, got out and went and sat in the Polonez. Chrostowski, who remained seated between the two commandos in the Mercedes guessed that their chief was using the other car's radio system to discuss information or instructions. Every now and then, other cars with civilian number plates would drive up and then depart after apparently intense discussions. It lasted an hour or more. Chrostowski said, 'I felt that they might be settling my fate as well.'

When they eventually left Bemowo, Chrostowski was driven to Nowolipki Street, where his ground-floor flat had been burned out mysteriously in September. The *komandosy* handed him over to two plain-clothes men on the pavement outside. They asked Chrostowski to take them into the flat with a woman caretaker as a witness. He didn't know what to expect.

Once inside, the plain-clothes men, who expressed astonishment at finding it gutted by fire, explained that they were there to guard him until the kidnapping case came to trial but on condition that he remained in the flat. Chrostowski refused and signed a note to this effect at their request. Taking this — apparently with some surprise, according to Chrostowski — the two plain-clothes men departed. He then slipped out, leaving a light on, got into a friend's taxi, and was driven, lying down, to St Stanisław's where he arrived half an hour after Wende. That night he slept in the priests' house, much as Fr Popiełuszko used to, under the protection of volunteer guards.

Waldek Chrostowski's return was the only good news on the fifth day that ended without official indication of progress in the search for Fr Popiełuszko and his kidnappers. Earlier, at his weekly press conference at noon, government spokesman Jerzy Urban had amplified his remarks of the day before, describing the abduction of Fr Popiełuszko as a political provocation and an act of banditry designed to destroy positive processes initiated by the government — the normalisation of relations with some Western countries, the process of renewal and good relations between Church and State. He would not suggest who might have committed the crime, he said, but it was a matter of supreme concern to the State authorities.

When I asked the spokesman about a possible connection between the priest's abduction and Chrostowski's burnt-out flat, his reply was unusual: 'I ask you not to try to solve this case on your own.' Replying to a question about the earlier abductions in Toruń — a subject never previously mentioned by the authorities — Urban said that investigations into those cases had been dropped some two weeks earlier. 'In some cases,' he said, 'the fact of an abduction was not confirmed, while in others, the culprit or culprits were not identified.' It seemed an odd coincidence that enquiries which might have been of assistance in Fr

Popieluszko's case should have been halted only weeks before the priest's abduction in similar circumstances.

Wednesday, 24 October, began with the release of a statement which the underground leaders of Solidarity and its chairman, Lech Wałęsa, had signed at a secret meeting two days earlier. The kidnapping of Fr Popieluszko, they said, showed that terror and blackmail were being employed as permanent methods of political struggle. Then — in its first day-time communiqué on the investigations — the Ministry of Internal Affairs announced that all persons identified as owners or users of the type of Fiat involved in the kidnapping and who had been in the Toruń area at the time of the abduction had been detained for questioning. The Ministry picked out five people for special mention, giving only their first names and the initial letter of their surnames: two taxi drivers and a mechanical engineer from Bydgoszcz, an unemployed woman tailor from Warsaw and Grzegorz P., described as a Ministry of Internal Affairs functionary from Warsaw.

Shortly after 7 pm, I received a phone call from one of the government spokesman's assistants who said that the Minister wished to speak to me. Jerzy Urban told me that since my report on the previous day's press conference had been very fair, he wanted me to know, ahead of the 7.30 pm TV news, that all but one of those detained earlier for questioning had been released. Grzegorz P. of the Ministry of Internal Affairs had been placed under arrest for wilfully absenting himself from duty on 19 October, for making a false entry in the travel record of an official car and for failing to provide a convincing alibi. I asked the spokesman whether he thought there was any hope of finding Fr Popieluszko alive. He thought there was none.

The government spokesman's tip-off was soon confirmed on the television news, which also revealed that Waldemar Chrostowski was about to be shown a number of cars including the one probably used in the abduction.

The scenes at St Stanisław's that night were remarkable. Lit up inside, the church glowed in the darkness as crowds of people came and went, taking turns to maintain the vigil of prayer for Fr Popiełuszko's safe return. Lights outside the church illuminated the flowers and banners that adorned the iron railings enclosing the churchyard. The distant mutter of the rosary and the hymns of supplication were carried by loud-speakers into surrounding streets.

The churchyard, as usual, was busy with people exchanging information under the watchful eyes of volunteer church stewards maintaining security. What we did not notice immediately was that plain-clothes men of the Ministry of Internal Affairs were also there, waiting next to cars parked outside the railings. It was only when we spotted Edward Wende moving between those cars and the priests' house that we realised he must be negotiating Waldek Chrostowski's departure from the presbytery to inspect the cars the authorities had assembled.

We did not see Chrostowski or Wende leave but when the SB cars moved off in a column, we followed, all the way to Aleje Ujazdowskie, the handsome avenue where General Jaruzelski had his Prime Ministerial office. There the cars turned right and disappeared behind a building which I learned only later housed the Investigations Bureau of the Ministry of Internal Affairs.

Not many minutes later, having driven round the block, we entered a superior apartment house opposite the Foreign Ministry, climbed the stairs to the top floor and from there gazed down from the staircase window onto the Investigations Bureau yard.

Seven or eight light-coloured Fiats were drawn up in a line and quite a large number of men stood at various distances away from them, like prospective customers at a car mart. We had a fine view but couldn't hear what was being said and soon left.

Chrostowski did pick out the kidnap car, but not immediately. He quickly eliminated all except two cars, but found it hard to choose between them because they both looked exactly the same on the inside. Not having seen much the previous Friday night, he could only rely on memories of what he had heard. He therefore asked the police to open the car doors and boot lids and slam them shut. That did not help. Finally, he asked them to switch on the engines and Chrostowski immediately pointed to one of them. 'This is it,' he said. And when the police asked how he knew, he said he recognised the sound of an engine in perfect running order.

This answer puzzled the police but they told Edward Wende later that his client had, indeed, picked out the right car; it usually wore the number plates WAB 6031.

By nightfall on Wednesday, 24 October, it might have seemed fair to an outside observer to say that investigators had made great progress in the five days since Fr Popiełuszko had been kidnapped. The announcement by the Ministry of Internal Affairs that one of its own men was under arrest was something few could have imagined.

This, however, did not alter the belief in Poland that the Ministry was incapable of telling the whole truth. And in fact the truth was that not one but three of the Ministry's officers were already under arrest. And the testimony of the Ministry's own witnesses suggests strongly that those three officers could have been taken into custody much earlier if evidence in the police's possession had been recognised for what it was.

# 17

# Behind the Scenes[1]

It was the car proved to be the downfall of Grzegorz Piotrowski and his two lieutenants. That is scarcely surprising given that the policemen on duty outside the church in Bydgoszcz on the evening of the abduction had noted that the Fiat's number plates had been changed.

This fact was not yet known to the general public, but the early official communiqués suggested that the authorities had pursued this clue from the start.

On Saturday evening, less than 24 hours after the crime, the first public announcement of Fr Popiełuszko's abduction said that the priest's car had been followed out of Bydgoszcz by a car wearing false plates, KZC 0423.

The second communiqué on Sunday evening described the kidnappers' car as a 'light-coloured Fiat 125' and said that a search was continuing for the three occupants of an 'ash grey Fiat 125' seen in Bydgoszcz on Friday wearing the false plates KZC 0423.

The climax, apparently came on Monday evening, after a meeting of the special operations group set up two days earlier under the leadership of General Zenon Płatek to coordinate the investigations. The meeting itself, which took place in Department Four and lasted roughly from 6 to 7 pm, produced nothing remarkable. But afterwards the group's deputy chairman, Colonel Zbigniew Jabłoński, Director of the Criminal Investigations Bureau of the MO (the uniformed civil police) took the General aside privately. He told him that it had been confirmed in Bydgoszcz — which he had just visited — that a car with number plates WAB 6031 had been seen there on Friday, that it was the same car as that seen later with the false KZC plates, and that the car belonged to the Ministry of Internal Affairs. Jabłoński had written it all down on a sheet of paper, which he handed to General Płatek.

To judge from his testimony in court, the General's reaction was swift. He said he immediately summoned Pietruszka, told him that 'a car from our department' had been seen in Bydgoszcz on the 19th, and instructed him to get hold of Piotrowski. He also phoned his superior, General Władysław Ciastoń, and asked for an urgent meeting. When Piotrowski appeared shortly afterwards with Pietruszka, the General challenged him: 'You were seen in this car in Bydgoszcz.' Piotrowski had replied that there must be some misunderstanding. Płatek told Pietruszka to take him away and get a statement out of him.

Piotrowski went away and composed his statement in about thirty minutes. It claimed that on the morning of Friday, 19 October, feeling tired and out of sorts, he had decided to seek some recreation by taking an official car without permission and driving to the Toruń area to go mushrooming. This he did, largely in the woodlands between Toruń and Bydgoszcz, until dusk, when he decided to drive into Bydgoszcz. On the way, he picked up two men who were heading into town to hear Fr Popiełuszko preach. Piotrowski said he took them to the church, went in himself to confirm that the priest was there, but then drove back to Warsaw, reaching home between 9.30 and 9.40 pm (just when Fr Popiełuszko had begun his journey home from Bydgoszcz). Piotrowski said that his wife and a neighbour could confirm the time of his return. The neighbour, Hanna Bandurska, did confirm it, but withdrew her testimony later.

General Płatek would describe the statement as 'suspicious, to say the least'. He even said when first interrogated as a

witness (on 19 November) that Piotrowski had been taken into
custody there and then.

This would have made sense but it was not true. For the rest
of Monday evening, Department Four was the scene of intense
consultations. These were described only sketchily in subsequent testimony at the trial. But the impression was that the
speed with which the General had reacted to Colonel Jabłoński's
information had been replaced by a calmer consideration of
what could be done. General Płatek phoned Bydgoszcz to
instruct that the two policemen who had seen the suspect car
outside the church should report for questioning at the Ministry
in Warsaw on Tuesday the following morning. This was the first
time the General admitted to even knowing of their existence.
Adam Pietruszka was sent to look at the car to see if it had any
of the features described by Waldek Chrostowski in his statements to the police in Toruń.

At one point, to judge from later testimony, there was a suggestion that Piotrowski joined Pietruszka, Płatek and General
Ciastoń in the latter's office on Monday evening. And at the end
of the Monday, Piotrowski was even allowed to go home. (This
was the night when Waldek Chrostowski took part in a reconstruction of the kidnapping and his own escape from
Piotrowski on the Bydgoszcz-Torun road.)

The next morning, the two officers from Bydgoszcz
reported to Generals Płatek and Ciastoń in Warsaw. They told
them how they saw a car with WAB 6031 number plates and
three men inside parked near the church of the Polish Martyrs
in Bydgoszcz early in the evening of Friday, 19 October, and
how later they noticed that the same car or one very similar and
with the same or similar three men was parked near the church
with different number plates, KZC 0423. The two policemen
were unable, according to General Płatek, to provide anything
approaching a detailed description of the three men. They were
asked to write a full report.

Captain Piotrowski, meanwhile, had not been idle. He
dictated a letter to his secretary, Barbara Story, applying for the
issue of four pairs of handcuffs. She typed it up for him and he

left the office with it. But only hours later, after completing an amplified version of his statement of the night before, Grzegorz Piotrowski was escorted by General Płatek to the office of the Minister, General Kiszczak, around midday.

According to Płatek, Kiszczak asked Piotrowski if he had taken part in the abduction of Fr Popiełuszko. Piotrowski said he had not, adding pointedly that he was, first and foremost, an SB man. Kiszczak had then ordered that Piotrowski be taken for interrogation to Colonel Zbigniew Pudysz, the Director of the Investigations Bureau of his Ministry. According to Piotrowski the Minister asked him what had happened to Popiełuszko. 'I didn't answer. He informed me that I was being arrested...'

That is how official sources record the detention of Grzegorz Piotrowski on suspicion of taking part in the abduction. Coming only three and a half days after the crime was committed, it was an achievement of which any police service in the world would be proud.

But from any dispassionate viewpoint, the above record had two serious shortcomings. First, it contained no mention of what was done for the two and a half days that preceded Colonel Jabłonski's intervention with the information about the kidnap car on Monday evening. Second, on Saturday night, almost exactly 24 hours after Fr Popiełuszko's body had been dropped into the Vistula, General Zenon Płatek, Director of Department Four, was told by telephone from Toruń everything about the kidnap car that Colonel Jabłoński told him on Monday, everything except the fact that the car belonged to his own department.

The investigations began for General Płatek at 7 on Saturday morning, when he said he received a phone call at home from Police Headquarters in Toruń with news of the abduction. He said he was told then that Waldemar Chrostowski's first statements to the police indicated that the priest had run off into the woods. This was a gross misinterpretation of what Chrostowski had said, but it apparently determined what the General said he did next. While still on the phone to Toruń, he gave an order, among others, that a search for Fr Popiełuszko should be organised with all available manpower and tracker dogs in the woods where he had been seized. From that moment until the middle of Saturday evening, the General's testimony revealed a surprising lack of interest in tracing the kidnappers' car. It happened to be parked in the Ministry yard beneath his office but did not, apparently, catch his eye as he rushed into his office before 8 am.

The General summoned all his deputies that Saturday, including Adam Pietruszka, Piotrowski's superior. They all told him they knew nothing about the abduction of the priest. Grzegorz Piotrowski, as head of the section with a special interest in Fr Popiełuszko, was also called in by the General and he too said he knew nothing of it. He assured General Płatek that neither he nor any other member of his section had been to Bydgoszcz the previous day.

In the absence of his superiors who had yet to reach the office — General Władysław Ciastoń, Deputy Minister and Head of the SB, and the Minister himself, General Czesław Kiszczak — Płatek took a number of key decisions. He instructed Pietruszka and Piotrowski to carry out investigations in Warsaw. He appointed two colonels, Longin Iskra and Romuald Będziak, to sort, analyse and distribute all incoming information. And he sent two other senior officers — they were Colonels Stanisław Luliński and Wacław Głowacki — to Toruń with instructions to keep him personally informed of progress in the investigations there.

His own appointment soon afterwards to head the special operations group presumably ensured that General Płatek was kept informed of all developments. His testimony suggests that investigations on Saturday morning and afternoon consisted largely of studying Chrostowski's statements to the police, of intensive searches for the missing priest in the areas of Górsk and Przysiek and of alerting the police throughout the country to what had happened. He was busy in consultations with Generals Ciastoń and Kiszczak, Płatek said, making phone calls to a number of Bishops, and remaining constantly in touch with the police in Toruń. But at no point did Płatek mention either a search for the kidnappers' car or any evidence in the possession of the police that might lead to the discovery of that car.

Yet the first mention of the car was made in the first public announcement of the priest's abduction on State television early that evening when it said that a vehicle with false number plates KZC 0423 had followed the priest's car out of Bydgoszcz. That communiqué had been prepared among others by General Płatek.

The General never said precisely where this information came from or how he knew the plates were false. In court, three months later, all he would say was that the 'information from Bydgoszcz' about a light coloured Fiat with KZC number plates seen near the church came in 'during the evening hours'. ·

If that information had come from the policemen who had been on duty outside the church, he would presumably also have been told that the car, when first seen, had had Warsaw plates, WAB 6031; and that in itself would have justified the conclusion that the KZC plates were false. General Płatek, however, gave no indication that he had been told any such thing, raising the question of how he knew the KZC plates were false. That is one of several questions that were never properly answered. But there is clear evidence that the General was given the answer within hours of the announcement of Fr Popiełuszko's abduction.

After leaving the office at 11 pm on Saturday night, General Płatek said he took some sleeping tablets to ensure a good night's rest before another busy day. In Toruń, meanwhile, Stanisław Luliński, the younger of the two colonels the General had sent there, came across a message from Police Headquarters in Bydgoszcz which he felt should be reported to General Płatek immediately. It said that a light grey Fiat with WAB 6031 number plates and three men inside had been seen on Friday evening outside the church in Bydgoszcz during Fr Popiełuszko's visit. Half an hour later, the message said, the same men were seen in 'the same or a very similar car', but the number plates were different: KZC 0423.

The reason for Luliński's excitement was simple enough; he knew that the WAB 6031 number plates belonged to a car used by the Department Four section in which he worked, the section headed by Grzegorz Piotrowski. At the time, however, 'he felt sure' that the WAB plates seen in Bydgoszcz were forgeries produced for criminal purposes. Luliński said he did not mention the reason for his excitement when he pressed Colonel Głowacki — his senior by age — to phone General Płatek and tell him about it.

Głowacki readily complied and got through to the General at his home late on Saturday night, having failed to catch him at work. He told him that he had 'urgent information' about cars seen outside the church in Bydgoszcz the previous evening and read out the message received from the police there. At this point, Głowacki testified, Płatek had excused himself for a couple of minutes, explaining that he had been asleep and needed to write it all down. When he returned to the line, Głowacki repeated the message and read out the number plates a second time. According to Luliński, who was watching and listening during the call, Głowacki did this very distinctly and clearly.

The way now appeared to be clear for the Director of Department Four to establish whose car bore the number plates WAB 6031. According to Głowacki, however, General Płatek gave him no instructions whatsoever.

Early on Sunday morning, after General Płatek arrived at the Ministry, Grzegorz Piotrowski was called in to work urgently by Adam Pietruszka. It was shortly after 8 am. On reaching the Ministry, Piotrowski said, he was told by Pietruszka that his car had been seen in Bydgoszcz, that its number plates were known and yet it was still parked in the Ministry yard for all to see. Piotrowski's immediate reaction was to drive the car off the premises, intending to find somewhere to change the number plates yet again. On the way, he saw Chmielewski waiting at a bus stop, picked him up and drove on to a wooded area at

Powsin on the southern outskirts of the city. There they replaced the WAB 6031 plates with others reading WAE 938B (Piotrowski explained, they always had alternative plates in reserve). According to Chmielewski, Piotrowski said that Pietruszka had ordered him to change the plates.

General Płatek said nothing about this incident. Early on Sunday afternoon, however, the General said he was told by Pietruszka that the KZC plates were false. Plates with those letters were not yet in use; they were due to be introduced in the town of Kalisz in a year's time. This admission in court was remarkable as the General had already approved a statement that the plates were false in the nation-wide communiqué broadcast the night before.

The kidnap car, with new number plates, was parked in the Ministry yard when Colonels Luliński and Głowacki drove in later that Sunday afternoon on their return from Toruń. Between 6 and 7 pm, they went to General Płatek's office hoping to report to him personally. In the General's absence — he said he was with his superior, General Ciastoń, for the entire afternoon and early evening — they found the office occupied by Adam Pietruszka and another Deputy Director. Głowacki delivered a report from notes, mentioning, among other things, that he had already told General Płatek the previous night about the Fiat with WAB plates and KZC plates being seen in Bydgoszcz on Friday evening. He said he again read out both number plates clearly and in full.

Luliński then read out and handed to Pietruszka a handwritten report on the mission to Toruń which consisted of general comments on the conduct of the investigation but did not mention anything about the Fiat with the changed number plates. Luliński and Głowacki would explain later by saying that it was not their brief to report on the specifics of the investigation, and, anyway, they had already told General Płatek the night before. Moreover, as Luliński would say in court, that sort of information would normally have been passed on to Warsaw immediately. But was it passed on to Warsaw and, if so, what happened to it?

On Sunday evening, however, the second television communiqué prepared by General Płatek betrayed no hint of any firm clue about the ownership of the car seen in Bydgoszcz. It might have been different, of course, if he had been in his office when Luliński and Głowacki turned up to report and if he had heard from them, face to face, what they said they had told him the night before.

General Płatek gave his first recorded account of what Colonel Głowacki told him over the phone when interviewed as a witness on 19 November. His memory of the call was distinctly different from that of the two colonels he had sent to Toruń. As a result, Captain Piotrowski and his two lieutenants were able to spend the weekend misleading the investigation. Only when Colonel Jabłoński, Director of the Criminal Investigations Bureau of the MO, provided the full information to General Płatek informally at around 7 pm on Monday evening, did he spring into action.

# 18

## Covering Up

At 8 am on Saturday morning, roughly eight hours after helping to drop Fr Popiełuszko's body into the waters of the Vistula, Leszek Pękala was back at the Ministry of Internal Affairs calmly filling out a form reporting how much petrol had been used the previous day. As agreed with Piotrowski, he recorded Cracow as the destination, not Bydgoszcz. Having done that, Pękala went home.

Waldemar Chmielewski didn't reach the office until shortly after 10 am, and then only after Piotrowski had sent a driver to tell him to come in. Unable to find his boss, he reported sick to the Ministry's duty doctor and was sent by ambulance to the nearest outpatients' department. There he underwent an electrocardiogram and was diagnosed as suffering from a sharp rise in blood pressure and debility. Returning to the Ministry hours later, Chmielewski was briefed on the investigation by Piotrowski, who said that what Chrostowski had been telling the police in Toruń didn't amount to much because it was confused. Chmielewski was not convinced. 'Any moment now,' he said, 'it will be our turn.'

Piotrowski urged Chmielewski to relax but he must have realised by now that Leszek Pękala was the stronger, more reliable of his accomplices. He sent Chmielewski to get Pękala, after which Chmielewski simply sat in Piotrowski's office watching his boss come and go. When Pękala eventually turned up, Piotrowski went through the same routine of reassurance and advised both of them to make sure they watched the announcement of the abduction of Fr Popiełuszko on the main TV news bulletin that evening.

For Chmielewski, this made matters worse. Watching at home, he was appalled to hear that a police cap badge had been found next to the car from which Fr Popiełuszko had been taken. Since the uniform and cap were still in his flat, he quickly checked and found that the badge was, indeed, missing. He would have to replace it with one from the cap that he kept with his uniform in the home of his wife's parents.

On Sunday morning, Chmielewski was on his way to visit his in-laws when Piotrowski saw him at the bus stop and picked him up as he was driving out to Powsin to change the number plates of the car. After doing that, Piotrowski dropped Chmielewski at the in-laws' flat but said he couldn't wait. Chmielewski made his own way back to the Ministry with the replacement cap badge.

Later that morning, the three met in the small café or bar next door to the Moskwa cinema on Puławska Street at the foot of Rakowiecka, a short walk from the Ministry. They did so, they said, because they suspected that their offices and even the corridors might have been bugged. The group made plans to obstruct the investigation by placing misleading phone calls to the police and to certain Bishops. Piotrowski also suggested demanding a ransom for Fr Popiełuszko's safe return.

The chronology now becomes hazy but it is certain that Piotrowski and Pękala drove some distance away from the Ministry — to the area of Czerniakowska Street — and used an inter-city phone box to call one of the Bishops. It turned out to be a source of great amusement for the two of them. Piotrowski demanded a ransom of US$50,000 for the priest's return and said that further instructions would be given in a church in Kalisz. Piotrowski told Pękala that the Bishop's secretary who took the call reacted with an incoherent gulp and replaced the receiver. They were still laughing about it,

Chmielewski said, when they got back to the office, where they composed an anonymous ransom demand. It said:

> There were police in K [meaning Kalisz]. If you want a happy ending, place a notice in the personal columns of *Kurier Polski* on the 25th of this month saying:
>
> 'Young lady, 25, pretty, would like to meet gentleman up to 50, businessman.'
>
> Will then indicate place to leave the money. Prepare $50,000 in tens and twenties. No police. There will be no second chance.[1]

Chmielewski, who later described this letter as infantile, went home at about 1 pm and returned between 5 and 6 in the evening. By then he was extremely nervous, and told Piotrowski that he believed he was being followed. Piotrowski told him to stop worrying and go home, but Chmielewski was not reassured. 'I was still convinced that someone was on my tail.'

Piotrowski was having no such trouble with Leszek Pękala. It was Pękala who volunteered to post the ransom demand, addressed to Bishop Miziołek, from Poznań on Monday. It was Pękala who phoned the police in Toruń on Sunday evening after the TV news had reported the search for three people seen in Bydgoszcz in an ash grey Fiat with false number plates. On Piotrowski's instructions, he told the police that he lived in Toruń and had seen a light grey Fiat with three men inside on that very night on Fordońska Street, Bydgoszcz. The car had pulled up outside a gate, which one of the men had entered only to re-emerge dressed in a policeman's uniform. Pękala told the police that he found this so curious he had noted the number plate. It was WAE plus four digits — 'not the numbers of our car' but near enough to create confusion in the investigations. When the police asked for his name, he said he had run out of coins and rang off.

According to Pękala, his boss told him one or two similar calls would be made by a woman.

By Sunday evening, Piotrowski had told Pękala that the

number plates of their car — WAB 6031 — were 'already known'. He had also confided that he was happy with the composition of the special operations group. In a conversation later that night, according to Pękala, Piotrowski disclosed that 'they keep on asking whether the body will be found' and that he found these questions laughable or tedious.

One other piece of testimony provides a clearer picture of why Piotrowski was feeling so scornful. Beata Marszczak, a 23-year-old typist employed in another part of the Ministry, testified that she and Piotrowski met on Sunday in the Wilanowska Café in Wilanów, close to the palace of King Jan Sobieski, in the southern outskirts of the capital. Piotrowski, she said, had talked about the priest's abduction. 'Beata, I'll tell you the truth. I had a hand in it but I didn't do it… If I had to do it again, I certainly wouldn't get involved, because I don't like inconsistent people at higher levels who say "Go for it, lads" when the going is good, but wash their hands of it all when things get tricky and it looks as though someone will have to pay for the consequences.' The typist said that these words were almost identical to those used by Piotrowski, who told her he had said the same thing to one of the Directors. He hadn't named him but the man had apparently shouted back at him: 'What do you think you're playing at, Comrade?'[2]

On Monday morning, the kidnap car was taken to the Ministry garage by the driver employed by Piotrowski's section, Wojciech Kaczorowski. He said Piotrowski handed him a document that morning, suggesting that he look after it since he might find it useful. This puzzled Kaczorowski for although he didn't read it carefully he could see that the document was an expired travel permit and there was no need for Piotrowski to hand it to him. Kaczorowski jotted instructions for the mechanics on the back of it and left it inside the car next to the gear lever.

Leszek Pękala, meanwhile, was on his way by train to Poznań from where he would post the ransom letter to Bishop Miziołek before returning to Warsaw. He did not see Piotrowski or Chmielewski that day.

When Chmielewski reached the office, Piotrowski told him that there was no need to worry and the men who made up the special operations group headed by General Płatek were 'decent people'. But when Piotrowski asked him to phone a number which he had written down for him, Chmielewski said he wouldn't because he still felt that someone was following him.

Piotrowski's secretary, Barbara Story, on the other hand, simply obeyed when her boss told her to go to a telephone box and phone the duty officer at the national headquarters in Warsaw of the MO, the uniformed civil police. She was instructed to say that she and her husband were in the Toruń area when their car broke down late the previous Friday night. They were trying to flag down a car for assistance when they saw a light-coloured Fiat approaching. This car slowed down but once it drew level with them, accelerated away. Story told the police that she and her husband had been able to get a look at the three occupants; they had realised on Sunday evening that the men answered the descriptions broadcast in the TV communiqué. Story testified that she had given the police the car's registration number but couldn't remember it any more. It seems possible, however, that Barbara Story's phone call had a close link with something Chmielewski did later in the day.

Piotrowski showed Chmielewski a car number plate written down on a piece of paper; it was WAE 8031, not much different from WAB 6031. He asked Chmielewski to get some of his colleagues to help him find how many permutations of the number they could find, how many different number plates they could make up by switching the figures around. When Chmielewski asked why, Piotrowski said the number had been seen in Bydgoszcz. Chmielewski and colleagues readily complied and found more than a hundred possible combinations.

This seems to have been the last job Waldemar Chmielewski did for Grzegorz Piotrowski. Only hours later on Monday, Colonel Jabłoński of the Criminal Investigations Bureau — the body which Piotrowski had said was on their side — delivered to Department Four evidence leading to the arrest of the Captain and his two accomplices. But, even after that evidence was presented, Piotrowski was still able on Monday night to phone Colonel Luliński and tell him to return to Toruń the next day on the instructions, he said, of General Płatek.

It had been Colonel Luliński, when in Toruń on Saturday, who had first seized on the report that a car carrying the number plates WAB 6031 had been seen outside the church in Bydgoszcz and had insisted that Colonel Głowacki tell General Płatek about it immediately. When he reached Police Headquarters in Toruń on Tuesday, however, Luliński could find no trace of WAB 6031 on the list of cars being sought in connection with the abduction. Instead, Luliński found another number, WAE 8031, the number Chmielewski and colleagues had been juggling with on Monday, it also had the same three letters as the number that Pękala had phoned in to the police on Sunday night, without revealing the digits. Perhaps it was also the number Barbara Story phoned in to the police on Monday morning.

On this evidence, it appears that Captain Piotrowski had been trying to replace WAB 6031 on the list of 'most wanted' number plates with WAE 8031. But it is difficult to see how he could have done it without an accomplice or accomplices in Toruń.

Mention of Colonel Adam Pietruszka has been deliberately kept to a minimum in this chapter in an attempt to demonstrate that everything Piotrowski and his two accomplices did to avoid detection was what one might expect them to have done without advice or encouragement from their boss. In all but one instance — the changing of the kidnap car's number plates on Sunday morning — this proved to be the case. Piotrowski would testify, however, that Pietruszka was behind virtually all their moves. And most of the evidence against the Colonel came from Piotrowski alone. This applies not only to what Piotrowski alleged Pietruszka had said or suggested during the Department Four discussions about Fr Popiełuszko before the crime, but also to what he claimed the Colonel did immediately after it.

Piotrowski said that early on Saturday morning, he had gone to Pietruszka's office and handed the Colonel the 'W' pass he had travelled with the day before. The first thing Pietruszka had wanted to know, he said, was whether Popiełuszko was 'retrievable'. He was visibly shaken, Piotrowski said, when he told him that that was 'now beyond me'. When Pietruszka asked whether they had been seen or left any clues, Piotrowski said they hadn't.

But that same morning Piotrowski assured General Płatek, in Pietruszka's presence, that he had not left Warsaw the previous day and didn't know what had happened to Fr Popiełuszko.

While incriminating Pietruszka, Piotrowski was also exonerating Płatek. This was more than once a feature of his testimony. On Sunday morning, for instance, when he and Chmielewski changed the car's number plates, Piotrowski said he did so on the orders of Pietruszka; he did not mention General Płatek.

As for his attempts to mislead the investigation, Piotrowski said that Pietruszka was behind virtually all of them. It was Pietruszka, he said, who suggested that something should be done to give the impression that Fr Popiełuszko was still around and who welcomed the idea of demanding a ransom. It was Pietruszka who advised him not to discuss the case with the others in their rooms, which were probably bugged. It was Pietruszka who recommended that phone calls be made to the police in Toruń, to National Police Headquarters and the prosecutor's office in Warsaw.

Piotrowski also said that Pietruszka had pressed him at some point on Sunday to say where Fr Popiełuszko was and to set him free. He had replied that as far as he knew Popiełuszko was to be found in the Vistula. According to Piotrowski, Pietruszka reacted with shock and stopped asking what had happened to Popiełuszko. At around 10 pm that night, Piotrowski told Pękala that he was tired of being asked whether the body would be found. Pękala, when asked by a judge if Piotrowski had named anyone in particular, said he could only remember Pietruszka.

Most of the evidence against Pietruszka came directly from Piotrowski or from witnesses reporting what Piotrowski had told them. That is why the testimony of Colonel Luliński about his second trip to Toruń was so valuable to the prosecution. His discovery that WAB 6031 had been supplanted by WAE 8031 on the list of number plates confirmed something he believed he had witnessed two days earlier, but had not mentioned to anyone else.

When on Sunday evening Luliński's colleague Colonel Głowacki presented an oral report to Adam Pietruszka, repeating what he had told General Płatek over the phone about the number plates WAB 6031 and KZC 0423, Luliński testified that he saw Pietruszka write the letters and digits down and then write something on the first group. It looked, he said, as if he was altering the numbers. Two days later, when he found that WAB 6031 had become WAE 8031, he was struck by how easy it was to change a B into an E and a 6 into an 8. Głowacki would confirm that Luliński told him about it when he got back from Toruń.

This was the first testimony against Adam Pietruszka that originated from someone other than Piotrowski, and had the additional virtue for the prosecution of coinciding neatly with testimony from Chmielewski and Piotrowski. Chmielewski testified that Piotrowski asked him to see how many different combinations he could make out of WAE 8031. And Piotrowski testified that on Sunday Adam Pietruszka had shown him how the figures making up a car registration number could be switched into various permutations.

It all fitted together so well that it almost sounded too good to be true. Another 12 days would pass before Adam Pietruszka would be placed under arrest and charged. In that time, presumably, more evidence against him accumulated, but it does not seem to have been the testimony of Colonel Luliński that occasioned the arrest. Luliński testified for the first time the day after Pietruszka was charged.

So what was the catalyst for Pietruszka's arrest?

# 19

# The Party Line

Away from the corridors of power the excitement of Wednesday evening — the announcement of an arrest followed by the identification parade of potential kidnap cars — created an atmosphere of expectation. A sense that the pace of investigation was quickening persisted throughout Thursday despite the exclusion of foreign media from a news conference the government spokesman gave at noon.

Jerzy Urban told official Polish journalists that the police believed they had identified the car in which Fr Popiełuszko had been abducted. In the boot of the car, strands of hair had been found which corresponded in some features to samples of hair found in the priest's flat. The same car had been picked out by a sniffer dog that had been shown clothing belonging to the priest and to his driver, Waldemar Chrostowski. It was also one of two cars, the spokesman claimed, that Chrostowski had picked out at the identification parade the previous evening. (They did not admit that Chrostowski had selected just one, recognising it because of its finely-tuned engine.) The car identified, Urban said, was that used by Grzegorz P., the man now under arrest.

Urban also announced that General Kiszczak, the Minister of Internal Affairs, was now supervising the investigation and would report personally to the public on the outcome. This presumably meant that he was taking over from General Płatek, of whose existence the Polish public had yet to be told. Urban's announcements, though, left one with the impression that once Kiszczak was in charge, the investigation began to produce results.

The truth was somewhat different, and much remained unknown at the time. We did not know that Grzegorz P. had been taken into custody around lunchtime on Tuesday (not Wednesday) or that his two accomplices had also been detained. Waldemar Chmielewski's first interrogation began at 2.40 pm on Wednesday afternoon.

Had we known, we would have treated more sceptically the Wednesday announcement that five people, including Grzegorz P., had been detained for questioning. And our verdict would have been scathing if we had known that one of the five, a Bydgoszcz taxi driver by the name of Wieslaw Warzocha, had been tricked into going to Police Headquarters as late as 11.30 that morning to be searched and interrogated as a suspect in the Popiełuszko case, then escorted to the remand cells. (Released more than an hour later, he discovered that 15 litres of petrol had been drained from the tank of his car.)[1] The announcement of the detention of the five was not an honest statement of progress, it was a public relations fabrication to delay the moment when the authorities would have to admit what they already certainly knew — that the crime had been committed by three of their own men. The authorities also needed time to agree on their public line.

The first sign of the political stance to be taken could be found on closer examination of what Jerzy Urban told Polish colleagues at the Wednesday noon news conference. He gave an assurance that the case was 'in particularly good hands' and that everything was being done to catch all the culprits and bring to light the circumstances of the crime. The government, Urban said, wished to express its appreciation to the Ministry of Internal Affairs and its staff whose 'self-sacrificing efforts' had led so quickly to the detection of 'the presumed culprits'. Only minutes earlier he had said that he was unable, in the interests of the investigation, to say how many other persons were under suspicion 'because it is not known at the moment how many people took part in the abduction'.

This, of course, was absurd. Chrostowski had said there were three assailants and the authorities had already claimed to be searching for three suspects. By midday on Thursday, three men had already been under arrest for roughly 24 hours. Urban's performance was an excellent example of news management, combining revelation with deception, while introducing a theme that was to be developed in the days to come: the claim that the Ministry which employed the three culprits was blameless, and deserving of praise and gratitude.

The spokesman's message was immediately challenged by the appearance of a Solidarity leaflet issued the day before accusing the state authorities of creating 'complete anarchy in the organs of justice and law and order'. If those responsible for the deaths of Grzegorz Przemyk and Piotr Bartoszcze and for the attack on the charity at St Martin's Church had been punished, the leaflet said, this act of terror against Fr Popieluszko would not have been possible. 'Regardless of who it was who hired the "unknown assailants", responsibility rests with the organs of law enforcement operating in this system.'

By this time, fears that Fr Popieluszko was dead were being taken more seriously. If one man was under arrest and being interrogated, why were the authorities no nearer to finding the missing priest? Cardinal Glemp voiced those fears in an appeal for prayers he issued that day on his return from a brief visit to East Berlin. 'Not having any sign that Fr Popieluszko is alive,' he wrote, 'we are afraid that a murder of the kind seen in countries afflicted by the plague of terrorism may have been committed in Poland.' The Cardinal's message insisted that as far as was humanly possible, everything to do with 'this shameful act' should be brought to light.

That evening, the main television news bulletin led with a series of reports which seemed to indicate progress in the investigation. They included Jerzy Urban's announcement that the kidnap car had been identified and news that the Ministry of the

Interior now knew who had kidnapped Fr Popiełuszko. A Ministry communiqué said three people were under arrest — Grzegorz P. and two 'accomplices'. An intensive search for the priest was continuing, it said, in the area of Toruń and also Włocławek, a place not previously mentioned. The communiqué added, however, that in view of the need to conduct various procedures, including the confrontation of suspects and witnesses, detailed information about the enquiries would not be revealed for two or three days so as not to compromise the investigation.

The bulletin went on to broadcast Cardinal Glemp's statement in full. This, in itself, was remarkable; usually the Primate's words were subject in the official media to misrepresentation rather than reproduction. But this was a moment when the authorities needed to create a semblance of national unity; quoting the Primate word for word was the most convenient way of borrowing the Church's prestige to convey such an impression.

Some viewers may even have hoped that they were witnessing a change of heart on the part of the authorities. Sadly, they were wrong. For when they broadcast the Cardinal's fears about murder, General Kiszczak and his team already knew that Fr Popiełuszko was dead, and that he had died at the hands of three members of the secret police. At 12.40 pm that day, Thursday, 25 October, Waldemar Chmielewski had taken his interrogators to the dam at Włocławek from which he said that Fr Popiełuszko had been dropped into the Vistula.

Six days after the abduction, General Kiszczak could not have doubted that the priest was dead, but with the search for the body just beginning, he needed time to prepare for the public moment of truth. He was no doubt worried about the reaction. This was an unprecedented political crisis made worse by Chmielewski's testimony to prosecution interrogators that day that a police patrol had stopped the kidnap car close to the dam at Włocławek on Friday night but allowed it to continue when Piotrowski produced the 'W' pass.

By Thursday evening, General Kiszczak and, of course,

General Jaruzelski, knew who had kidnapped Fr Popiełuszko, what they had done to him and where he was to be found. And by coincidence, they learned the last details one day before the Central Committee of the Party was due to convene in Warsaw for a plenary session or 'plenum' to discuss, of all things, 'the strengthening of the State, the development of socialist democracy and the consolidation of the rule of law, public order and social discipline'. The sort of meeting that was usually largely ignored was now the object of national scrutiny.

The members of the Central Committee, some 250 Party bosses from all over the country, took their seats on Friday morning in the huge headquarters on the street called Nowy Świat (New World). At the same time, several miles away one of Solidarity's most respected leaders, its regular spokesman Janusz Onyszkiewicz, gave a press conference on the grounds of the priests' house at the church of St Stanisław Kostka in Żoliborz. Any chance that Fr Popiełuszko was still alive, he said, was slim. He and his colleagues were quite sure that he had been kidnapped by the SB.

Onyszkiewicz emphasised that he was not suggesting the abduction had been carried out on the orders of Generals Jaruzelski or Kiszczak. It could, he said, have been the work of a group acting on its own. It could also be an element in a power struggle inside the Ministry or higher. Onyszkiewicz did not doubt that the authorities would try to find the guilty men, but since the results of the investigations could be politically damaging, there could be no certainty that the whole story would ever be told.

First reports from the Party plenum did indeed suggest a determination to uphold the law. In a brief opening speech, General Jaruzelski had asked the Central Committee to adopt a statement 'condemning the act of dangerous banditry which has so disturbed public opinion in our country'. He said that the Party had to fight against everything that violated elementary norms of legality and in so doing also dealt a blow to 'the Party's policy and its leadership'. The General did not mention Fr

Popiełuszko by name; it was the Party, apparently, that he saw as the main casualty.

An eight-point declaration adopted by the Central Committee at the end of the day condemned 'the dangerous and provocative crime of abducting Fr Jerzy Popiełuszko', and called for the rapid identification and punishment of the 'direct and possible indirect perpetrators of the crime'. This was the first official admission that those who committed the crime may have had the backing of others.

The declaration made two other demands: that the public be systematically informed of progress in the investigation, and that the Political Bureau conduct a special review of 'Party and professional supervision' in selected areas of social and political life, but particularly internal security. Having raised the possibility that discipline and loyalty to the Party leadership were not all that they should be in the Ministry of Internal Affairs, the Central Committee went on to express 'complete confidence' in the Ministry and its staff, led by General Kiszczak. The existence of what the declaration called 'a few criminals, provocateurs and agents of an evil cause' did not alter the fact that both the uniformed police and SB were doing a good job and deserved the respect and trust of the public.

The Party and society, it said, should resist attempts by 'enemies of People's Poland' to exploit the crime and play on people's emotions in order to disturb the peace and the country's internal stability.

Without doubt, the unidentified 'enemies' were Solidarity, in particular the Workers' Solidarity Committee at the Huta Warszawa steel works, which had called for a strike on the coming Monday if Fr Popiełuszko wasn't back by then. Ironically, Fr Popiełuszko himself, the victim of the crime the Central Committee was supposedly condemning, also qualified for the title of 'enemy' in the minds of the Party faithful because of his association with the steel works and Solidarity. His defence of Solidarity had cost him his life at the hands of three officers employed to defend the Communist regime who were now condemned as 'agents of an evil cause'.

This statement was typical, betraying no sympathy for the victim, only concern about damage to the Party. It was also characteristically dishonest. When it demanded that the public be kept informed of progress, the Central Committee had just been addressed by General Kiszczak and given information which was being studiously withheld from the public. It was only through the BBC's subscription to the Party's theoretical journal *Nowe Drogi* (New Roads) that I discovered the Minister had even spoken at the plenum; I read the text of his speech, among others, in a verbatim record of the meeting published early the following year.[2]

General Kiszczak told the Committee that Fr Popieluszko's kidnappers were three officers of his own Ministry. He named them, providing brief biographical details, and said that Waldemar Chmielewski had admitted on Thursday that the priest's body had been dropped into the Vistula at Włocławek. A search had been going on there ever since. There was a fear, Kiszczak said, that the priest 'may no longer be among the living'.

The General conceded that it was possible that others apart from the trio under arrest had been involved. So far, he said, there was nothing to suggest that the crime had been sponsored by anyone from the Ministry of the Interior, but it was his impression that the kidnappers had set out to cast suspicion on the Ministry by deliberately leaving a police cap badge at the scene of the crime.

General Kiszczak spoke with greater certainty when he declared that the only people whose interests were served by the crime were 'our enemies', who were using the crime 'to launch a new campaign of lies and slander, revive anti-State activities and rebuild illegal structures', by which he meant the Solidarity underground.

In a speech closing the first day's proceedings,[3] General Jaruzelski announced that General Kiszczak would be addressing the nation on television the following evening. That was as much as we were told by the official media. His brief address, however, discovered later in *Nowe Drogi*, seemed to suggest that he was deeply upset by the crime, not because of the harm done to Fr Popiełuszko but because he knew the Party would be blamed for it. It was 'cynical manipulation by our opponents', he said, to associate the Party with the crime.

'The crime that has been committed is a misfortune for us. It has given the enemy something else to feed on. All this is sad and painful, but it ought not to put us in the position of defendants in the dock or induce a state of depression or panic. As we have shown repeatedly in the past, we are capable of getting through difficult and onerous times in the profound conviction that history is on our side.'

General Jaruzelski told the Central Committee that he would seek the cooperation of the Church 'so as not to allow events to develop in an unpredictable way'. But while noting that the Church and the Primate usually behaved with discretion, the General recalled that a priest, Fr Zych, had been convicted not long ago as an accomplice in the murder of a Warsaw policeman, Sergeant Karos. 'But it never entered our heads to generalise and say that all priests are potential murderers.'

Whether this was a genuine warning to the Church not to generalise about the SB or just tough posturing is a moot point. It is a fact, however, that Fr Zych, who served in a parish outside Warsaw, did not take part in a murder. He was convicted of harbouring some teenage boys who had jumped on the police sergeant on a Warsaw tram in January 1982 as part of their response to martial law, a campaign to steal policemen's pistols. In the ensuing struggle, the sergeant's pistol went off with fatal results.

It is also a fact that hardline attitudes to the Church were not extinct in the Central Committee. In a remarkable speech never delivered but placed on the record of the plenum, Stanisław Łowicki, a senior blue-collar worker from Bytom, accused the Church hierarchy of reluctance to accept the constitutional separation of Church and State. 'The clergy don't want to give up the fight against the socialist system and never will... We have many examples of this: Fr Jankowski and many others like him... At the sixth plenum of the Central Committee I said that counter-revolution comes out of the Church. I say it again today. Correct me if I'm wrong.'[4]

Comrade Łowicki's speech, which went on to demand that the country be 'purged of its native foes' such as Kuroń, Michnik and Bujak, was not exceptional. It contradicted the declared policy of General Jaruzelski, certainly, but it would be echoed in attitudes and actions in the days, weeks and months to come.

The Church, which seemed to understand the authorities better than they understood the Church, was ready for trouble. As the Central Committee was ending its first day's work, Cardinal Glemp went to St Stanisław's where he told the congregation at the end of evening Mass what he had learned of Fr Popiełuszko's final hours of freedom in Bydgoszcz. He called for a Christian response to the crime 'without any impulse for revenge, without any hatred'.

The Primate's visit to St Stanisław's, however, was not entirely successful. At a meeting in the crypt with steel workers who made up the guard protecting Waldek Chrostowski, he was publicly scolded by their leader, Seweryn Jaworski, for going ahead with his visit to East Berlin after the announcement of Fr Popiełuszko's abduction. His reputation suffered again that evening when he advised Solidarity representatives to remove their information centre from the ground floor of the priests' house as soon as possible so as not to give grounds for police intervention.

Late that night, the government news agency, PAP, issued a commentary which was clearly inspired by the Central Committee's secret deliberations. It accused 'past masters of provocation' whom it named — Jaworski, Kuroń, Wujec, Romaszewski and Onyszkiewicz — of occupying the priests' house at St Stanisław's against Church wishes. Their purpose, it said, was to fill people with hatred, to provoke demonstrations and to bring about clashes at any price.

This was an exceptionally revolting piece of official Communist journalism. Its author, who preferred to remain anonymous, claimed that political has-beens were homing in on the tragedy in the hope of recouping their losses. 'One gets the impression that these people are finding it difficult to conceal their joy beneath their mourning garb.' It went on to claim that it was not yet clear who had kidnapped Fr Popiełuszko and maybe even killed him or what their motives were. This was a convenient lie. The authorities had already announced that they had the kidnappers but had not made public everything they knew.

Besides insults and more than one reference to the possibility that Fr Popiełuszko was dead, the commentary, which duly appeared in the papers the following morning, also carried the thinly veiled threat of a return to martial law:

> It is a foul thing to feed on tragedy... Political provocations which seek to profit from public distress over the tragedy of the Żoliborz priest... can lead only to conflicts and clashes. The authorities will make sure that the country remains at peace. The only question is whether it will be necessary to pay a high price for that peace once again.

None of this frightened anyone; it merely exposed the authorities' failure to understand either the mood of the nation and its relationship with Fr Popiełuszko. But the commentary also demonstrated something else: after being caught in the wrong and on the defensive, Generals Jaruzelski and Kiszczak were not going to say 'sorry', they were preparing for the attack.

# 20

# Kiszczak's Half-Truths

On Saturday afternoon, Janusz Onyszkiewicz gave his last press conference at St Stanisław's before he and his colleagues left the premises at the Primate's request. He revealed that at an identification parade earlier at the Rakowiecka prison, Waldek Chrostowski had identified Fr Popiełuszko's three kidnappers — Pękala by sight, and Piotrowski and Chmielewski, whom he had never seen clearly, by their voices and the way they talked. Chrostowski had been accompanied by his lawyer, Edward Wende, on this, only his second excursion from the safe haven of St Stanisław's since his return from Toruń on Tuesday evening.

Onyszkiewicz, of course, was one of the small group of Solidarity activists who were condemned in that morning's papers as 'masters of provocation'. The authorities, no doubt, had been particularly irked by the fact that much of what he had suggested to journalists on Friday had been confirmed later by General Kiszczak in his speech to the Central Committee. Fr Popiełuszko had, indeed, been abducted by SB officers and his chances of survival were worse than slim.

As for Onyszkiewicz's suggestion that the crime could have been the work of a group acting on its own or part of a power struggle in the Ministry of Internal Affairs or even higher, it was too early to say. The Central Committee, however, had already dismissed the kidnappers as 'a few... agents of an evil cause', and General Kiszczak, while conceding the possibility that others had been involved, had told the Committee that nothing so far suggested that the crime had been sponsored by anyone inside his Ministry. By the time the General began his address to the nation at 8 on Saturday evening, that was no longer true.

On Friday evening, Waldemar Chmielewski had informed his interrogator that Piotrowski had told him and Pękala several times that 'his superiors' had agreed to their operation against Fr Popiełuszko. 'He didn't name anyone, though, and we didn't ask.' On Saturday, Chmielewski went further. 'It emerged from our conversations with Piotrowski that our activities against Popiełuszko had the agreement of his immediate superiors. Piotrowski didn't say exactly who. All he said was that we had the *placet* [agreement] of the directors... that the matter was on the record. We took this to mean that senior bosses knew about it [Note the plural].'[1]

Pękala testified that Piotrowski managed to create in him and Chmielewski 'a profound conviction that the plan was accepted very high up, even if it did not exclude the possibility that the kidnapped priest could die by accident'. The phrase 'very high up' presumably also signified more than one superior officer.[2]

It seems likely that General Kiszczak knew at least part of this when he spoke before the television cameras on Saturday evening. The general public, however, knew hardly anything except that three men were under arrest for kidnapping Fr Popiełuszko. Only one, Grzegorz P., had been identified as an officer of the Ministry of Internal Affairs. The General had a captive audience thirsting for information and hanging on his every word. But he told them less than he had told the Communist Party's Central Committee.

General Kiszczak said it was his difficult and bitter duty to announce with great regret that Fr Popiełuszko's kidnappers were three young officers from his own Ministry, whom he named. Most people had believed this from the start and it was good to hear it confirmed publicly. But that was all the General would give his audience in the way of new, hard fact. The fact that a search for the priest's body in the waters of the Vistula had been going on since Thursday afternoon was withheld.

'Unfortunately,' the General said, 'I cannot at this moment provide information or even a sufficiently credible conjecture as to the fate of the kidnap victim. The suspects are giving extremely different testimony under interrogation, changing it or withdrawing it time and again. So far, they are refusing to reveal many important details which could facilitate the search for Fr Popiełuszko. One plausible hypothesis of the investigation is that the kidnap victim is dead.'[3]

As the General well knew, this was a virtual certainty and he referred to that possibility more than once. 'The organiser of the abduction,' he said, was claiming that he had personally taken the priest's life. Nonetheless, the General appealed to everyone to help find the priest 'if he is still alive'. He also suggested that one reason why the three suspects kept changing their evidence could be because they realised that 'if found guilty they could be sentenced to the supreme penalty'. By this time, however, neither Chmielewski nor Pękala was changing or withdrawing evidence; they were both consistently adding to it.

General Kiszczak said that the kidnappers had 'deliberately' left a police cap badge at the scene of the abduction to point the finger of suspicion at his Ministry. He quoted Piotrowski as saying under interrogation that his motive for the crime was the fact that the authorities were so ineffectual in the face of Fr Popiełuszko's 'blatant political activity'. He did not mention that this was precisely the complaint of the OAS, the Anti-Solidarity Organisation involved in previous kidnapping incidents in the Toruń area, investigations into which had only recently been dropped by the local prosecutor.

General Kiszczak said that there wasn't yet enough evidence to discount or confirm the possibility that others had been involved in organising the abduction of Fr Popiełuszko, but this was the subject of particularly intensive enquiries. 'Was there a hidden inspirer of this crime and if so who? Was there someone who shielded those who committed the crime, and if so who?' The answers, the General promised, would be shared with the public. This was an advance on what he had told the party plenum, and his talk of 'a hidden inspirer' primed the public for an announcement.

Having failed to tell the whole truth himself, General Kiszczak proceeded to warn 'the enemies of people's power' not to 'manipulate' the truth. 'It is wrong to take one isolated incident and draw baseless, general conclusions from it... It is wrong to identify the criminal act of individual officers of the Ministry of Internal Affairs with the security apparatus as a whole... I warn the enemies of our State... not to try to exploit this human tragedy. They should not push an overexcited section of society into activities which carry the threat of unpredictable consequences.'[4]

The broadcast made it near impossible for anyone to go on believing that Fr Popiełuszko would return. And for that reason, the General's warning to 'enemies' was strikingly out of place. For most people, the loss of the priest was a matter of personal as well as national grief, and the mood in Warsaw was subdued. There was not the slightest hint of any inclination to demonstrate or provoke street clashes. While in the immediate aftermath of the abduction there had been a call for a strike at the Huta Warszawa steel works on the coming Monday, the mood had changed.

In Gdańsk, at the end of Sunday Mass at St Brigid's, Lech Wałęsa counselled calm. Speaking no doubt because of Kiszczak's warning, he said that if people chose to demonstrate at the monument to slain workers outside the shipyard gates, the authorities 'would use their clubs against us or open fire. I think that road is doomed to failure from the start. We are just as strong, though, at our places of work or on our knees in prayer...'

In Warsaw, in keeping with their own propaganda, the authorities paid no heed to that. They despatched police columns, backed by water cannons, to the area around St Stanisław's in Żoliborz. It was the last Sunday of the month and the regular Mass for the Homeland was to be said in the absence of Fr Popiełuszko.

The police were witness that evening to the largest congregation they had ever seen there, some 40,000 to 50,000 people from all over Poland. They filled the side streets around the church and the little park that faced it, listening intently as loudspeakers relayed a recording of Fr Popiełuszko's voice and the last words he uttered from the altar in Bydgoszcz on the night he was kidnapped. The police, of course, heard those same last words as well as the call for prayers during Mass for those who were the enemies of the missing priest.

When Mass was over, it took half an hour or more for the crowds to disperse quietly under the watchful gaze of the police. When someone threw leaflets into the air a rebuke was delivered swiftly over the church's loudspeakers.

Earlier that day, Karol and I listened in the BBC office to the voices of the missing priest's parents — Marianna, seventy two, and Władysław, seventy four — recorded on tape the day before at their home in Okopy in northeastern Poland. While I stayed in Warsaw for General Kiszczak's broadcast, Karol and his friend Jerzy Kisielewski had driven to Okopy to get some idea of the background from which Fr Popiełuszko had emerged.

What they found was a household of religious piety. They were shown photographs of the future priest on the day he made his First Communion. His father described with pride how his son had said he wanted to be a priest when he was only five, standing next to the coffin of his sister, Jadwiga, who died at the age of two. Most remarkable, perhaps, was the mother's account of how she had first heard on television of her son's abduction a week earlier and how her husband, when she told him, had cried out that 'bandits have thrown him into the river'.

The father's anguished cry was virtually confirmed by the authorities on Monday morning when they announced that police frogmen were searching for Fr Popiełuszko in the waters of the Vistula at Włocławek. A communiqué from the Ministry of Internal Affairs said that one of the kidnappers claimed that the priest had been thrown into the river near Toruń, while the other two said he had been abandoned in the waters of the reservoir at Włocławek, where a dam across the river controlled the flow of the Vistula westwards and northwards to the Baltic. So far, the communiqué said, the frogmen had failed to find the priest. Strong currents were making their work difficult and dangerous, but the search was being continued by teams with special equipment. Another member of the kidnap trio had been taken to the area that day.

The announcement was another stage in the authorities' measured release of information designed to prepare the public for the bad news to come. One immediate effect, though, was to prompt speculation that Fr Popiełuszko's body had already been recovered. After all, why would the authorities have announced on Thursday that they were going to withhold details of their enquiries, only to break their silence by revealing where exactly they believed the priest was to be found before he was even found? A West German television crew, which rushed to Włocławek after the announcement, was kept at a distance of several hundred metres from the dam but reported that police activity seemed to be continuing.

At his regular press conference at noon on Tuesday, the government spokesman, Jerzy Urban, stated categorically that Fr Popiełuszko had not been found either alive or dead. He said that the chief accused, Grzegorz Piotrowski, had changed his testimony and was now claiming the priest had been abandoned not in the Vistula but somewhere else, alive. The two lieutenants, on the other hand, had each said that the priest's body was to be found in the Włocławek reservoir, where several dozen police frogmen were continuing their search. The waters were being dragged with weighted nets.

This added little to what was known, but Urban made up for that with a statement he knew no journalist could resist.

It is General Kiszczak's theory that someone else is behind the kidnappers. If this is true, then it is clear that the kidnappers are counting on help from their protectors. They are saying nothing about them during the investigation. Special security measures are being applied with regard to the three men under arrest so as to make it impossible for anything to happen in this case such as happened in the case of President Kennedy's assassination or in the West German prison in the Baader-Meinhof case. The special security measures are connected with the theory that the kidnappers could have accomplices who are capable of a great deal. Their food is being served in a special way and their guards have been doubled.

Independent, underground sources were to report later that security measures on the second floor of Block Three of the Rakowiecka prison, where Piotrowski, Pękala and Chmielewski were being held, were indeed exceptional. The lights in their cells were never switched off, officers were sitting outside their cell doors, fully armed ZOMO riot police were stationed at either end of the long, oblong floor in which the staircase occupies the centre, and a guard with a guard dog was in position at the entrance below.

Western journalists in Poland were sometimes accused of paying too much attention to what Jerzy Urban had to say, but this could not be ignored. To suggest that Fr Popiełuszko's kidnappers were in danger of being killed as was Lee Harvey Oswald, President Kennedy's presumed assassin, while in police custody in 1963, or that an attempt could be made to rescue them from prison as Andreas Baader, one of the founders of the terrorist Red Army Faction, was rescued from a West German gaol in 1970, implied that the supposed accomplices of Piotrowski, Chmielewski and Pękala were powerful enough to stage a murder or a rescue mission in defiance of the Jaruzelski government.

True or false, this gave a more serious complexion to the claim that the abduction of Fr Popiełuszko was a political provocation against the government. And Urban added an interesting note: that the search for 'possible inspirers' of the priest's abduction was being conducted not only in the kidnap investigation but 'by studying various other phenomena in Poland'. No hint of what these 'phenomena' might be would emerge until years later. The spokesman was asked, however, why the recent Central Committee meeting had expressed confidence in General Kiszczak but not his predecessor as Minister of the Interior, General Mirosław Milewski, the member of the Party Politburo still supposedly responsible for political supervision of the Ministry's work. Mr Urban provided no direct answer, noting merely that the Central Committee had decided to review Party supervision of security matters.

All such thoughts, however absorbing, disappeared at 7.30 pm with the main television news bulletin. The solemn garb and demeanour of the presenter made it obvious that the moment had come.

> The Ministry of Internal Affairs announces that late this afternoon, as a result of intensive searches by specialist teams of police divers, the body of Fr Jerzy Popiełuszko was found in the waters of the reservoir at Włocławek and brought to the surface. His remains have been taken to a forensic medicine centre for postmortem examination. The State authorities remain in constant contact with representatives of the leadership of the Polish Episcopate. On the instructions of the Minister of Internal Affairs, intensive enquiries continue with the main aim of determining who if anyone inspired the abduction of Fr Jerzy Popiełuszko and the taking of his life.

I was alone in the office when the news came through but by the time I had written a short piece and put it over by telephone to London, I had been joined by Karol. We set off by car along the familiar route to Żoliborz and the church of St Stanisław Kostka. We parked some distance away because, as usual, there was no space closer. As we walked towards the church, the voice of a priest, floating out over loudspeakers, grew louder with every step. He was trying to comfort the congregation inside the church and the growing crowd outside. Fr Jerzy, he said, was a martyr who had given his life so that they could live. At that moment, however, they seemed beyond consolation, numb with the shock that comes with a death in the family.

The priest intoned the opening phrases of their favourite patriotic hymn, 'Boże coś Polskę', normally sung with gusto at the end of Mass, especially the Masses for the Homeland. They joined in but their voices were weak and some were crying.

In Gdańsk, Lech Wałęsa issued a statement. 'Let there be silence throughout Poland, the quiet of mourning and also of hope that this death can help us build social peace.'

# 21
# Return to Żoliborz

The next morning, the Communist daily, *Trybuna Ludu*, reported that the Party Committee at the Ministry of Internal Affairs had passed a resolution approving the expulsion of the three kidnappers from Party ranks. It also claimed that that the crime had been timed deliberately to follow the 40th anniversary of the SB and Civil Police, the celebrations of which, it said, had demonstrated that its officers were 'meeting with friendliness and good will on the part of the public'. In the circumstances, it is difficult to imagine a more provocative lie.

In striking contrast, the four leaders of the Solidarity underground in the Warsaw region issued a statement assuming a share of responsibility for the death of Fr Popiełuszko. The men who had managed to elude the SB for almost three years — Zbigniew Bujak, Viktor Kulerski, Konrad Bielinski and Zbigniew Janas — put their names to a searching examination of the national conscience which declared that 'we are all guilty'. It would be hypocritical, they said, to lay the blame exclusively on the men of the SB. The bitter truth was that Solidarity activists, Warsaw workers and intellectuals and Church authorities had failed to protect Fr Popiełuszko because they had failed to stand up openly against increasing acts of terror. If there had been proper resistance, they said, then maybe the murderers would not have had the courage to do what they had done.

Experience had taught these officers that they could act with impunity.

In a nation that had so often shown itself capable of heroic resistance against all odds, it might have seemed harsh to say 'we are all guilty'. But few could quarrel with the analysis. For years, not one officer had been punished for violence against citizens, not for shooting protesting workers in Gdańsk and Szczecin in December 1970, for beating demonstrators in Radom in the summer of 1976 or for opening fire and killing miners at the Wujek colliery in December 1981.

> Every officer knew and saw that he was free to beat and to kill with impunity. This only encouraged them. They were embold-ened also by verdicts handed down by the courts... The judges who recently acquitted the murderers of Grzesia [Grzegorz] Przemyk now have the blood of Fr Jerzy Popiełuszko on their hands...
>
> We repeat: Officers of the security apparatus feel that they are beyond punishment. This is not altered by any of the dec-larations made so unsparingly these days by their superiors, nor is it changed by the search for scapegoats. It can be changed only by the sustained, daily resistance of all of us against law-lessness and banditry...[1]

The Church was already resisting a move by the authorities to dictate where Fr Popiełuszko should be buried. The priest's body had been taken for the postmortem not to Warsaw, as most people had expected, but to Białystok, chief city of his native province in the northeast. The plan, clearly, was that he should be buried quietly in Suchowola where he went to school and served on the altar. The Church, however, wasted no time in making sure that Fr Popiełuszko would not be buried in obscurity. A document in Church archives, signed by the priest's parents and dated 30 October, the evening the authorities announced the recovery of the body, authorised a delegation of the Metropolitan Curia to take their son's remains back to St Stanisław's in Warsaw.[2]

The next day, the Primate and the Curia completed virtually all arrangements for the funeral. Two men were chosen to represent the Church during the postmortem, defence lawyer Jan Olszewski from Warsaw and a forensic medicine specialist, Dr Edmund Chruscielewski from Poznań. Two priests were appointed to bring the body back to the capital after the post-mortem. The eleven-member committee which the Primate had appointed to organise the funeral decided that Fr Popiełuszko would be buried on Saturday, 3 November, in Warsaw's most beautiful cemetery at Powązki after a Requiem Mass at St Stanisław's at which Cardinal Glemp would officiate and preach.

The committee included supporters and friends of Fr Popiełuszko: Bishops Miziołek and Kraszewski; Fr Król, Chancellor of the Curia; Prof. Klemens Szaniawski of Warsaw University; and Karol Szadurski, an engineer from Huta Warszawa — but its decision was challenged and reversed the following day. A small delegation from the parish, accompanied by Fr Popiełuszko's mother, handed the Primate a petition requesting that the priest be buried at St Stanisław's. Fr Bogucki, the parish priest, sent a similar request from his hospital bed and in the evening it was announced that the Primate had agreed; Fr Popiełuszko would be buried in the yard of the church where he used to preach.

It was an appropriate day for such a decision, the feast of All Saints, a national holiday in Poland when people flocked to the cemeteries in their thousands with flowers for the graves of family and friends. On Friday morning, the feast of All Souls, two priests of the Warsaw Curia — Fr Grzegorz Kalwarczyk and Fr Edward Żmijewski — set off for Białystok in separate cars to bring back the body of Fr Popiełuszko. Fr Zmijewski had with him my bright red 'idiot's' camera, which Karol had asked me to lend to 'someone' the day before.

As the priests drove north and east, I joined a small group of parishioners gazing through the railings as workmen dug Fr Popiełuszko's grave in the corner of the church grounds where, for more than a year, a makeshift shrine had honoured the memory of Grzegorz Przemyk. His funeral in May the previous year had been organised by the priest who was now dead. It was a perfect autumn day. The sky was a clear blue, the air was crisp and fresh, and the trees that fringe the little park were losing their last golden leaves.

In Białystok on Friday crowds of people were waiting outside the forensic medicine centre when Fr Kalwarczyk and Fr Żmijewski arrived with Fr Popiełuszko's family and Jacek Lipiński from Huta Warszawa. They found the gates locked and it took considerable negotiations with the local prosecutor, with police officers and doctors before they were finally allowed in by a rear entrance. To judge from the detailed report compiled by Fr Kalwarczyk, he was more shocked than he had expected when he was admitted to the dissecting room along with Fr Żmijewski and Lipiński for purposes of identification. He was told by a doctor who had taken part in the postmortem that he had been shocked not so much by external signs of beating but by the internal damage to the abdominal cavity. Never before had he seen such injuries.

Fr Popiełuszko's face looked so different now that it was difficult to confirm that this was his body. When the mouth was opened to check teeth against dental records, they saw that the tongue had been reduced to a pulpy mass. To eliminate any doubt, Fr Popiełuszko's two brothers were invited in to assist. The elder brother, Józef, was too upset to speak, but the younger, Stanisław, remembered that his dead brother had two birth marks or moles on his chest which resembled a couple of extra nipples. They looked and they were there. Józef signed the document of identification.

An official photographer took several pictures of the corpse, but when Fr Żmijewski tried to do the same he was stopped by a police officer. Fr Kalwarczyk, taking out pen and paper, asked for the officer's name. The officer complied and gave his place of employment, with a blush, as the Ministry of Internal Affairs. Fr Żmijewski was allowed to take his pictures.

Three Sisters of Charity then dressed Fr Popiełuszko for burial. On his soutane they pinned three badges — one of the Black Madonna of Częstochowa, another bearing the inscriptions Solidarity and Huta Warszawa, and the third showing St Stanisław's Church and the words Mass for the Homeland. Over that, the nuns dressed him in a long white alb and a red chasuble. In his hands they placed a crucifix which also bore the name of Solidarity and the rosary beads sent to him as a present by Pope John Paul II.

After a laboratory assistant had done some cosmetic work on Fr Popiełuszko's face, using only powder, the body was placed in the oak coffin lined with metal which Fr Kalwarczyk had brought from Warsaw. This was then carried into another room and parents and family, in the presence of a doctor, were brought in to see the body. Bishop Edward Kisiel of Białystok said the traditional prayers for the dead before the lid was placed on the coffin. At the insistence of Frs Kalwarczyk and Żmijewski, the police affixed only paper seals around its edges. Some of the many priests who were present during these final moments carried the coffin out into the open air where a huge crowd carrying flowers and lighted candles had managed to get into the grounds and had been singing hymns for more than an hour. Laymen took the coffin from the priests and carried it at arm's-length high above their heads through the dense throng to the hearse waiting outside the gates.

Fr Kalwarczyk, who sat in the passenger seat of the hearse, remembered the leaving of Białystok:[3]

More than 200 taxis and cars joined the cortege spontaneously and accompanied us to a point beyond the city limits. The drivers blared on their horns. One could hear the wail of sirens. The streets, especially those close to the forensic laboratory, were crammed with people. Some held lighted candles or the votive candles normally placed on graves. Others carried flowers, others were weeping or kneeling on the street as they said farewell to Fr Jerzy. Even the man driving the hearse was crying. Most of the people held their hands high in the air making the V sign with their fingers. There was also a crowd of youngsters who ran behind the hearse. All the way to the boundary of the Archdiocese we passed groups of people bidding farewell to their compatriot. And all this took place in the rays of the setting sun.

At the edge of the Archdiocese, in the village of Żółtki, the cortege halted and we all got out of the cars. Together with a large group of local people... we knelt on the roadway... and said the Angelus and Eternal Rest... Having said goodbye to the Bishop, we set off more quickly for Warsaw... There were six cars in the cortege. Every few kilometres we passed police cars standing at the roadside, but no one stopped us. Whenever we passed through larger townships we switched on the flashing lights...

In Warsaw, we were joined near Dzierżyński Square by a police car which led the way to Żoliborz. After crossing the bridge over the Gdańsk Station, the police car turned left and a policeman controlling the traffic tried to get us to do the same. But Fr Żmijewski in the lead car drove straight on to Paris Commune Square and turned left onto Krasińskiego. Waiting for us there were tens of thousands of people. Passing through a lane edged by crowd barriers, we entered the small square in front of the church... The bells began to toll...

I was there when the cortege arrived, standing on the balcony above the front entrance of the church, next to a tiny nun who could barely see over the balustrade. Something passed over the crowds as the cars approached, a sound like a sigh or a collective intake of breath. And as the leading cars drew to a halt, windows were lowered and arms and hands emerged in the V for victory sign.

'There's Waldek,' the nun said, to herself as much as to anyone else. Below us, Waldemar Chrostowski waited at the gates of the churchyard. As the coffin entered the grounds there was a pause as Chrostowski took the place of one of the bearers. The coffin was then carried into the church and placed on a catafalque before the high altar.

It was about 6.40 in the evening. Within an hour, as the first of many thousands of people queued to file past the coffin, the Ministry of Internal Affairs made an important announcement.

Two more men had been taken into custody, it said, on the instructions of the Minister, General Kiszczak. One was the Deputy Director of a department, Colonel Adam P. The other was the head of a section in the Warsaw City Office of Internal Affairs, Lieutenant Colonel Leszek W. At the same time, the communiqué said, the Director of the same Ministry department, Brigade General Zenon Płatek, had been suspended from his duties by the Minister for 'lack of sufficient supervision'.

I remember speculating that a clean-up could be underway in the Ministry of Internal Affairs. After all, the authorities had stated repeatedly that they would continue intensive investigations into the possibility that others, as yet unknown, had instigated the abduction and murder of Fr Popiełuszko. The fact that a Deputy Director of a department had been detained indicated that the search had gone higher. Would it go higher still?

It did not. The fact that General Płatek was named in full meant that there was no intention of treating him as a suspect. Within two days, Adam Pietruszka would be placed under arrest, but Leszek Wolski would be released for lack of evidence. The search for 'hidden inspirers' was effectively over before the priest had been buried in his grave.

# 22
# The Funeral

By a sad accident of history, Saturday, 3 November, 1984, was the day of another momentous funeral, that of Mrs Indira Gandhi, Prime Minister of India. She too had been assassinated for political reasons. It was my fear that the world's news services, and in particular television, would devote far more attention to her obsequies and very little to those of a relatively obscure priest from Warsaw. Of course, a sense of protocol alone would determine that a Prime Minister with a distinguished name celebrated in the history of the twentieth century would take precedence over someone of no secular rank and with a name that few could spell, let alone pronounce. And the pictures from Delhi might also be considered more colourful and more dramatic than those expected from Warsaw.

But it did seem possible that the funeral of Fr Popiełuszko might be of greater historical consequence. He was being buried in the capital city of a Soviet Bloc State, the first admitted victim of the Communist secret police, in the presence of countless thousands of people openly proclaiming with banners and slogans their love for him and their support for the illegal Solidarity trade union movement, which he had championed. This was 1984, not 1989.

Regardless of other events, the priest whose death, in the words of the Pope, was of great moral significance, was laid to rest as a national hero and martyr by a grieving but defiant people, in a demonstration of patriotic fervour that the Communist government could never dream of evoking. For that reason it was a moment of historic significance.

They filed past the coffin in their thousands throughout the night. Thousands more travelled to the capital from all over the country in the hours of darkness by car and train. At St Stanisław's, confessionals were set up in the churchyard and priests and penitents alike shivered in the cold. The doors of the church were supposed to be closed at 4 am so that final preparations could be made for the funeral. Shortly before then, Jacek Lipiński left the church to see how many people were still waiting to file past the coffin, but he had to go by car; the queue stretched round the block and out of sight. The church was finally cleared and closed, he told me, at 5.30 am. Fr Popiełuszko's parents took a last look at their son and the coffin was sealed.

Nobody can say for sure how many people attended the funeral on that bright, clear but chilly morning. Only an aerial view of the entire district of Żoliborz could have afforded a proper measure of the multitude. Long before 11 am, when the Primate was due to begin saying the Requiem Mass, we had been forced to park the car miles away because of the crowds streaming towards the church. I remember noticing how a large number of people ahead of us, mainly young men, kept entering the apartment houses ringing Paris Commune Square, a few minutes walk from the church, and wondering why. The reason became clear later when I looked up from where I was standing, close to the grave, and saw them standing on the roof tops, silhouetted against the sky. Others were perched in leafless trees.

My own estimate was that at least a quarter of a million people attended the funeral of Fr Jerzy Popiełuszko. Some said hundreds of thousands, others said a million. But the occasion was so big that it was possible to be 'there' when standing several streets away.

The altar for the Requiem Mass was set up on the balcony where I had stood the night before and where Fr Popiełuszko had said many a Mass for the Homeland in summertime. Beneath it in the forecourt of the church, his coffin lay on the catafalque. Places were reserved nearby for the dead priest's family, Solidarity notables including Lech Wałęsa, Jacek Kuroń and Adam Michnik, for foreign diplomats, and the head of the nominally Catholic, pro-government Pax organisation, Zenon Komender. At the altar, the Primate Cardinal Glemp was assisted by four Bishops and eight priests, including the parish priest, Fr Bogucki, who had left his hospital bed to be present.

Inevitably, the reports from Warsaw that day were of the funeral of a martyr for Solidarity. Two years had passed since Solidarity had been made illegal by Act of Parliament, but today it was as if that had never happened. Countless banners bearing the outlawed name and the names of the towns, factories, universities, institutes, even the scout troops from which they came, could be seen wherever one gazed over the heads of the densely packed crowds.

But there were others for whom Fr Popiełuszko was not just a Solidarity priest. A doctor spoke passionately about his defence of the life of the unborn child. A nurse recalled how he had revived, virtually from nothing, the Church's mission to the medical profession. Cardinal Glemp in his sermon saw Fr Jerzy as an example of someone who lived for others and not for himself.

> He was simply devoted to people, and they through him grew closer to God. That was why he was the object of such universal and spontaneous love. As he said himself, he did not seek regard for himself, he did not want to attach the faithful to himself, he simply wanted to bring closer to them the beauty of God and the truth of the faith. It is true that when it came to the social application of divine truths he was resolute and demanding. He was continually accused of making his preaching of Church teaching too political. This is a matter I will not discuss in the course of a religious funeral at a moment of deeply felt grief. The time will come, for sure, when it will be the subject of objective discussion and analysis, for... love

for one's homeland, as a form of love for one's neighbour... is not just an abstraction, it finds ways of expressing itself socially. Fr Popiełuszko loved his country with a great love, a love that had not been modernised by fashions for permissiveness or relative values, but one that was recognised in traditions handed down from generation to generation...[1]

Some of my journalist colleagues didn't like to be reminded that Fr Popiełuszko was against abortion, as if that complicated the image of the Solidarity priest, which was otherwise perfectly acceptable in the West. Cardinal Glemp, however, was right to present the full picture. Fr Popiełuszko was, first and foremost, a Catholic priest, and it was in response to a call for a Catholic priest, any Catholic priest, that he had been sent to administer the sacraments to striking workers at Huta Warszawa in August 1980. The workers took him for what he was and now, at his funeral, he was addressed by his friend, the steel works engineer Karol Szadurski, both as a priest and a liberator. 'Fr Jerzy,' he asked, 'can you hear the bells of freedom ringing?'

The distinguished actor Andrzej Szczepkowski, speaking on behalf of the actors who had regularly assisted at the Masses for the Homeland, said that 'the faith of our fathers is the unchanging foundation of patriotism' and that 'this fearless, young priest' was now assured of entry into 'the triumphal assembly of Polish martyrs'. The voice and the language of this speaker, those of classical drama, preceded the more direct but stirring words of the Solidarity leader, Lech Wałęsa, making his first speech in public since the imposition of martial law.

... To the roll-call of those who have died for Poland, to the list of names to be seen on the memorials of Warsaw, Poznań, the Coast and Silesia, we are adding the name of a Warsaw priest, a son of the countryside of Białystok, a chaplain of the workers. Fr Jerzy fell victim to a wave of violence and hatred, which he always confronted with goodness and truth. Over the coffin of our brother let us swear never to forget this death. Let us keep for ever the memory of Fr Jerzy and his teaching...

A good man and a courageous one, a splendid priest, pastor and champion of the nation's cause, he bore witness all his life to the unity of Church and Nation. From August 1980 to the last days of his life, from Huta Warszawa to Gdańsk, Bytom, Jasna Góra and so many other sacred Polish places and finally to Bydgoszcz, he was Solidarity's companion, preaching the word of God and the teachings of the Holy Father, conducting an untiring prayer for the intentions of the homeland. Poland, which has such priests and a self-sacrificing people displaying loyalty and solidarity, has not perished and will not perish.

We bid you farewell... swearing that we will never give in to violence... and that we will respond to lies with truth and to evil with good... Rest in peace. Solidarity lives because you gave your life for it.[2]

Fr Bogucki's opening words were equally memorable: 'It seems to me that I see before me the whole of Poland, the real Poland that believes in God, Catholic Poland... Poland which wants freedom and its own national identity.'[3] There was a great deal of truth in that, but not all in that massive congregation were either Catholics or even believers.

There was thought, of course, about the future. Fr Bogucki hoped that Fr Popieluszko's death would give birth to a greater good for the Church and for Poland. Earlier, Cardinal Glemp had stated precisely what was wanted. 'Would that Poles... did not have to meet in tears at the grave of a priest and martyr. Would that they could meet instead at the table of dialogue to agree on their aspirations for peace. This is what the Church has been advocating for a long time.'

There was no good reason at that moment to believe that the authorities would ever respond favourably to the pleas of the Church or of Solidarity. But when the funeral was over and as the huge crowds made their way home, one thing that could be said for certain was that Solidarity was alive. A column of many thousands of people, still carrying their standards and banners, made its way on foot from Żoliborz back into the city centre.

On reaching the Mostowski Palace, otherwise known as the Warsaw City Office of Internal Affairs, they found it surrounded by a guard of ZOMO riot police, who remained unmoved when invited by the crowd to throw away their sticks and 'come and join us'. One of that crowd recorded later that as the train taking mourners home to Cracow began moving out of Central Station amidst the chanting of 'Solidarity' and the flashing of V-for-victory signs, he noticed Russians in a Soviet train on the other side of the platform gazing with incredulity at the scene, their noses pressed against the windows.

The following day, as thousands of people continued to file past Fr Popiełuszko's grave, the BBC office was able to report that according to completely reliable sources, the priest's body, when recovered from the Vistula, was not only gagged and bound hand and foot, it was also trussed. A rope tied round the ankles bent the legs backwards and upwards as it was extended up the back and looped around the neck like a noose. Any attempt to straighten the legs would have tightened the rope around the neck.

This cruel detail, yet to be revealed by the authorities, was enough, no doubt, to dampen what remained of the sense of euphoria produced by the glorious funeral of the day before. Nonetheless, there came a sign the next day that Fr Popiełuszko's death could indeed give birth to a greater good for Poland.

On Monday, 5 November, Mr Malcolm Rifkind, Minister of State at the United Kingdom's Foreign and Commonwealth Office, was at the start of a three-day official visit to Warsaw, the first by a British minister since martial law had been imposed in December 1981, when he found time to go with his wife to St Stanisław Kostka's and lay a wreath on Fr Popiełuszko's grave.

Moving away from the grave, Mr Rifkind took questions from a small group of journalists and I asked him whether he had any plans to meet what I described as representatives of independent opinion in Poland. Certainly, he said, because Britain had relations with the people of Poland, not just its government. And this he did, meeting four representatives of the outlawed Solidarity movement on British Embassy premises. They were Tadeusz Mazowiecki, a future Prime Minister, Bronisław Geremek, a future Foreign Minister, Janusz Onyszkiewicz, a future Defence Minister, and Krzysztof Śliwiński, a future Ambassador.

This was the first time that a visiting minister or representative of a Western government had chosen to have talks not only with the government but with members of the Polish opposition. To the dismay of General Jaruzelski's government, Rifkind set a standard which would be emulated by practically all Western ministers and representatives who were to visit Poland in the future. It marked the moment when Solidarity was shown to have gained in the West the official recognition it was denied at home.

# 23

# Recriminations

In the weeks that followed the funeral of Fr Popiełuszko, Solidarity and its supporters made clear their determination to exercise greater public control over the State security apparatus if only through the publication of more information. That was what the leaders of the Warsaw underground had called for in their statement on the last day of October. But the day before that — the day the priest's body was recovered from the Vistula — a group of workers and intellectuals meeting in Wrocław had gone further, announcing the formation of a new Human Rights Defence Committee. They said that the increasing brutality employed since December 1981 to suppress Solidarity and any opposition to the government had created a situation in which the police services were beyond the control not only of the public but of the political authorities as well. This, they said, could lead to a terror comparable to that of the days of Stalin and had to be resisted.

The authorities were quick to respond. On the day of the funeral, the official press carried a lengthy comment by Jerzy Urban on reports that committees similar to the one set up in Wrocław were planned elsewhere and that they intended to operate openly. The government spokesman bluntly ruled out any chance that such 'self-styled organisations' would be allowed to operate openly or semi-legally and alleged that the people behind them — he named Gwiazda, Wujec, Onyszkiewicz, Romaszewski and Kuroń — wanted 'once again to take the road to confrontation'.

Committees similar to the one in Wrocław — Urban described them later as 'anti-State structures' — did indeed spring up in Cracow, Warsaw, Szczecin and Toruń but they were declared illegal almost as quickly as they appeared. That did not mean that they fizzled out. Like Solidarity, declared illegal in 1982, they moved underground, printing and publishing information on the security services and the legal and judicial system. Underground publishing was nothing new but there now came a fresh resolve to work the presses with even greater focus and regularity. And this added impetus to the development of underground journals such as *Praworządność* (The Rule of Law), the equal in intellectual content of some of the West's weighty current affairs periodicals.

This was the moment, I believe, when Solidarity began to demonstrate a renewed confidence that it had won the moral and political arguments and that, in spite of grievous losses and setbacks inflicted by police repression and violence, it could never be defeated. The authorities, on the other hand, were struggling to cope with being found out by a crime they could not hide. They disowned the crime, certainly, and this was received well by distant Western observers, but they had to contend with the widespread belief inside Poland that they were ultimately responsible. This was made eloquently clear by an open letter to General Jaruzelski, a copy of which reached the BBC office in Warsaw on the Monday after the funeral.

It had been written by Professor Edward Lipiński, the grand old man of Poland's socialist economists, a former member of the Party who in 1976 had helped found KOR, the Committee for the Defence of the Workers. Now, at the age of 96, he told the General that the murder of Fr Popiełuszko had taken away whatever remained of his moral legitimacy to exercise authority over the Polish nation.

You, Sir, are a faithful disciple of the theoreticians of socialist communism... Their idea of social peace is based on loyalty to three principles: violence, lies and enslavement... Anyone who thinks that freedom and pluralism are a condition of social progress is not only your political adversary, he is also, in your eyes, a deadly enemy whom it is right to destroy and even kill... It is in this spirit that the army, the police and the apparatus of the security service are reared... These murderers from the security service had to be trained, instructed and coached in bestiality over a long time. But the responsibility for this is borne by those who control this sinister process of education. We want to believe that it was not you, General, who ordered the murder of Fr Popiełuszko, but it is you who bear responsibility for it. It is on your conscience... The time has come for you to go...[1]

But far from 'going', General Jaruzelski was about to assume a new responsibility. Although General Kiszczak had told the Internal Affairs and Justice Commission of the Sejm that his Ministry employed only men and women of unimpeachable moral character 'dedicated to the Party and the socialist State', it was decided in the Politburo that the Prime Minister himself should take over the job of supervising Party work in the Ministry of Internal Affairs. The Politburo restated its confidence in the Ministry but did not explain why, if it was so confident, it felt the need to ask General Jaruzelski to take on yet another chore.

General Mirosław Milewski, the career SB man replaced as Minister of Internal Affairs by the career soldier Czesław Kiszczak in the summer of 1981, had been the one man in the Politburo responsible specifically for supervising Party work inside the Ministry until now. Why had he lost this job now? Were Western journalists wrong to wonder whether his dismissal had something to do with Fr Popiełuszko's murder? Jerzy Urban thought they were. It was shameful, he said, that members of the Party leadership should be named in sensational articles groundlessly imputing some sort of link with the crime.

What the spokesman did not say (and very possibly did not know) was that General Milewski was already under investigation for his alleged role in a sensational international smuggling operation involving the Ministry of Internal Affairs and some Polish criminals — a scandal made public only six years later.

As for the investigations into the priest's murder, the last announcements of substance came in the days immediately after the funeral, when Adam Pietruszka was charged with aiding and abetting the crime while Leszek Wolski was released for lack of evidence against him. General Kiszczak had then told the Internal Affairs Commission of the Sejm how Fr Popiełuszko had been overpowered and bundled into the boot of the car before being driven to Włocławek and thrown into the Vistula. And the chief of the Ministry's Investigations Bureau said it seemed likely that the priest had been throttled by the pressure of hands or a rope on his neck or been suffocated by something over his mouth which stopped his breathing. From then on the flow of information had dried up.

It was at this moment, when the public was very much in the dark, that Minister Urban chose to cast doubt on the evidence of Waldemar Chrostowski, the key witness in the coming trial. At one press conference, he made the apparently innocent remark that it was difficult to believe that a man who was handcuffed and gagged could escape from 'professionals' by jumping from a speeding car. A week later, he offered another 'curious detail': it had been discovered that the locking pins on the handcuffs placed on Chrostowski's wrists had been filed down. This, Urban claimed, explained how Chrostowski had been able to escape: the handcuffs had been placed on him only symbolically, and he was able to remove them. This meant that the reliability of Chrostowski's evidence had to be checked. After all, the spokesman noted, there was still that nagging doubt about his jumping from a car moving at 100 km/h.

These were not innocent observations and were demonstrably groundless. As was later shown conclusively, Polish handcuffs were so badly made that they could not be closed properly or even opened unless their locking pins were filed down. In fact, most police handcuffs were in the same condition as those used on Chrostowski. The spokesman was equally wrong to question the manner of Chrostowski's escape, something already confirmed by investigators. Jerzy Urban was trying to muddy the waters, knowing that a public starved of information could be fertile ground for rumour, insinuation and suspicion.

But the government spokesman was kept busy with a number of recurring questions week after week. One concerned the findings of the postmortem over which the forensic experts seemed unable to make up their minds. After producing provisional and then final reports, they eventually issued a final 'final' report. In this, they said that there was no evidence to suggest that Fr Popiełuszko had drowned (i.e. that he was alive when dropped into the water), but that they were still unable to say for certain whether the priest was dead when dropped from the top of the dam or 'on the border line between life and death'. The verdict was that Fr Popiełuszko died from suffocation or asphyxiation caused by a combination of factors: the gag in his mouth, the sticking plaster wound round his head to keep it in place, and the rope secured to his feet and then looped round his neck in such a way that any movement would tighten it like a noose.

That report emerged slowly but there was no progress in the other matter of consuming interest: the search for any others involved in the crime. In his broadcast to the nation three days before the priest's body was found, General Kiszczak himself had asked whether there was a 'hidden inspirer' (note the use of the singular), and had promised to tell the public if there was. And just over a week later, it was announced that one man, Colonel Adam Pietruszka, had been placed under arrest. That proved to be the last of the arrests, but since the public was told repeatedly that the search was continuing, people could be forgiven for expecting more. On two occasions, wittingly or unwittingly, the authorities seemed to feed this public appetite.

On Monday, 19 November, it was announced that a veteran, hardline Communist, Kazimierz Mijal, had been arrested following his return to Poland after 18 years of voluntary exile, during which he had waged a propaganda war against the Communist regimes in Poland of Władysław Gomułka and his successors, mainly from Albania and Belgium. The government spokesman was questioned at his regular press conference the next day about a possible link between Mijal's return and the murder of Fr Popieluszko. To this and to a similar question the following week, Mr Urban's consistent reply was that there was no evidence of any link. But he did not hesitate to add, first, that Mijal's political tracts had suggested that the murder of Fr Popieluszko had been justified since it was the result of the government's 'alliance with the Church' and, second, that the authorities did not exclude any possibility when it came to finding possible instigators of the crime. All of this seemed to suggest that an active search was continuing.

On the last day of November, however, an official announcement produced a response from the Western press which the authorities found unacceptable. Two officers from the Ministry of Internal Affairs and their driver had been killed in a road accident when returning to Warsaw from Cracow and Tarnow in the south, where they had conducted investigations arising from the murder of Fr Popieluszko. Their car had been hit head-on by a heavy lorry overtaking in the opposite direction.

The news, not surprisingly, gave rise to speculation by Western journalists suggesting that perhaps it wasn't an accident, that the officers had learned too much about the 'hidden inspirers' of the murder and had been eliminated to stop them talking. After all, it was not unknown, in Soviet practice at least, for the lorry to have been used as a murder weapon. The Polish authorities should have known what to expect but Jerzy Urban took great exception to the speculation, which he said was groundless. The officers, he said, had been enquiring into side issues. All their materials had been rescued from the crashed vehicle, the lorry driver had not tried to escape and was under arrest. It was clearly an accident. When I suggested to the spokesman that the speculation was justified in view of repeated references by the authorities to the possible existence of 'protectors' and 'inspirers' who were 'capable of a great deal' (to quote his own words), he gave a remarkable reply: 'If there was anything in this accident to suggest that someone was killing officers investigating the case of Fr Popiełuszko, then perhaps, in the interests of the investigation, we would not have announced it... Since we have announced it and since we say it was a pure accident, you should believe it...'

This was too much to ask of many in Poland, for whom disbelieving Urban was almost a matter of principle. The authorities knew this and clearly understood that the public wanted the exposure of more 'hidden inspirers'. There came a time when Jerzy Urban suggested that maybe we would learn more only at the trial. The accused, he said, might feel more inclined to tell the truth when they faced the threat of the death penalty.

General Jaruzelski offered similar thoughts when addressing an exclusive conference of leading Western journalists invited to Warsaw to hear the government's point of view. It was the sort of occasion to which resident foreign correspondents such as myself were never invited. Speaking on 28 November in the splendid setting of the Jabłonna Palace just north of the capital, the General announced that the investigation into the abduction and murder of Fr Popiełuszko was completed, that the indictment was being drawn up, and that the trial would probably begin in December.

Then he came to the difficult part. People, he said, kept asking who 'the inspirers' were. So far, he didn't know, but the search continued. However, he said, if the trial itself failed to provide an answer, the authorities wouldn't succeed in inventing any inspirers either. The General thought that anyone facing the threat of the supreme penalty should say so if they had received any instigation or instructions.

The General's words were puzzling. On the one hand, the investigation was completed; on the other the search was continuing for 'the inspirers'. He seemed also to be saying that if the trial failed to expose any inspirers, there was nothing the authorities could do about it and that would be the end of that.

One has to wonder why General Jaruzelski felt the need to say these things. Was it possible that General Jaruzelski was simply preparing his audience, and through them the world, for the fact that nobody else would be revealed as a 'hidden inspirer'? Worse things had been done in the name of reasons of State.

# 24

# Nailing Pietruszka

Behind the scenes the interrogation of suspects and witnesses had continued and the evidence had accumulated, particularly against Adam Pietruszka. But that evidence does not make it clear why he was taken into custody on 2 November and not earlier or, indeed, later. Early testimony from Chmielewski and Pękala must have raised suspicions about Pietruszka, but it was only after his detention that much of the serious testimony against him was recorded. His arrest, in fact, seems to have prompted a flood of statements incriminating him. And this itself raises questions: was this evidence new to the investigators or was it well known to them but not officially recorded until General Kiszczak, who had taken personal charge of the investigation, decided that Pietruszka had to be prosecuted?

Consider the evidence against Colonel Pietruszka before his arrest. Under interrogation on Friday and Saturday, 26 and 27 October, Waldemar Chmielewski said that Piotrowski had claimed first that the planned abduction had been agreed to by 'his superiors' — which could have meant Pietruszka, Płatek and Ciastoń — and second, that it had the approval of his 'immediate superiors' and 'the Director's office', indicating Pietruszka or Płatek, or both. Piotrowski, Chmielewski said, had not given names.

On Sunday, 28 October, Chmielewski discarded the plural

'superiors' and testified that Piotrowski had claimed to have been ordered by his 'immediate superior' to change the car's number plates. On Monday, Chmielewski repeated the phrase when he recalled how Piotrowski had gone to see his 'immediate superior' to discuss what would happen if Fr Popiełuszko should die. Though he stressed that he could not be sure whether Piotrowski had actually talked to his 'immediate superior', it was obvious that he was talking about Pietruszka. It also seems unlikely that Piotrowski would have said that he was going to see his immediate superior, rather than simply saying Pietruszka. It was Chmielewski who chose the words 'immediate superior' in the hope, perhaps, of not incriminating the Colonel, who had got him his job in Department Four.

That was all Chmielewski had to say on the subject before Pietruszka's detention on 2 November. But the next day, that of Fr Popiełuszko's funeral, the young lieutenant discarded the previous, guarded terminology. He named Colonel Pietruszka without apparent hesitation as the man who, according to Piotrowski, had agreed to the planned operation against the priest, had discussed the possibility that the priest would die, had provided the 'W' pass, had ordered Piotrowski to change the kidnap car's number plates on the Sunday morning after the murder and had warned him that their offices were probably bugged.

This was not watertight testimony, consisting, as it did, of a repetition of what Piotrowski claimed as the truth. But for the investigators it was a vast improvement on what he had said before, particularly since it coincided with new testimony from others which tended to suggest that it was true. There was something odd, though, about the way the new evidence came in.

Colonel Pietruszka was taken into custody on Friday evening, 2 November. Only a few hours earlier, at 3.30 that afternoon, interrogators recorded a statement by Beata Marszczak, the 23-year-old Ministry typist who met Piotrowski in the cafe at Wilanów on the Sunday after the murder. It is unclear why the Investigations Bureau chose to interview her at that precise moment, but her first-hand account seems to have led the way. In reply to unspecified questions, she said that on 19 October (the day of the priest's murder) she had visited Piotrowski's section and while there had heard his secretary, Barbara Story, tell someone on the phone that 'as regards Grzegorz Piotrowski's absence, Colonel Adam Pietruszka knows all about it'. Marszczak said she could see that Piotrowski's office was empty and she thought nobody was in the office of his deputy, Janusz Dróżdż, either.

On the face of it, this was perfectly plausible. But why did it come from this typist rather than from Barbara Story, Captain Piotrowski's 36-year-old secretary, who had already been interviewed three times? Whatever the answer, Story confirmed Marszczak's testimony the next day, saying that Piotrowski had told her that Pietruszka knew the reason for his absence or where he was. When General Płatek had phoned before noon asking for Piotrowski or his deputy (who was in Gdańsk), she had told him that Pietruszka knew the reasons for Piotrowski's absence. This, she said, was what Beata Marszczak had heard her saying.

On the same day, however, Piotrowski's deputy, Janusz Dróżdż, produced evidence concerning Barbara Story, which dated back to the day her boss, Piotrowski, was taken into custody. On that day, Tuesday, 23 October, all members of Piotrowski's section were instructed to submit statements on what they did on 19 October. Janusz Dróżdż was to collect the statements and deliver them to General Płatek by three in the afternoon. Now he testified that when he took the statements to Płatek's office he found Adam Pietruszka in the absent General's chair.

According to Dróżdż, Pietruszka examined the statements but raised objections to two of them on the grounds that they were too long, clearly marking in the margin the passages he thought should be removed. The statements objected to were those by Barbara Story and Zbigniew Stromecki, and the passages earmarked for deletion both recorded that early on 19 October, Grzegorz Piotrowski had told them that Pietruszka would know where he would be that day. Dróżdż said that Pietruszka had ordered him to tell Story and Stromecki to rewrite their statements omitting the passages indicated and to destroy the originals. After Story and Stromecki had complied, Dróżdż said he put the originals through the shredder.

On Sunday, 4 November, the day Adam Pietruszka was placed under formal arrest, Barbara Story confirmed the testimony of Janusz Dróżdż.

Finally, on Monday, 5 November, interrogators recorded the testimony of Stanisław Luliński that he and Wacław Głowacki had told Pietruszka on the Sunday after the crime that a car with WAB 6031 number plates had been seen near the church in Bydgoszcz on Friday night. Pietruszka, Luliński said, had written the number down but seemed to be altering the letters and digits. Two days later, when he went back to Toruń on Piotrowski's instructions, he discovered WAE 8031 rather than WAB 6031 on the list of suspect number plates.

On the three days that followed Adam Pietruszka's detention, then, investigators quickly acquired crucial evidence which indicated that Pietruszka not only knew about Piotrowski's trip outside Warsaw but had suppressed this knowledge and even altered evidence from his own staff which showed that Piotrowski's car had been seen outside the church in Bydgoszcz on the night Fr Popiełuszko had been abducted.

All this was certainly enough to justify the decision to take Pietruszka into custody and charge him with aiding and abetting the crime. Remarkably, though, most of it came in after Pietruszka's detention. This is not to say that the facts of this evidence could not have been known to investigators before Pietruszka's detention. What it does suggest, however, is that once the decision to detain the Colonel was taken, the formal registration of evidence against him was organised with considerable skill and speed.

Taken together, the evidence against Pietruszka looked persuasive with two caveats.

On 5 November, Luliński also testified that his colleague Colonel Głowacki had told General Płatek by phone the night after the murder that a car with WAB 6031 number plates had been seen outside the church in Bydgoszcz and that the same or a very similar car had been seen again with KZC 0423 plates, which the General had described as false in the television announcement of the abduction a few hours earlier. Why did investigators ignore this while concentrating on evidence against Pietruszka?

The second caveat concerns reasonable doubts about the events of Tuesday, 23 October, when Piotrowski was taken into custody and all members of the section were instructed to gather in Pietruszka's office. Pietruszka might be expected to have been present at such an important meeting in his own office, but he was not. Equally curious, if not more so, is the fact that the six people present at the meeting who later testified about it in court were far from unanimous about what was said or who was there.

According to Janusz Dróżdż, the chief anti-Pietruszka witness in this instance, the members of Piotrowski's staff were joined by Generals Płatek and Ciastoń, the Deputy Minister. Ciastoń, he said, announced first that Piotrowski had been taken into custody and then told them all to write statements of their movements on the day of the crime.

Of the six witnesses to the meeting, three didn't even mention that Ciastoń was there. They were Płatek, Pękala and Chmielewski. Even more strikingly, only two witnesses — Janusz Dróżdż and Zbigniew Stromecki — testified that Ciastoń had announced that Piotrowski had been detained. This important and probably shocking development was not mentioned by Pękala, Chmielewski, Płatek or Barbara Story. She said she didn't hear any such announcement.

There may well be an explanation for these discrepancies, but it is not obvious. It is hard to understand how Pękala and Chmielewski could have failed to mention that they had been told that Piotrowski was in custody when their testimony indicated clearly that they had been in a state of considerable alarm, induced by the fact that their boss was nowhere to be seen and they didn't know where he was. Ciastoń's reported announcement would surely have removed their doubts. But as Chmielewski's testimony made clear, his fears continued for two days after the Tuesday meeting and for one day after his detention on the Wednesday. 'I thought the boss had disappeared and that he was doing something against me and Pękala so as to avoid responsibility himself... From the moment we were told to provide statements I was convinced that he had escaped and would try to act against us. It was only on 25 October, when I heard that Piotrowski was under arrest, that I decided to tell the truth...'[1]

It is impossible to reconcile this statement with Dróżdż's claim that General Ciastoń had told the staff that their boss had been taken into custody. It is difficult, in fact, to believe anything said about the Tuesday staff meeting, except that everyone was asked to submit a statement on what they did on 19 October.

An undeniable fact, though, is that the entire episode, as presented by Janusz Dróżdż, was used by the prosecution to incriminate Adam Pietruszka while depicting Generals Płatek and Ciastoń as senior officers simply doing their job.

To add to the confusion, not all of the testimony from Chmielewski or Pękala supported the view that Adam Pietruszka was the only senior officer involved in the crime. Under interrogation on 6 November, for example, Chmielewski, as though warming to his theme of incriminating the Colonel, recalled an occasion before the trip to Gdańsk when Piotrowski had returned to his office looking 'very pleased' and announced that 'Pietruszka had to square the whole business with Ciastoń'. The business in question, Chmielewski said, was that of Fr Popiełuszko.

This sort of testimony should surely have been seized upon by those supposedly searching for 'hidden inspirers' of the crime. But Chmielewski would be persuaded later to say that he was mistaken. Nonetheless, it is difficult to understand how this young officer, who otherwise seemed so alert to the needs and discipline of the SB, could have been so rash as to name the head of the SB in connection with the operation. Unless he was honestly reporting what Piotrowski had told him.

Pękala, on the other hand, seemed from the start to be firmly wedded to the belief that they were involved in a much bigger operation, planned and approved 'very high up'. In the week that followed Pietruszka's detention and arrest, he was slower than Chmielewski to name the colonel and more inclined to spread responsibility among the senior ranks. When Piotrowski had said that their operation had been approved higher up, he told interrogators, 'it was my personal feeling that this phrase "higher up" stood for one of the Deputy Ministers... and besides, he actually gave the name of one of the Deputy Ministers...'[2]

Pękala refused to name this Deputy Minister, but since there were several Deputies, he need not have had General Ciastoń in mind. While pointing the finger more firmly at Pietruszka as the week progressed, Pękala maintained that it was his clear impression that 'top people' were also involved. He said that Piotrowski had named three people with whom he had reached agreement before the operations against Fr Popiełuszko and to whom he had reported afterwards. But of these three, Pękala was willing to name only Adam Pietruszka. And according to Pękala, Piotrowski said that Pietruszka was 'decidedly in favour of causing the death of Fr Popiełuszko' while 'others were still hesitating'.

Leszek Pękala, it seems, was less cautious than the SB-trained Chmielewski. His testimony sometimes seemed contradictory, particularly on the subject of naming names. But he obviously believed that Colonel Pietruszka was not the only senior officer involved in or aware of the crime. All signs suggest that those conducting the investigation were content to ignore this and concentrate their efforts against Pietruszka and nobody else.

Not all of these efforts were so successful. One which came to light during the trial cast suspicion not only on Pietruszka but on others, including General Płatek. It concerned the travel permit signed by Pietruszka with which Piotrowski and his lieutenants drove to Bydgoszcz on 19 October.

According to Wojciech Kaczorowski, the 30-year-old driver employed by Piotrowski's section, his boss handed him an expired travel permit on the morning of Monday, 22 October, which he had left near the gear lever in the car and to which he had given no further thought.

The next day, when everyone in the Ministry was talking about the previous Friday's events, Kaczorowski went to the workshops to check on the car, noticed the date on the document when he picked it up and became, as he put it, intrigued. Kaczorowski said he showed it to Barbara Story back at the section, who said she was unable to confirm that the signature on the document was that of Adam Pietruszka. Two days later, he said, he showed it to another member of Piotrowski's staff, Colonel Józef Maj, who said it was, indeed, Pietruszka's signature and advised him to take the document to the Director. Kaczorowski said he had lacked the courage to do as Maj had suggested. But after another delay of at least one day, he persuaded Maj to take the document to General Płatek himself. In their testimony on what happened next, the General and Colonel Maj could not agree.

After receiving the document from Kaczorowski, Colonel Maj said he had put it in his locker, in the presence of another, unidentified officer, for safekeeping overnight before taking it to Płatek the next day. This, most probably, was Monday, 29 October. Maj said he watched Płatek examine the document, noticing that it left him in something of a state, and left.

Płatek's testimony was strikingly different. He had given Maj a telling off, he said, first for taking such a long time to take the document to him, and second for delivering it in such a grubby, crumpled condition 'as if it had been rescued from the throat of a dog'. The General also said he had complained that the permit had been tampered with and altered.

Maj consistently denied that Płatek said anything of the sort. He also maintained that when he handed the document to the General it was in exactly the same condition as when Kaczorowski gave it to him.

The General's complaint, however, was a serious one. In its original state, as filled out by Piotrowski, the permit carried the travel date of 19 X, i.e. 19 October. But according to Płatek, the document handed to him by Colonel Maj bore signs of something having been written in and then erased in front of the 'X'. He had therefore taken it immediately to the Investigations Bureau. As became clear at the trial, the figure 'I' had been inserted in front of the Roman ten, making the date 19 IX, or the month of September instead of October. This would have exonerated Pietruszka on the charge of having authorised Piotrowski's journey to Bydgoszcz.

Later, though, a documents expert testified that the 'I' had been erased 'by mechanical means'. Why was it erased? Possibly because it was established that no permit was issued for anyone from Piotrowski's section to travel outside Warsaw on 19 September. Possibly, also, because the forgery could have been exposed by comparing the ink used to insert the 'I' with that used initially by Piotrowski. In fact, the documents expert told Piotrowski that such a comparison was impossible because of the way the erasure had been carried out.

What did the court make of all this? In effect, nothing. When the lawyers representing the priest's family and Chrostowski suggested that Płatek and Maj should confront each other in court, the presiding judge disagreed. In the end, the court concluded that Pietruszka was sufficiently incriminated without the puzzle being solved.

While that may well have been true, it is a mystery why neither the investigators nor the prosecution nor the court thought fit to ask who was lying, General Płatek or Colonel Maj. Here surely was an opportunity to identify any 'hidden inspirers', if they existed. If Płatek was telling the truth about the travel permit, the document had been tampered with before Maj gave it to him. But if Maj was telling the truth, the alteration was effected and reversed when the document was in Płatek's hands.

The court may have been interested simply in nailing Pietruszka alone, or perhaps it was keen to avoid a public airing of any discord over the case in Department Four.

Grzegorz Piotrowski, perhaps out of mischief, crowned it all on the last day of the trial when he told the court that he didn't think he had handed the document to Kaczorowski anyway. 'If I'd had the permit for the 19th in my hand I would have destroyed it for sure... to cover our traces.'

Such contradictions shed doubt on much of the evidence offered by the prosecution, and tend to elevate the case from a mystery to a deliberate mystification, calculated to confuse the most objective observer while securing the authorities' chief objective: limiting the potential damage to the Communist regime.

# 25

# Płatek's Excuses

Throughout November, Adam Pietruszka steadfastly maintained his innocence. He denied ordering Piotrowski to change the kidnap car's registration plates on Sunday morning, telling interrogators that it was not until the evening of Monday, 22 October, that he was told that the car had been seen in Bydgoszcz on the night of the crime. This suited General Płatek, who never mentioned the switching of the number plates and insisted that he was first told about the car on the Monday by Colonel Jabłoński of Criminal Investigations. How, then, did Płatek explain the testimony of two of his own officers that they had informed him in a phone call from Toruń on Saturday night that the car with the tell-tale number plates had been seen outside the church in Bydgoszcz when Fr Popiełuszko was there? To that there is no satisfactory answer, only a record of his statements under questioning which tended to cast doubt on his competence or his honesty.[1]

When first questioned as a witness on 19 November, the General in essence denied what Colonel Luliński had told investigators two weeks earlier. Głowacki had indeed phoned him, he said, but he had spoken of three cars with Warsaw number plates being seen in Bydgoszcz. Głowacki had not passed on any precise numbers because the only thing known about them was that they began with the letter W, signifying Warsaw.

Confronted at his next interview on 23 November with Głowacki's testimony which confirmed that of Luliński, General Płatek repeated that he had not heard the Colonel spell out any Warsaw number plates. He could only suppose that if Głowacki had read out a Warsaw number plate, he must have done so when he himself was answering another call from Department Four's duty officer. Further, he had not left the phone to find pen and paper, as had been suggested, since they were always available next to his telephones.

Obviously, the General had changed his story from one interview to another but his interrogators seem to have left it at that. At his third interview on 28 November, there was no mention either of the kidnap car or the testimony of Colonels Luliński and Głowacki, and General Płatek was able to speak at length about the workings of his department, pointing out among other things that Adam Pietruszka was responsible for supervising the work of Grzegorz Piotrowski. Pietruszka's behaviour 'during the critical days', he said, did not indicate that he could have been involved in a scheme to kidnap Fr Popiełuszko.

This was the day on which General Jaruzelski told visiting journalists that the investigation was over and the indictment was being prepared. In the days that followed, Adam Pietruszka may well have wondered why he faced conviction while Płatek managed to change his story and still survive.

On 4 December, Pietruszka changed his own testimony, finally admitting that he had, indeed, ordered Piotrowski to change the car's registration plates on Sunday morning. But he had done this, he said, because General Płatek had called him into his office and told him he had seen a car with WAB 6031 plates parked in the yard, that a car with those same plates had been seen in Bydgoszcz the previous Friday evening, and that he, Pietruszka, should do something about it because the car belonged to Piotrowski's section.

Later, Pietruszka repeated his account, adding the detail that Płatek had even checked a register of Department Four cars in his secretary's office and found that the car in question was

Piotrowski's. The General had told him to do something about it so that there would be no 'unwanted speculation'. Pietruszka said he couldn't be sure but the General may have added 'until the matter is cleared up'.

Pietruszka's testimony, if true, clearly incriminated General Płatek. It suggested that he had been lying to interrogators and raised the distinct possibility that Płatek had heard every letter and digit of the car number plates read out to him over the telephone by Colonel Głowacki on Saturday night.

This was enough, it seems, to persuade investigating officers that there was room for another interview with the suspended Director of Department Four. General Płatek presented himself at the Ministry's Investigations Bureau at the seemingly unusual time of 9 pm on 5 December, the day after Pietruszka's revelations. He had decided, he said, to amplify his previous testimony.

Dealing first with the evidence of Luliński and Głowacki, the General changed his story yet again. He said he did not rule out the possibility that they had passed on information about the WAB 6031 number plates, but since his concentration had been disturbed by a simultaneous call from a Director of a Department, he may have failed to memorise precisely what Głowacki had told him. And besides, he said, he had received so many pieces of information and made so many decisions since first hearing of the abduction of Fr Popiełuszko that it had been extraordinarily difficult to recall the course of conversations or their timing.

Once again, General Płatek had changed his testimony. The call from Głowacki, it now transpired, had been interrupted not by a duty officer but by a Director of a Department, a far more important personage. But that was a mere refinement compared with the new emphasis that the General placed on the possibility that his memory had failed him under stress. One may question why he had to 'memorise' what Głowacki said when he could have written it on the note pad which was ever ready next to his telephones at home. But the General's failing memory would stand him in good stead.

The General seemed less assured, however, when confronted by Pietruszka's damaging testimony about the events of Sunday morning. He said he had asked Adam Pietruszka to try to clear up the question of the WAB 6031 car, instructing him to inspect the car in the garage and to take statements from the staff of Piotrowski's section. 'All orders given to Pietruszka aimed at clearing up how WAB 6031 came to be used to commit a crime. I had the authority to give orders in the case as Pietruszka's superior and as the officer coordinating activities.'

The General said nothing about what he did or said on Sunday morning, ignoring Pietruszka's allegations. At the same time he provided his interrogators with a striking example of the confused or failing memory he had been talking about. The inspection of the car was ordered not on Sunday but on Monday evening. Statements by members of Piotrowski's staff were collected on Tuesday, not on Sunday.

It is difficult to imagine how the officers or prosecutors who listened to the General found it possible not to press for a direct reply to the allegations of his former deputy; that was the last time he was questioned on the record before the trial.

Adam Pietruszka incriminated himself, of course, when he admitted ordering Grzegorz Piotrowski to change the number plates of the kidnap car. Why he did so can only be guessed at but it seems likely that he wanted to incriminate Zenon Płatek.

By early December, when he made his allegations, Pietruszka must have known that the testimony accumulated against him left little hope of an acquittal. He may even have been shown some of the General's testimony.

In November, for instance, Płatek had given Pietruszka a good reference, so to speak, but his praise had been too faint to override a clear, underlying suggestion that Pietruszka had been less than forthcoming about the report Luliński and Głowacki had brought back from Toruń. Pietruszka may well have decided that there was no point in protecting someone who was helping to convict him.

That said, it was impossible to confirm that Pietruszka was telling the truth because no one else was present at his alleged meeting with the General. No one, equally, could prove that Pietruszka was lying.

As for Płatek, it was he who constantly raised questions about his truthfulness by frequently changing his testimony. And it is difficult to find any objective reason for believing Płatek rather than Pietruszka, apart from the fact that the General was a witness for the prosecution and the Colonel was one of the accused. This is not to say that Pietruszka was innocent, only that he believed he deserved protection too.

The indictment in the case of the abduction of Fr Jerzy Popiełuszko was completed and signed by the Toruń District Deputy Prosecutor, Zygmunt Kołacki, on 10 December, five days after General Płatek's final interview with interrogators.

It was a remarkable document, for it made no mention of what the General had said under questioning.

Indeed, it contradicted him by simply reporting as a fact that Colonel Luliński had urged Colonel Głowacki to tell the General without delay about the car with Departmental plates seen in Bydgoszcz. It continued:

This they did in a telephone conversation with Z. Płatek late that night. This information formed the basis for activities aimed at determining whether the Department's official Fiat 125p with WAB 6031 registration plates really was used on 19 October and if so, by whom and for what purpose, and whether the car was actually in Bydgoszcz...
On the orders of Z. Płatek, section head Grzegorz Piotrowski provided a written statement on this matter...
On 23 October, G. Piotrowski was detained...[2]

This sequence of statements may have created the impression that General Płatek had got his man thanks to honest, straightforward police work. If that was the intention, as it seems to have been, the authorities were telling an enormous lie, largely by omission.

One of the indictment's most glaring omissions was its failure to mention that it was Colonel Jabłoński of the Criminal

Investigations Department of the MO — the civil police as opposed to the SB the secret police — who had forced the resolution of the case by handing Płatek written confirmation on the Monday evening that a Department Four car had been seen in Bydgoszcz. Why was this crucial fact omitted? Maybe because its inclusion would have raised questions about General Płatek's performance: if he had been told about the car on Saturday night, why did it take him until Monday evening to act?

Equally important was the failure to mention Adam Pietruszka's testimony that it was Płatek who had told him on Sunday morning to do something about the car then parked in the Ministry yard because it had been seen in Bydgoszcz and belonged to Piotrowski's section. One would have thought that prosecutors who stated as a matter of fact that the General was told about the car on Saturday night might have seen some virtue in Pietruszka's claim.

But according to the indictment, it was Pietruszka who ordered Piotrowski to change the plates, having learned on Sunday morning from an unidentified source that the car had been seen near the church in Bydgoszcz.

More surprising still was the indictment's claim that Pietruszka failed to pass on what Luliński and Głowacki had told him on Sunday evening about the car being seen in Bydgoszcz. If General Płatek had been told about the car by Głowacki on Saturday night, as the indictment said, there was no need, presumably, for Pietruszka to tell him again. And there would have been even less reason to repeat the information if, as Pietruszka alleged, he had been told about it by the General on Sunday morning.

It seems clear that the authors of the indictment went out of their way to avoid all such considerations and exclude anything that might incriminate General Płatek. But their version of events, just like his, fails the test of serious scrutiny. The evidence supports the suspicion that the General tried to stage a cover-up. The indictment reads like a cover-up for him.

# 26

# *Góra*

Nearly a hundred people were allowed to attend the trial in Toruń. They were issued with official passes bearing their names and on each of the twenty six days the court was in session they had to present these and other identity documents at two separate check points and have their bags or pockets searched by the so-called 'anti-terrorist brigade' before being admitted to the court room.

Among them were members of Fr Popiełuszko's family and his friend, Waldemar Chrostowski, the families of the accused, representatives of the Ministry of Justice and the SB, five priests, three law academics and twenty five journalists, only six from Western news organisations.

These six had apparently been chosen by the authorities because they were either native or bilingual Polish speakers. It might seem that this arrangement made sense given the alleged shortage of space in the court room, but for those excluded it was professionally disastrous. News organisations don't send correspondents to foreign capitals at great expense in order to copy or rewrite the work of others. But that, in effect, was what the rest of the Western media corps, including the BBC, was expected to do.[1]

The frustration of excluded reporters was not, however, the most important result of the authorities' policy. It meant that the Polish public, which listened in great numbers to the news bulletins of Western broadcasting stations, received less than the usual coverage and analysis on the most important and complex event for some time. The authorities obviously did not want everything said in court to be open to public scrutiny. The work of Jacek Ambroziak is a case in point.

A lawyer by training, Ambroziak was accredited as the representative of the press office of the Catholic Episcopate. His reports, which amounted to a very full though not a verbatim record of what was said in court, were published in the Church's regular *Pismo Okólne* or *Circular Letter*. Though published with considerable delay, this provided those not in court with their first real opportunity to understand the context from which the headline stories emerging from Toruń came. And yet, when Ambroziak's work was reproduced in *Tygodnik Powszechny*, the Catholic weekly published in Cracow, the authorities censored large sections on the grounds, presumably, that details of this allegedly open trial were too sensitive to be seen and read by the Polish public.

One might have thought that this trial had nothing to hide. After all, the Minister of Internal Affairs, General Kiszczak, had already outlined to the Polish people what Piotrowski and his accomplices had done to Fr Popiełuszko. It only remained for the court to fill in the details, present the evidence, reach a verdict and pass sentence.

But there was a fourth man in the dock, Colonel Pietruszka, Deputy Director of Department Four, who stood accused of aiding and abetting the crime. As the trial began, the general public had little idea about Pietruszka's alleged role but the records of the investigation offered evidence that the role of Pietruszka's immediate superior, General Płatek, seemed just as suspect. The authorities were sensitive because they faced two trials: one to prove the guilt of the men in the dock, and a second to disprove or discredit any suggestion that others, further up in the hierarchy, were involved. But they also faced two substantial difficulties. The first was General Płatek's pretrial testimony which seemed so unconvincing as to be virtually incriminating. Płatek had to be protected if the stain of guilt was not to spread higher.

The second problem was the fact that Fr Popiełuszko's family and Waldemar Chrostowski, whom the court recognised as auxiliary plaintiffs or accusers, were represented by four distinguished defence counsel: Andrzej Grabiński, Jan Olszewski, Edward Wende and Krzysztof Piesiewicz, all of whom could be said to be 'opposition' lawyers. Olszewski was one of the authors of the statute of NSZZ Solidarność, the Independent Self-governing Trade Union Solidarity. He and Grabiński were advisers to the Union's Warsaw region leadership until the imposition of martial law. In the three years since then, all four had defended Solidarity activists and other political opponents of the regime.

In this trial, their role was to represent the interests of their clients while complementing the case against the accused. As such, they carried on their shoulders most of the hopes that justice would be done. But their difficulties began before the trial got underway. The speed with which the case was brought to court left them little time to become acquainted with the 16 volumes of documents and 30 sound and video recordings assembled by the investigation.

As the trial began on 27 December, however, the lawyers were undoubtedly better informed than the representatives of the Church and the Western media. And it would have taken remarkable intellectual acuity for any of the latter, with no knowledge of the details of the investigation, to have concentrated on the reading of the indictment when the four accused were there to be seen for the first time. Moreover, when first Pękala then Chmielewski and Piotrowski took the witness stand, the journalists in court could not ignore the details of the crime as described in their own words by the three men who had committed it.

However, those details were not, apparently, of supreme concern to the authorities or the court, presided over by Judge Artur Kujawa. For them, it seems, the overriding concern was to ensure that anything Piotrowski, Pękala or Chmielewski had said about the role of senior representatives of the Ministry other than Pietruszka was very deliberately questioned and withdrawn.

This process began on the second day of the trial and proved to be a striking demonstration of how the three guilty men, with the encouragement and prompting of the presiding judge, were able to withdraw almost everything they had said previously about their crime having the approval of 'top people', the 'top brass', the 'top leadership'.

All those expressions are translations of one small but versatile Polish word, *góra*, meaning hill, mountain, or mountain top but also, in common parlance, things and people above you either in rank or location or both, as in 'the bosses upstairs'.

The attempts to clear the *góra* began with the questioning of Leszek Pękala. He had testified that he had been sure that Piotrowski's planned operation against Fr Popieluszko had been accepted 'very high up' even though it might end in the priest's death; that Piotrowski had said they would be rewarded mightily in their careers 'as long as the body was not found'; that Piotrowski had told them before the trip to Bydgoszcz that the decision that Popieluszko should die had been taken; that it had been approved 'higher up'; and that he took this to mean that approval had been given by one of the Deputy Ministers.

When asked to confirm or deny passages from pre-trial testimony read out in court, Pękala repeatedly denied any intention to kill Fr Popieluszko, but confirmed that Piotrowski had said that the operation had been approved 'at Deputy Minister level'. Piotrowski, he said, had named one of the Deputy Ministers.[2]

This prompted the presiding judge, Artur Kujawa, to intervene. Accusing Pękala of inconsistency, he pointed out that he had named Pietruszka alone as the one who had agreed to the priest's death but, on another occasion, claimed that Piotrowski had named a Deputy Minister as well. Could he explain?

Pękala, as if on cue, now readily denied that Piotrowski had told him he had the agreement of a Deputy Minister. His boss had named one of the Deputy Ministers in connection with Fr Popiełuszko, Pękala said, but he had misunderstood what had been said.

Judge Kujawa, not satisfied with this, asked Pękala whether it was possible that the Deputy Minister had been named in connection with 'other matters connected with Fr Popiełuszko'. Pękala agreed. When Piotrowski named the Deputy Minister, he said, it could have been in quite another context about something perfectly legal. Shortly afterwards, when Pękala complained of tiredness, Judge Kujawa ordered a four-day adjournment.

That, however, was not the end of it. When the court reassembled on Wednesday, 2 January 1985, Pękala was reminded of yet another piece of his pre-trial testimony claiming that before, during and after the operations of 13 and 19 October Piotrowski had said he had squared their plans with persons upstairs and delivered reports to them. He had named three names, among them Adam Pietruszka.[3]

When Pękala said that Piotrowski had delivered a report 'upstairs', he was asked, did that mean Pietruszka? 'I was sure it meant Pietruszka,' Pękala replied, 'and from the impressions Piotrowski created it emerged that some Deputy Minister could have known about it.'

'Impressions?' queried Judge Kujawa, intervening at yet another crucial moment.

'Well, he didn't say it straight out,' Pękala explained, 'but it emerged from the context and that's what I took it to mean.'[4] That marked the end of Pękala's grilling on the subject. The suggestion was that his claims about 'top brass' involvement were based on impressions and misunderstandings. But, at the end of it all, Pękala still believed that it had been perfectly reasonable for him, or anybody else, to deduce that a Deputy Minister had known about the operation against Fr Popiełuszko. And he never withdrew his claim that Piotrowski had named a Deputy Minister, even though Judge Kujawa persuaded him to reconsider the context in which this happened. Nor did Pękala withdraw his claim that Piotrowski named three persons, including Adam Pietruszka, with whom he had discussed the events of 19 October.

It seemed that Pękala's testimony was perfectly acceptable to the court when it incriminated Adam Pietruszka but was subjected to meticulous scrutiny and criticism when it cast suspicion on others.

It was the same with Waldemar Chmielewski. When he took the stand, questions about the 'top brass' emerged once again but they were largely overshadowed. As Chmielewski began his own account of the crime, it became obvious that he was suffering from a nervous facial tic, a spasmodic twitching of the right cheek, and that his speech was seriously affected by a stammer. When Judge Kujawa asked how long he had suffered from this disability, Chmielewski replied 'since all this, since being arrested'. In obvious distress several times at the witness stand, and allowed to give part of his testimony sitting down, Chmielewski, nonetheless, gave a detailed and coherent account of the crime and revealed who he thought was informed of the plan.

He said that Piotrowski had told him and Pękala early on that he had discussed with Pietruszka the possibility that Fr Popieluszko might die of a heart attack and that a decision had been taken that they would have to dispose of the body should this happen. Piotrowski had also said that the decisions had taken some time because it had been necessary to get it agreed with 'the top brass'. Chmielewski said he understood this to be a reference either to the Director of the Minister's Office or to one of the Deputy Ministers. Piotrowski, he explained, said that the decision had been taken in connection with 'the matter of the corpse'.

This was a remarkable piece of testimony, potentially more damaging than anything Pękala had said earlier. Chmielewski was saying that knowledge of the operation, including the possibility of Fr Popieluszko dying, could have reached the office of the Minister himself, General Kiszczak, as well as a Deputy Minister. Moreover, the sequence of events he described — first the discussions between Piotrowski and Pietruszka, then the decision from the 'top brass' — suggests that the 'top brass' referred to those more senior than Pietruszka.

Chmielewski did not name any names apart from that of Pietruszka in court. But before the trial, as we have seen, he had quoted Piotrowski as saying that Pietruszka had had to secure Deputy Minister Ciaston's agreement.[5] When this passage was read out in court (at the request of Andrzej Grabiński, representing Fr Popiełuszko's family), Chmielewski confirmed his understanding that Pietruszka had had to get the matter agreed with the 'top brass'. At this point, Judge Kujawa intervened for a brief but pointed exchange:

> Kujawa: Was the term 'top brass' used or was a name named? Chmielewski: I just treated it in terms of rank.
> Kujawa: Where did you get the name from? Or was it a matter of conjecture on your part?
> Chmielewski: Yes.
> Kujawa: Who was Pietruszka's immediate superior?
> Chmielewski: Director Płatek.
> Kujawa: But in your testimony just read out you didn't name Director Płatek, you named the Deputy Minister.
> Chmielewski: I took the term 'top brass' to refer to the Deputy Minister; that's why I named him.

Asked by the second judge, Maciejewski, whether Piotrowski had actually named the Deputy Minister or whether it was conjecture on his part, Chmielewski agreed that it was his conjecture. He had caved in.[6]

But that does not mean Chmielewski's original testimony was outlandishly wrong. Oddly enough, when Grzegorz Piotrowski himself took the witness stand on the seventh day of the trial, he told the court that Department Four could not have taken that decision on its own. He also said that he had indeed named General Ciaston as someone informed of the planned crime, confirming Chmielewski's testimony, which Judge Kujawa had seemingly sought to undermine.

Piotrowski recalled how he had told Pękala and Chmielewski

that 'the bosses' were taking into account the possibility that the priest would die. And when wondering who these 'top brass', the *góra*, might be, he said he had believed that the decisions could not have been taken at Department level. Somebody higher up, one of the Deputy Ministers, must have been involved. 'It was then that I named Ciastoń. After all, I knew how decisions took shape in our department. They were always cleared with the leadership of the Ministry.'

About one hour later, however, Piotrowski proceeded to say in effect that the crime against Fr Popiełuszko was an exception to the rule. Before the trip to Gdańsk on 13 October, he said, Adam Pietruszka had given him to understand — without tangible proof but quite unambiguously — that 'top brass' were involved. Maybe, Piotrowski added regretfully, it would have been better if there had been 'no such top brass'.

At this point, Judge Kujawa jumped in to ask whether the 'top brass' meant Adam Pietruszka alone. 'I know that now,' Piotrowski replied. 'Then I thought otherwise.'[7]

At this moment, no doubt, the SB officers in court probably exchanged knowing glances if not smiles. And with good reason. Grzegorz Piotrowski, on whose words both Pękala and Chmielewski had based their belief in the involvement of 'top brass', was testifying that Adam Pietruszka had deceived him into thinking more senior officers were involved, that he had misled Pękala and Chmielewski into believing the same thing, that it was all a misunderstanding. With the help of the presiding judge, the chief villain was stating categorically that there was no 'top brass' but Pietruszka.

Piotrowski said more on this in answers to later questions from the judges and prosecutor. He said that nobody had told him in so many words that Fr Popiełuszko had to die. The planned operation had been approved by Adam Pietruszka, he said, but to name any other names would be to incriminate innocent people. Judge Maciejewski asked pointedly if Piotrowski could have acted 'without the inspiration of Adam Pietruszka'. Certainly not, he replied. It was impossible to do anything without the knowledge of one's superiors. And besides, 'it's difficult to call it inspiration; it was a task entrusted to me'.

When Judge Kujawa asked when it was that the accused had realised that 'top brass' approval didn't exist, Piotrowski said his first doubts had set in after he got back from Bydgoszcz.

A couple of immediate, follow-up questions from Kujawa helped him explain how. Hadn't Adam Pietruszka warned him to be careful because eavesdropping equipment had been installed? the judge asked. Why then the bugging if the 'top brass' had approved the operation? Piotrowski agreed. 'I knew then there was something wrong.'

With the presiding judge and the alleged murderer working so well together, the lawyers for the auxiliary plaintiffs were no doubt keen to pursue the matter with Piotrowski. But when Judge Kujawa enquired if they had anything to ask the accused, Piotrowski quickly announced that he wanted to exercise his right not to answer questions from them. 'I know these gentlemen well,' he said, 'and I know what they will ask me about.'

Uproar ensued, with Andrzej Grabiński protesting that the accused had no right to discriminate against one side in the case. Piotrowski's lawyer maintained that he did. The State prosecutor agreed but said the court should decide. After an adjournment, Judge Kujawa ruled that he could not force Piotrowski to answer.

This was yet another success for Grzegorz Piotrowski, who had been allowed to destroy the normal sequence of court procedure the day before.

# 27

# Piotrowski Attacks

It was on the eighth day of the trial that proceedings took an unexpected turn. Grzegorz Piotrowski had just completed his opening statement which included not only an account of the crime but an explanation of his motives.

Speaking with confidence, Piotrowski denied suggestions in the indictment that he had hated Fr Popiełuszko and acted out of frustration. His attitude to the priest, he insisted, had been one of 'cold indifference'. Knowing that 'this once very average chaplain' was 'engaged in something beyond his capabilities', it was his duty, he said, to expose and counteract his activities inspired by Western centres of subversion, his contacts with Western embassies, his countrywide trips to encourage the integration of underground Solidarity organisations, and his 'criminal activities'.

Piotrowski did not specify immediately what these activities were, but he claimed later that the sum of 60 million zloties belonging to the Mazowsze (Warsaw) Region of Solidarity was deposited with Fr Popiełuszko immediately after the introduction of martial law. These monies, he said, had been distributed by the priest shortly thereafter, but some 4.7 million had gone missing in mysterious circumstances. Two receipts signed by Zbigniew Bujak, leader of the Warsaw region underground, proved to be forgeries and one of them was the work,

Piotrowski said, of Jerzy Popiełuszko. These allegations were never proved or substantiated. Indeed, Adam Pietruszka would say that if true, he would have known about them, but he did not.

That, however, seemed to be of no importance. Piotrowski said that when he saw that the Church reacted with indifference to the priest's activities and when he realised that the report that Fr Popiełuszko would be sent to Rome was fiction, he decided to take action outside the law to ensure the lesser of two evils. 'I was not a man without fault,' he said, 'but neither I nor Pękala nor Chmielewski would be in the dock now if the law had been the law for Jerzy Popiełuszko.'

Piotrowski's account of the crime itself was remarkable for one significant omission. He declined to comment on the final phase of Fr Popiełuszko's fight for his life, that ill-defined period between the departure of the kidnap car from the filling station outside Toruń until his bound and gagged body was placed for the last time in the boot of the Fiat. Piotrowski said nothing about those bouts of intense violence when — according to Chmielewski and Pękala — he had used the wooden stake to rain blows on the helpless priest. Piotrowski did testify, however, that until he saw the forensic report, he had believed that it was he who had killed Fr Popiełuszko.

When Piotrowski had finished, the presiding judge invited him to talk about an exhibit Fr Popiełuszko was said to have set up inside St Stanisław's to mark the fortieth anniversary of People's Poland. He responded with relish.

The exhibit, he said, featured photographs mainly of rioting and disturbances. It was after he had shown them to Płatek and Pietruszka, that the latter had commented that 'only the grave could straighten out a rogue like that'. Piotrowski claimed not to have attributed much importance to this remark, believing it to be more an expression of the SB's impotence. He personally was exasperated by the fact that such a provocative exhibit should be staged in a church.

Piotrowski rejected Judge Kujawa's suggestion that the priest's activities infuriated him.

I'm one of those placid, good-tempered people it's difficult to upset. Anyway, as far as the relationship between Jerzy Popiełuszko and me is concerned, I knew that his attitude to the authorities was one of hatred. I can also say that he had the same attitude to those who sit at the judges' bench. But my attitude to him was one of indifference. I never even thought of him after 4 pm. Popiełuszko was a matter of indifference to me. He broke the law and what irritated me more was the fact that the rule of law could do nothing about it...[1]

Was this the cue Judge Kujawa had been waiting for? 'We must get to the reasons for this operation,' he announced, '... we must turn to the documents of the case brought against Jerzy Popiełuszko in the Warsaw District Court...' He then read out selected passages from the indictment served on Fr Popiełuszko in July. As we know, the case was dropped by the authorities in August under the latest amnesty and was, presumably, a thing of the past, but Judge Kujawa proceeded to quote references to 'the Jaruzelski junta', the 'Sovietisation of the homeland' and the 'Communist dictatorship'. These phrases were taken not from anything the priest had said in sermons but from the thousands of alleged Solidarity underground leaflets supposedly discovered in his private flat on Chłodna Street.

The patience of the defence lawyers, notably Edward Wende, who had assisted the priest throughout the investigation against him, was wearing thin as Judge Kujawa quoted from other documents supposedly confiscated during the search of the Chłodna Street flat.

One was a letter said to have been written to Fr Popiełuszko by Jerzy Giedroyc, editor of *Kultura*, the Polish language monthly published in Paris, confirming the receipt of certain materials. The second was an associated document supposedly reporting critical questions put to Primate Glemp about his attitude and his public statements. When Kujawa added his own comment — were the Primate's calls for peace and reconciliation not in keeping with the Gospel? — and went on to quote a passage about the Primate's attitude to Solidarity, Jan Olszewski intervened, protesting that he couldn't tell what was in the documents and what was merely the presiding judge's commentary. Edward Wende added that the documents should not be accepted as evidence because it had never been established who had written them.

The lead prosecutor and Piotrowski's defence counsel disagreed. And it came as no surprise when Judge Kujawa ruled that the documents must be admitted as evidence to make clear what Piotrowski meant by his 'attitude of indifference' to the priest.

Olszewski had already pointed out that reading the documents at this moment would break up the normal process of the trial when the accused had not completed his testimony. Events would prove him right, but he could hardly have foreseen what would happen next.

Ignoring for the moment a request from Piotrowski's lawyer for a five-minute adjournment for consultations, Judge Kujawa began reading out another document — a statement allegedly written by Piotrowski inside the Rakowiecka gaol on 26 October 1984 (one week after the murder) on his motives for the crime. This was yet another indictment of the murdered priest, accusing him of further crimes. Piotrowski wrote that Fr Popiełuszko had been directly involved in organising 'illegal structures'(the Solidarity underground), that he had assisted and had contact with those in hiding, that he had organised underground printing shops and the distribution of illegal publications, and that besides making hostile utterances in public, he had sent abroad information that was damaging to the Polish People's Republic.

Piotrowski's statement was an indictment also of the methods employed by the authorities to neutralise Fr Popiełuszko. The effects, he said, were 'inversely proportional' to the efforts involved. He cited as a typical example the release of Fr Popiełuszko after one night in the cells in December 1983. Grown men, he wrote, had wept like children when they heard the news.

Since the lifting of martial law, Piotrowski said, Jerzy Popiełuszko had been involved in opening up channels of underground communication and training new cadres for 'future surges of social activity'. He claimed that many SB officers had come to believe that legal methods amounted to no more than tilting at windmills, while the Ministry leadership was irresolute, unable or unwilling to force the Episcopate to do something about Fr Popiełuszko's activities. And, chillingly, Piotrowski wrote that he was one hundred per cent sure that if a call had gone out a week earlier for those willing to 'have a go' at Popiełuszko, there would have been no shortage of SB volunteers.

A few months earlier, Piotrowski wrote, 'one member of the Ministry's leadership' had said that since the enemy was not too choosy about their methods, 'we should adapt accordingly'. This, along with a growing sense of impotence, had given birth to the idea of intimidating and tormenting Fr Popiełuszko by means of physical violence and mental stress.

There was a postscript to the statement: 'On a document suggesting effective action against Fr Popiełuszko within the law, Minister Kiszczak wrote a note, "Would readily agree, but…"' Piotrowski offered 'No comment.'[2]

As soon as Judge Kujawa finished reading, Edward Wende said that the disclosure in court of material connected with previous proceedings against Fr Popiełuszko violated the regulations of the Code of Criminal Proceedings. His protest was ignored, as the judge declared a 30-minute adjournment.

Piotrowski's statement fitted in with government claims that the crime was 'a provocation' against the national leadership. While accusing the priest of crimes never even mentioned by the authorities, Piotrowski openly blamed the leadership, specifically Kiszczak, for lacking the courage to act decisively against the priest. The statement also echoed the sentiments of the anti-Solidarity police organisation, the OAS, which had carried out the Toruń abductions earlier in 1984. For the authorities, this was good news, for it absolved them implicitly of involvement in the crime.

When the court reconvened, Judge Kujawa kept the focus on the Church. He asked whether the documents in the case against Jerzy Popiełuszko were known to the accused. Piotrowski said they were, adding that the questions and answers read out earlier by the judge came from a document recording details of a meeting between the Primate and priests of the Warsaw Archdiocese which had circulated among the clergy and throughout the capital.

This was the document dismissed by Fr Popiełuszko in his diary as a malicious forgery. Judge Kujawa's mention of it now presented Piotrowski with another opportunity to attack the Church.

He had misled the court, he confessed, when he said that his attitude to Jerzy Popiełuszko had been coldly official; it wasn't. On the contrary, he was so passionately devoted to his job that he could not keep calm when, for example, Fr Zych, the priest convicted, as he put it, for the murder of the Warsaw policeman, was transferred from prison to a monastery following pressure from the Episcopate. How could one stay calm, he asked, when it was impossible to submit to the Commission Investigating Hitlerite Crimes the facts of Bishop Tokarczuk's 'collaboration with the Gestapo during the Second World War', which had been reported in 'the Western press'.

Judge Kujawa allowed Piotrowski to continue with a series of outrageous but unchallenged allegations: that Archbishop Gulbinowicz of Wrocław had refused to hand over some 80 million zloties that didn't belong to him; that the Church got away with dozens of millions of zloties in unpaid taxes every year; that churches and other buildings were being erected illegally; and that during street disturbances in Gdańsk there was a walkie-talkie radio link from the demonstrations to Fr Jankowski's presbytery at St Brigid's. Piotrowski also bemoaned the fact that he and officers like him were able to be with their children only once or twice a month, 'and all because a few priests want to make trouble'. He ended with a warning that other witnesses and those in the dock, not to mention the prosecutors and judges, would all have their appointed places when and if that 'new surge' of which Jerzy Popiełuszko had spoken was to come about.

Having allowed Piotrowski to say as much as he wanted, Judge Kujawa quickly dismissed the protests of the auxiliary lawyers. Piotrowski answered questions from the judges and the prosecutor, Leszek Pietrasiński, for the rest of the day and part of the next, the ninth day of the trial, but still refused to take questions from Olszewski and his colleagues.

It is not improbable that Piotrowski felt pleased with himself. He had been shielded from the auxiliary lawyers and been permitted to slander not only the Church and some of its most respected prelates but also the priest he was accused of murdering.

Judge Kujawa prompted him yet again: 'What's all this about a jealous husband?' This was a reference to Piotrowski's opening statement in which he had said that one of his ideas had been to get hold of the priest and talk to him as if he [Piotrowski] were a jealous husband, recording it on tape. This, he thought, could persuade Popiełuszko that he was facing the vengeance of a jealous husband and the prospect of blackmail.

Piotrowski's reply might have come from a Graham Greene novel: 'I had information about Jerzy Popiełuszko's relations with a certain lady. I have proof of this — rendezvous, hotels, bars. I could even tell you the lady's name if the court so wished.'[3]

It is astonishing that Piotrowski's allegations were tolerated, even encouraged in court, and the Church responded tersely. The Press Bureau of the Episcopate announced on 11 January that it saw no reason to adopt an attitude to Piotrowski's slanderous utterances since they came from a person who, by reason of being on trial, bore no responsibility under the law for telling untruths.

There is no evidence to suggest that the authorities took Piotrowski's allegations seriously. The 80 million zloties which Archbishop Gulbinowicz was accused of refusing to return to their rightful owners belonged to Solidarity and was in the Archbishop's safekeeping, or so the general public believed. As for the alleged collaboration with the Gestapo during the Second World War, of Bishop Tokarczuk of Przemyśl, the 'Western press' which Piotrowski cited turned out to be *Settegiorni*, an obscure propaganda weekly of the Communist camp, published in Sicily and distributed to the embassies of socialist and Third World countries. Bishop Tokarczuk was admired not only for his support of Solidarity but for presiding over a diocese where 'illegally' built churches and chapels had tended over the years to appear overnight.

There was little doubt that what happened in court that day was a carefully coordinated performance between the accused, the prosecutor and the judge. Piotrowski, who had nothing to lose, was apparently authorised to put his hatred into words and lash out at the Church and Fr Popiełuszko in terms which the authorities never had the courage to use. Although they disowned Piotrowski and his colleagues in the dock, the authorities knew that in the eyes of many people, not only in Poland, they too were on trial. And Piotrowski was a useful servant. The man they would convict was in an ideal position to say for them that in the eyes of the regime neither the Church nor Fr Popiełuszko was innocent.

# 28

# Pietruszka's Defence

Among several disadvantages facing Adam Pietruszka as he sat in the dock flanked by uniformed policemen was one he may not have recognised — he looked the part of the conspiratorial SB bureaucrat pulling strings from behind a desk, the role in which the indictment had cast him. First newspaper pictures from the court room showed him wearing a distant expression, as if he were still struggling to comprehend what was happening to him. Pietruszka's greatest disadvantage, of course, was that he knew he would not be acquitted and that the evidence to convict him would come from fellow SB officers, mainly his former subordinates.

Adam Pietruszka's career had got off to a slower start than that of Grzegorz Piotrowski, who came from an SB family. Pietruszka was from a peasant family and graduated from a technical college in Poznań. For a few years he had worked in the management of the railways in Szczecin in the northwest, where he joined the uniformed police and the SB in 1961, aged twenty three. Only fourteen years later in 1975, was Pietruszka transferred to the Ministry in Warsaw as deputy head of a section. Piotrowski had made that transition from Łódź in only six years.

According to Piotrowski, Pietruszka was nothing if not quick-witted.

When Pietruszka took his junior colleague's place at the witness stand, he had far more to say about him. Piotrowski's arrival in the Department as deputy head of the section had caused discord, Pietruszka said. Piotrowski was very young and junior, in a section where majors and colonels predominated, and there was resentment at his rapid rise. After eighteen months, Piotrowski had been transferred to head another section and 'win his spurs' but had returned to head his old section after six months. He had a number of positive traits, Pietruszka conceded; he was dynamic and active, totally devoted to his work, and never said he was too tired or busy to do anything. Piotrowski always stressed his personal involvement in work, Pietruszka said, but devoted little time to what he was supposed to do, supervise others. Pietruszka said that given time Piotrowski had the makings of a fine boss, but he was also capable of wilful behaviour 'bordering on insubordination'. He also 'frequently reported on what he had already done', before telling his boss he was going to do it.

This was essential to Pietruszka's defence. Charged with inspiring the crime, he wanted the court to believe that this was not the first time Piotrowski had done something without telling him.

Pietruszka could perhaps have argued that he was being convicted before he had a chance to speak. He pleaded not guilty to all charges, declaring that they were based entirely on slanderous statements by Piotrowski. This was not precisely true. After all, the evidence assembled against him included independent testimony provided by officers other than Piotrowski or his accomplices. It is true, however, that most of the evidence against him came either from Piotrowski or from Pękala and Chmielewski quoting what Piotrowski had told them.

Pietruszka denied or explained all of the damaging comments attributed to him by Piotrowski. These included the alleged remark that it would have made 'a lovely accident' if Piotrowski had managed to smash the windscreen of Fr

Popieluszko's car on the return journey from Gdańsk on 13 October.

Pietruszka also denied suggesting that Fr Popieluszko could be pushed off a moving train. And the court failed to produce anyone other than Piotrowski to say he had heard Pietruszka making the suggestion. Leszek Wolski, head of the SB section at Warsaw City headquarters, said he never heard it at all.

The court nonetheless determined that Piotrowski was telling the truth, that Pietruszka was lying, and that Leszek Wolski's testimony was self-serving and unbelievable.

Ultimately, it was never demonstrated conclusively that Pietruszka had said the words Wolski denied hearing. And however much the people of Poland wanted to see Pietruszka convicted (and would have loved to see Wolski convicted as well), the fact is that the court accepted the minority version of what was said at the first two Department Four meetings convened to discuss the problem of Fr Popieluszko. Two out of three participants disagreed with Piotrowski's version; Pietruszka denied it and Wolski couldn't or wouldn't confirm it. But the court went with Piotrowski.

Pietruszka did admit responsibility for Piotrowski's trip to Gdańsk on 13 October, the date of the first attempt against Fr Popieluszko, but he insisted that he had sent him there on a job totally unconnected with the priest. He told the court that Piotrowski, who chose the date of the trip, was supposed to travel north accompanied only by Pękala, not Chmielewski.

The purpose of the trip, Pietruszka told the court, was to carry out 'external reconnaissance' for another operation. Piotrowski had taken Chmielewski with him, without Pietruszka's knowledge, and had changed the trip's purpose. Pietruszka claimed to have rebuked Piotrowski for doing this but admitted that he had enquired, nonetheless, how the visit had gone for him and for Fr Popieluszko. Piotrowski had said only that 'we didn't meet, we didn't manage it, we missed, there's no more to say'.

As for Piotrowski's trip to Bydgoszcz on 19 October, the day of the murder, Pietruszka maintained that he could not possibly have authorised it because he had sent Dróżdż to Gdańsk that day and it was a rule in the department that a section head and his deputy could never be absent at the same time. Besides, he said, he had not known that Fr Popiełuszko had gone to Bydgoszcz until the Saturday morning following his abduction.

The question of the permit authorising Piotrowski's journey on 19 October was far more difficult. Pietruszka insisted he had not seen the document until the investigation. He did admit, however, that the signature and the stamp on the permit were his. He was at a loss to explain this, he said, because he had not signed it. Nor did he know who was responsible for the attempted alterations to the permit.

More damaging still was Pietruszka's admission that Piotrowski had walked into his office early on the Saturday morning and handed him the 'W' pass, just as he was about to join General Płatek to discuss the priest's abduction. Piotrowski had told him he had got the pass from Pietruszka's driver, Wronski, but not where he had been with it. Pietruszka did not report this to Płatek, he told the court, for three main reasons. First, he had rejected any suspicion of Piotrowski because he couldn't accept that he could have done such a thing; second, because Piotrowski told General Płatek that he had not been to Bydgoszcz on Friday; and third, because of the discovery of the police cap badge at the scene of the kidnapping. This, Pietruszka maintained, had pointed to the possibility of 'a political provocation by the underground against our organs'.

It was General Kiszczak himself who had first made this claim in his broadcast to the nation a week after the abduction. General Płatek also claimed that he suspected the Solidarity underground had a hand in it. For the general public, however, such a suggestion was ridiculous. So too was Pietruszka's appeal to what can only be described as SB family values. He told the court that Waldemar Chmielewski's father who worked in Department Four was a very close friend, and that it was he, Pietruszka, who had got young Chmielewski his job there. For these reasons, he said, he could not possibly have allowed him to take part in an operation that involved shoving Fr Popiełuszko into a car.

Pietruszka's difficulties multiplied when it came to evidence of his behaviour in the days following the crime. When he finally admitted ordering Piotrowski to change the car's number plates on Sunday morning, he said he did so because Płatek had told him the car had been seen in Bydgoszcz. His purpose, evidently, was to incriminate the General as much as himself. To that end he also said that the General had told him to pretend that he first heard about the car on Monday evening, not Sunday morning. The court, however, was not interested in a case against General Płatek, only in convicting Pietruszka. The questioning intensified.

Knowing that Piotrowski had used the 'W' pass on Friday and that Piotrowski's number plates had been seen in Bydgoszcz that day, wasn't he suspicious? All Pietruszka could say was that he refused to suspect Piotrowski because he found it inconceivable that a colleague, someone whose job it was to protect the rule of law, should have done such a thing. As for the 'W' pass, he said he had not told Płatek about that because he was afraid of being implicated.

The case against him deepened when asked whether Piotrowski had told him that the priest had been thrown into the water.

> We talked about this several times every day. I kept asking Piotrowski what had happened to Popiełuszko. On Sunday he told me: 'They all keep asking me that. I don't know. Maybe he's floating in the Vistula.' And with a wave of the arm, he walked out. I took in what he had said and I was shocked. But it was so impossible for an SB officer to throw a priest into the waters that I didn't allow myself to think it. I thought it was absurd...[1]

Pietruszka admitted that he had done nothing with this information. However, the most damning feature of this testimony, was that by asking what had happened to Popiełuszko, Pietruszka seemed to be admitting knowledge that Piotrowski had a hand in the priest's disappearance. But the timing of the conversation is all important. Having stated that it took place on Sunday, Pietruszka almost immediately said that it happened on Monday, which would have been after the revelation was made. The court never found out.

Equally interesting is Pietruszka's claim that Piotrowski said 'they' kept on asking about Popiełuszko. Who were they? The prosecution did not ask.

If the case against Pietruszka was based largely on the testimony of Piotrowski, it was also supported by SB witnesses.

In statements about their contact with Piotrowski on the day of the murder, Barbara Story, his secretary, and another colleague had written that on leaving the office that morning, Piotrowski had said that Adam Pietruszka knew why he was absent, if anyone should ask. To make matters worse, Janusz Dróżdż, Piotrowski's deputy, had testified that Pietruszka had told him to get the two officers to shorten their reports, removing references to himself. Dróżdż had done this, shredding the originals.

Pietruszka denied this, claiming that another Deputy Director witnessed what was said.

But it was Pietruszka's misfortune that the allegations he was trying to refute were to be repeated by the three key witnesses several days later, after a procession of more than a dozen witnesses in the meantime had helped to erode whatever memory was left of Pietruszka's defence.

It is interesting, however, that Barbara Story was first questioned as a witness on Wednesday, 24 October, the day after she had composed her statement. But she said nothing about it then, or at two subsequent sessions on the following Friday and Saturday. It was one week later, the day after Pietruszka was detained, that she first testified that on the day of the crime, her boss had told her that Pietruszka would know why he was absent. It was on the Sunday that she first told investigators of Pietruszka's demand that her statement be cut down.

It is at least possible that the testimony of Story, as well as that of Dróżdż and Stromecki, was a convenient afterthought designed to incriminate Pietruszka as the sole 'hidden inspirer'. But perhaps they were simply not asked the right questions.

Apparently, it was the testimony of 23-year-old Beata Marszczak, the Ministry typist and friend of Grzegorz Piotrowski, that inspired the questioning. On Friday, 2 November, only a few hours before it was announced that Pietruszka had been detained, she said that on 19 October, the day of the crime, she had visited Piotrowski's section and heard Barbara Story telling someone over the phone that Piotrowski was not at work and that Colonel Pietruszka knew why. This was the first mention of the clue that led to such an accumulation of testimony against Pietruszka.

Among several questions prompted by Beata Marszczak's testimony, one has to ask why she was questioned in the first place?

What strength there was in Pietruszka's defence lay in his testimony that General Płatek knew on Sunday morning that the Department car had been seen in Bydgoszcz, something Płatek denied.

But Pietruszka struggled in the face of hostile questioning, although he did manage to slip in at least two remarks which, if noticed, could have raised questions about his immediate superiors.

For instance, in his account of how General Ciastoń sent him to look at Piotrowski's car in the repair shops, he recalled that the General had suggested he check whether the vehicle had been damaged, whether it was dented or buckled. This was an apparent reference to the fact that Fr Popiełuszko had pressed the lid of the car boot so hard that he had dented it from the inside, creating a five-centimetre gap where its upper rim joined the car frame beneath the rear window. Pietruszka, however, had been sent to the Ministry's garages on the night of Monday, 22 October, before any arrests had been made and before any damage to the boot lid had been discussed. So how could General Ciastoń have suspected any such damage? Presumably, only by being told about it by Piotrowski.

Another of Pietruszka's almost casual remarks contradicted

General Płatek. According to Pietruszka, (in testimony on 11 January), the sighting of number plates beginning with the letters KZC in Bydgoszcz reached the Ministry 'right from the start, in the very first reports', which probably meant between 7 and 8 am on Saturday morning. When first questioned as a witness, the General had said he first heard of the KZC plates when phoned from Toruń by Colonel Głowacki on Saturday night. But the General's official announcement of the abduction earlier that night had spelled out the letters and digits of the number plates, describing them as false.

It is surprising that two such close colleagues should have disagreed so clearly over a crucial piece of evidence.

But raising such questions was all Pietruszka could do. He had admitted that Piotrowski had been in possession of his 'W' pass on the day of the crime (while denying that he gave it to him). He had failed to explain how Piotrowski obtained the travel permit bearing his signature and stamp (while denying that he signed or stamped it). He had admitted that Płatek had told him on Sunday morning that a car with Piotrowski's registration plates had been seen in Bydgoszcz, and after confessing that Piotrowski had told him that Fr Popiełuszko might be in the Vistula. Pietruszka must have known that he would not avoid conviction.

But still he insisted on denying most elements of the prosecution's evidence as well as the main charges themselves.

What was the point of these denials when he had already admitted so much? Everything Pietruszka said in court — from his proud reference to being educated in 'the rigours of socialist humanism' to his acid exchanges with Jan Olszewski and Edward Wende and his contemptuous description of Fr Popiełuszko as one of those priests who 'wear the cross on their breast but carry hatred in their hearts' — placed him in the ranks of the *beton*, the concrete hardline Party loyalists. Everyone believed him guilty and wanted him condemned.

In retrospect, however, and at a distance of two decades, the case against Adam Pietruszka does seem strangely unconvincing. Can the word of one proven criminal, Grzegorz

Piotrowski, be taken as convincing proof that Pietruszka alone instigated the crime? Is it not just as possible that Pietruszka did indeed press Piotrowski into doing something more drastic than usual to curb the priest's activities, without ordering his murder?

Is it not possible even that this was a case in which policemen committed murder in the name of the authorities but without their sanction, and the regime simply felt obliged to protect them? And if so, was Pietruszka the only Department Four officer who tried to cover up the crime and delay its solution? Pietruszka was not innocent, but there are grounds for suspecting that he was framed to take all the blame, in order to protect others and the system they served.

In its bid to convict Colonel Adam Pietruszka, the court welcomed Piotrowski's testimony that it was impossible to do anything in the Department without one's superior officer knowing about it. Would it ask General Płatek when he appeared at the witness stand whether he knew what his chief deputy was up to before, during and after the crime? And if not, why not?

# 29

# Płatek

It would have made sense if General Płatek had followed his deputy, Adam Pietruszka, to the witness stand. They were, after all, the closest of colleagues and in the days following Fr Popiełuszko's abduction, they worked together in the 'operations group' set up to run the investigation. Their evidence was also closely linked. Pietruszka had claimed that the General had told him about the kidnap car's Ministry number plates on the Sunday morning. This was something that Płatek had never admitted. All the more reason, then, for the General to take the stand when Pietruszka's testimony was still fresh in the minds of those in the court room.

The prosecution waited, however, until 21 January to call General Płatek, seven days after Pietruszka had completed his testimony. In the meantime, seventeen other witnesses, including Waldek Chrostowski, three priests and eleven SB officers or employees, had come and gone. Their testimony, if not exactly blotting out the memory of what Pietruszka had said, managed to create distance between him and the General.

As a witness, Zenon Płatek was not expected by the court or the prosecution to demonstrate anything other than the guilt of the accused. In the eyes, however, of the auxiliary prosecutors and the general public they represented, he had a great deal to explain. After all, he had been suspended from duties as

Director of Department Four for failing to exercise 'proper
supervision' of his staff, while Pietruszka had been taken into
custody. People had a right to know how Płatek's fault differed
from the alleged crime of his deputy and to ask how it was
possible for one to inspire and cover up such an unusual crime
without the other noticing. The public, moreover, had yet to
learn what the General had told investigators before the trial.

A key, though understated, element in Płatek's case was his
claim to have been absent from his desk for long and crucial
periods of the early investigation, when Adam Pietruszka was
left in charge and, by implication, at liberty to tamper with the
evidence. This was particularly true of the Sunday, when the
General emphasised that he scarcely had time to give instructions to Pietruszka around 8 in the morning before he dashed
off in response to a summons from his superior, General
Ciastoń, and spent most of the day with him. It was during this
supposed absence that Pietruszka told Piotrowski to change the
number plates on the kidnap car. Later that day Pietruszka was
alleged to have suppressed what he was told by Colonels
Luliński and Głowacki and changed WAB 6031 to WAE 8031.
Płatek was similarly absent on the Tuesday afternoon when
Pietruszka was accused of ordering two members of
Piotrowski's staff to alter written statements which could have
incriminated him. Even on the day of the crime itself, General
Płatek claimed to have been out of the office all day, leaving
Pietruszka, as usual, in charge.

The General's absence at these moments was certainly convenient but he still had to clarify his testimony on two crucial
moments in the investigation. The first was Colonel Głowacki's
phone call from Toruń on Saturday night, in which he told the
General about the kidnap car and the Ministry number plates.
Płatek denied this but the indictment stated categorically that
the General was, indeed, told.

The second difficulty arose from Pietruszka's claim that
Płatek had told him on the Sunday morning about the number
plates. Płatek had always maintained that the first he learned of
this was on Monday evening, when Colonel Jabłoński of the

Criminal Investigations Bureau told him. But his position was now compromised by the prosecution's acceptance of Pietruszka's testimony as further proof of Pietruszka's guilt.

General Płatek tried to accommodate these difficulties in his opening statement by introducing elements never previously mentioned.

Głowacki's phone call, he repeated, had woken him up from a sleep induced by sedatives. The Colonel had asked whether he and Luliński couldn't return to Warsaw the next day, there being nothing very important to report apart from the fact that a car with KZC plates had been seen near the church in Bydgoszcz. Głowacki, however, had added that there was a report of another, light-coloured Fiat with a Warsaw number plate having been seen there too. When the department's duty officer had called on another line, Płatek said, he had ended Głowacki's call by ordering him to look into that Warsaw number plate and report back the following morning.

That was roughly a repetition of what Płatek had said in his first two interrogations, though he spoke then of three cars with Warsaw number plates, not one. Now he added something completely new:

> When I got up the next morning my thoughts returned to what Głowacki had told me about those Warsaw number plates. Somehow or other I had a fixed idea in my mind that it could be a provocation — this business of the Warsaw plates. And it seemed even more possible because I knew that Chrostowski had seen a little light in the [kidnap] car. He had also spoken about that shelf, and I thought that that could be the housing for a two-way radio and the light was part of it. But such radios can only be found in Ministry cars. This was just a loose association of ideas on my part.[1]

Suddenly, General Płatek was able, three months after the event, to remember in precise, self-analytical detail what he was unable either to remember or mention when questioned by investigators two months earlier. Płatek's revelation also helped him explain what happened on Sunday morning.

He had spoken about this moment only twice before. The first time, under interrogation on 19 November, he simply said that when he went into the office on the Sunday morning (after Głowacki's call), he had instructed Pietruszka and Piotrowski, 'in connection with the information obtained', to get in touch with Bydgoszcz and Toruń and try to establish who were the owners of 'those three cars', the three cars with Warsaw plates said to have been seen in Bydgoszcz. What, precisely, did this 'information obtained' consist of? Nobody seems to have asked.

The second time General Płatek spoke about the Sunday morning was on 5 December, when he was confronted with Pietruszka's testimony saying that the General told him then about the kidnap car's real identity. His reaction, as we have seen, had been to record a statement that made little sense.

The General's new, improved testimony in court said that he drove to the Ministry that Sunday morning in his own private car, arriving a couple of minutes before 8 am.[2]

> As I walked through the parking area… I noticed a car with WAB 6031 number plates and on reaching the office I asked the duty officer if our department had a car with such plates. He said it didn't. All the same, I checked for myself on the list kept under glass on the desk top and couldn't find the number. On the list was the official number plate of the car. I then asked if Director Pietruszka was available, and before that I had called for information from Colonel Głowacki. It was then that my superior phoned and asked me to go and report on the search for Fr Popiełuszko. In the meantime Pietruszka arrived and I gave him the information from Bydgoszcz. I told him how I had been walking through the Ministry yard and seen a similar car parked there. I instructed him to look into this, and to look into the matter of all the possible Warsaw number plates seen near the church in Bydgoszcz. Then I practically ran to my superior's office where I told him about all the overnight reports. I told him about the car with KZC plates, about the cars with Warsaw plates, saying that this was being looked into and that I had prepared detailed instructions…

This was, in effect, Płatek's apologia, his explanation of why he had been suspended but not accused. It was the first time he admitted seeing the car with WAB 6031 number plates in the Ministry yard and asking Pietruszka to look into it. He was now telling the court what he had never even hinted at in four sessions with investigators before the trial, and was thus confirming part of Pietruszka's testimony. But he was omitting to confirm that he had told Pietruszka that a car with those plates had been seen in Bydgoszcz and that the plates belonged to Piotrowski's section. He couldn't confirm that, because to do so would place him in the dock alongside Pietruszka.

Płatek's statement had not explained why the sight of those number plates in the Ministry yard on Sunday morning had concerned him. After all, the car had been there on Saturday morning when he had arrived following the news of Fr Popiełuszko's abduction. Why did he notice on Sunday what he didn't notice on Saturday? And why did he say that the car he noticed was 'similar'? Similar to what?

The obvious answer is that Colonel Głowacki had told him by phone the previous night that a car with WAB 6031 plates had been seen near the church and that the same car or one very 'similar' had been seen later wearing different plates, KZC 0423. The General, however, had consistently denied hearing any Warsaw number plate being read out during that phone call.

General Płatek appears to have spent most of Sunday with General Ciastoń, but he revealed nothing about their discussions. He concentrated more on what was part of the case against Pietruszka and a key element of his own defence.

> When I got back to my office, Pietruszka told me that the KZC number plate had turned out to be false. The word from Kalisz was that such plates would be introduced only in a year's time. I asked him about the WAB number plate. He said that there was no information on that score, Piotrowski was looking into it, but there were many such number plates and it all had to be checked out. I then asked him about Głowacki and Luliński, but Pietruszka told me that they had already left and that there

was nothing special in their reports. I asked about the WAB number and told him to check it out. At the same time I phoned Bydgoszcz and instructed them to verify the colour of the car, suggesting that officers of the Criminal Investigations section check out the notes and pass them on to me. That was Sunday evening. I returned home at 23.00.[3]

Płatek's claims don't really stand up to scrutiny. In court, on 21 January 1985, he was saying that he had told Pietruszka on the Sunday to look into 'the WAB number plates'. And yet, in the three months that had elapsed since that Sunday, General Płatek had consistently denied knowing anything about such number plates. His claim in court that he had given specific instructions on Sunday to Criminal Investigations was also new and it clearly anticipated the confirmation the very next day by Colonel Jabłoński of what Głowacki had told the General on Saturday night.

The court never heard Colonel Jabłoński's version of this moment because he was never called as a witness.

But the General's instantaneous reaction, summoning Pietruzka and demanding a statement from Piotrowski, is also questionable. How could the General be so quick to challenge Piotrowski if he had not already known that the WAB 6031 plates belonged to Piotrowski's section?

By the time the General concluded his opening statement, there were many questions waiting to be asked. The presiding judge asked him when he first began to suspect Pietruszka. 'Initially,' he said, 'I had no such suspicions and gave him a variety of instructions to carry out. But when I came to ask him "What about the car, what about Głowacki's report or what did Luliński have to say?" it seemed to me that he wasn't giving me much detailed information and that I was having to check many of these things out for myself, though I did go on giving him orders.'[4]

It would have been useful to ask the General at this point why he was now suggesting that he had considered the information from Głowacki and Luliński so important. After all, he initially denied that he was told it or heard it over the phone on Saturday night. And he still had to explain why he was so troubled by Piotrowski's number plate, having failed to hear it from Głowacki over the phone, when he saw it eight hours later in the Ministry yard.

An explanation of sorts began to emerge after the court read out the record of General Płatek's four interviews with investigators on 19, 23, and 28 November and 5 December. This was the first time that the General's ever-changing testimony on the subject had been made public. And as the minutes of each meeting, the product of several hours of interrogation, were read out almost without interruption, even the sharpest intelligence would have struggled to keep up.

Płatek attempted an explanation shortly after the reading was concluded. 'I was constantly tormented by the business of those WAB 6031 number plates,' the General said. 'They preyed upon my mind even after I provided my first testimony... On the night in question I was exhausted, I took some sleeping tablets, the telephone dragged me from my sleep, and at the same time the duty officer phoned. For all these reasons it could have escaped my notice and maybe at the time I didn't attach such weight to the information...'[5]

Essentially, Płatek was repeating the same old story. But by saying now that he could have underestimated 'the information', he seemed to be suggesting that there was more to Głowacki's call than he had previously thought or said.

On his second day at the witness stand, General Płatek confirmed under questioning by Judge Maciejewski that he had first been told about the car with KZC plates on Saturday evening 'before night time'. Asked then what exactly Colonel Głowacki had said about the car, Płatek gave an interesting answer:

I had been informed about the KZC plates earlier. Then information was passed that that car had been parked by the church. First to set off was a car apparently leading the way, followed by Fr Popiełuszko's car and behind that by the KZC car with the three men inside. He also gave me the information that there was a car with a Warsaw registration plate, WAB, but he didn't give me the digits.[6]

This was the first time Płatek had said that Głowacki had spelled out the letters of the Warsaw vehicle. Once again he was changing his testimony. When Maciejewski pointed out that Płatek had said something quite different in pre-trial testimony, the General responded quickly:

'Somehow or other this stuck in my mind. As soon as I woke up in the morning, the letters WAB were there in my head. It's difficult for me to explain it now.'[7]

The judge read out part of the General's signed testimony in which he said Głowacki had told him that the car had attracted attention because of 'the first letter' of its number plates, signifying Warsaw.

General Płatek responded just as vigorously: 'But I amplified this later, for that question was a constant source of disquiet for me and I came to the conclusion that I was probably told that the number plates began with WAB.'[8]

The word 'probably' is not normally accepted as incontestable testimony, but this court seems to have raised no objections. This was, in fact, a crucial moment, for General Płatek had finally hit upon an explanation of how he could deny hearing Colonel Głowacki tell him about the WAB 6031 number plates on Saturday night, but still react with concern on Sunday morning when he saw those number plates in the Ministry yard.

There are good reasons for not believing him. First, he had failed to mention it in any of four interviews with investigators. Perhaps he had no reason to until 4 December, when Adam Pietruszka testified that the General had told him on the Sunday morning about the kidnap car with the Department plates.

Second, even in court it emerged only under questioning during his time at the witness stand. He hadn't alluded to it in his opening statement. It was completely new, and perfectly tailored to meet his needs. If he had 'remembered' the whole number plate, he would have been obliged to explain why Piotrowski was not arrested sooner. If he had stuck to his original claim that he had been told only of a car or cars with number plates beginning with the letter W, he would have found it hard to explain the special attention that he paid to Piotrowski's car in a yard in which most if not all cars had plates beginning with W.

Leszek Pietrasiński, the lead prosecutor, rose to the occasion by asking the General what had made him notice the car. The General listed four things: very few cars were parked in the yard on Sundays; what had happened (presumably he meant the abduction) was serious; he remembered the previous night's 'conversation about the WAB car'; and he also remembered Chrostowski's testimony about the kidnap car's 'little light', which he suspected would only be found in a police car.

Practically every ingredient in this response was produced exclusively during the trial. This was a matter of indifference to the prosecutor whose benign questions offered Płatek an opportunity to explain himself without risk of being challenged.

The General was free to bolster his own position and undermine that of Pietruszka by repeating that his deputy had failed to pass on Luliński's and Głowacki's report about 'the WAB car', and by suggesting that he had locked away their written report so that he couldn't read it until Monday morning. He knew, of course, that the written report said nothing about the car.

Asked when he first began to suspect Pietruszka, the General sidestepped the question. 'He was my closest colleague, my deputy,' he said. 'He shared in many activities. It was difficult for me to suspect him. However, there were certain jobs I asked him to do which he carried out quite sluggishly. He was slow, for instance, in clearing up the question of the number plates. That prompted me to exercise a certain caution.'[9]

It was true, the General said, that he had escorted Pietruszka to the Investigations Bureau on 2 November, but 'I was not aware that I was taking him to be detained'. And he denied Pietruszka's allegation that on their way to the Bureau, they had agreed to say that they had first discovered conclusively about the WAB 6031 number plates on the evening of Monday, 22 October. Both, however, stuck to that line until Pietruszka changed his testimony to the Sunday morning version on 4 December.

A series of questions on the ransom demand followed but Płatek's imprecise answers were of no concern to the prosecutor, who was more interested in how Department Four had informed the Church about the activities of Fr Popiełuszko and other priests. The General said that the Secretariat of the Episcopate was ill-informed and evasive about what was going on and that it was his department's basic job to keep the Office for Denominational Affairs (headed by the Minister, Adam Łopatka) informed of every sermon or statement by Fr Popiełuszko. Prosecutor Pietrasiński then asked the court to 'authenticate' this testimony by reading out and including in trial documents a letter sent to the Primate, Cardinal Glemp, by Minister Łopatka on 2 May 1984 (discussed in Chapter 8) and other official complaints sent to the Episcopate in January and March of 1984 (Chapter 7). The presiding judge obligingly read out the documents and immediately called an adjournment.

This was not the first time that Judge Kujawa had jumped at the opportunity to read out official documents which presented the authorities' case against Fr Popiełuszko. He had even done so without request. Ten days earlier, Jan Olszewski had asked Adam Pietruszka whether he had supplied the material for the protest from the Office for Denominational Affairs accusing Fr Popiełuszko of belonging to a counter-revolutionary organisation with its centre at St Stanisław's. When Pietruszka claimed not to remember the details, Kujawa read out the official protest followed by the text of Fr Popiełuszko's sermon on the last Sunday of August, which allegedly contained proof of the counter-revolutionary organisation's existence.

For Jan Olszewski this must have been extremely annoying for he knew that the sermon contained no hint of counter-revolution and that it was an article in *Izvestiya* by its Warsaw correspondent that had first suggested it did. It was as if the presiding judge had been fitted with a tripwire mechanism to air the State's grievances against the dead priest whenever possible. As he had done before, Kujawa now called an adjournment at the very moment when Olszewski and his colleagues were anxious not only to protest against his intervention but to put questions to General Płatek.

It was only after a furious and lengthy legal argument and yet another adjournment that Andrzej Grabiński, representing Fr Popiełuszko's family, was able to question General Płatek. It was the beginning of the trial's most interesting and most penetrating cross-examination.

# 30

# A Witness Not on Trial

By the time Andrzej Grabiński began his cross-examination, General Zenon Płatek may well have believed that he had given a reasonably good account of himself. Now he would be questioned by men who were less well disposed towards him than the presiding judge and lead prosecutor.

Grabiński, who was quite brief, betrayed no particular aggressiveness, but his final question elicited a revealing answer: 'Did you check on progress in clarifying the matter of the WAB number plates?'

'I've already explained that,' the General replied. 'I asked about it and, to sum up, I asked other services to look into it. I thought that *since it concerned the section* [my italics] one ought to hand it over to other services.'[1]

Never before had he said that he knew the number plates were connected in some way with 'the section', a phrase that could mean only one thing — Piotrowski's section. And yet, the General had maintained throughout that this fact, which he now says prompted his request to Criminal Investigations, had been unknown to him until after Colonel Jabłoński had told him on Monday evening following the enquiries by Criminal Investigations.

Jan Olszewski now took over the cross-examination and worked his way slowly but deliberately towards the car.

Q: It was on the morning of 20th October, then, that you heard the news of the abduction of Fr Popiełuszko?

A: Yes, I was told by telephone that Chrostowski had said that Fr Popiełuszko had escaped into the woods. And that, more or less, is what the cryptogram said.

Q: Did this coded message say anything about any cars, or was there still no mention at that time?

A: Of course there was. Already there were orders out concerning the car that Chrostowski was talking about. The officer who reported to me said that he'd ordered road blocks in Toruń province.[2]

General Płatek had always testified that he had organised a large-scale search for Fr Popiełuszko in the woods near Toruń on the basis of the incorrect report, repeated here, that Chrostowski had said the priest had run into the woods. He had not talked of any search for the kidnap car until the Saturday evening, when the television announcement of the abduction spoke of the car with false number plates. Now, Płatek was claiming to have been told early on Saturday morning that the police had indeed been searching for the kidnap car described by Chrostowski and had even set up road blocks. It remained to be seen whether any of this was true. Jan Olszewski dug deeper.

Q:... Did you ask Bydgoszcz, which carried out the surveillance... whether the number plates of cars near the church had been noted down...?

A: I instructed Bydgoszcz to send full documentation and all details.

Q: And did you receive such a report?

A: I don't know, it's hard for me to answer that now.

Q: I beg your pardon, but a priest had been kidnapped. The information was very important, was it not? And you don't know whether it came in from Bydgoszcz?

A: There was information in the morning about the church service.

Q: What I want to know is whether you demanded the despatch of information about cars near the church, as provided by the people who had the area under surveillance.

A: The chief in Bydgoszcz told me that... these people were on their days off and he had difficulties getting them in.[3]

This was not the first or last time that General Płatek gave the obviously false impression that as Director of Department Four in the Ministry of Internal Affairs he was powerless to change with a mere snap of the fingers such humdrum arrangements as the shift patterns of junior officers in a provincial town. But Olszewski pressed on.

Q: You have said that you learned about the car and its registration numbers on Saturday night.

A: That's right, though the KZC numbering was known earlier.

Q: When did you learn that the KZC number plates... were false?

This was a good question. The original announcement of Fr Popieluszko's abduction, which Płatek claimed to have helped compose, had stated quite clearly on Saturday evening that the plates were false. So the General must have learned they were false before then.

Before Płatek had a chance to reply, however, the presiding judge, Artur Kujawa, intervened with an answer of his own: 'The witness has already explained that it was after he returned from his superior in the evening and after Pietruszka had taken Głowacki's and Luliński's report.'[4]

At this Płatek merely said: 'That's right.' But it could not have been right. Kujawa was saying that Płatek learned the KZC plates were false on Sunday evening, almost 24 hours after he had already told the nation they were false.

Oddly enough Jan Olszewski did not make this point. Instead, he asked how it could be that all the services involved in the investigation needed 48 hours to establish that number plates beginning with the letters KZC did not exist in Poland. The General gave another shockingly simple reply: 'It was Sunday and it was very difficult to find this out... we got hold of an appropriate official but it took time.'

Płatek's answer converted the possibility of concealment on the part of the investigating authorities into a matter of rank incompetence. The fact remains, however, that it was widely known on Saturday night that the KZC plates were false. Why then the insistence by the judge that it was only on Sunday that this became known? That depends on who knew the plates were false the previous day.

Two men fitted this category. They were Ryszard Mieszczyński and Jerzy Pacler, the SB men who observed the car outside the church in Bydgoszcz on Friday evening. If they reported that the KZC plates were false, they did so because they knew they had taken the place of the original plates, WAB 6031. They had no reason, however, to suspect that the WAB plates belonged to an SB section at the Ministry in Warsaw. It is possible that a report based on their surveillance, but unaware of its implications, reached the Ministry in a cryptogram from Bydgoszcz on Saturday evening and found its way at the last minute into the official announcement which General Płatek helped prepare.

There are solid grounds for believing that this is what happened. As mentioned earlier, the initial announcement said that Fr Popiełuszko's car had been followed out of Bydgoszcz by a Fiat wearing false number plates. Who else but Mieszczyński and Pacler had noted down the number plates and who else was in a position not only to watch the cars move off from the church but even follow them out of the city? And is it not possible that theirs was the brown Fiat that Marek Wilk said had followed him back into town after he had escorted the priest's Volkswagen Golf out to the road to Toruń?

If so, the television announcement carried deeply embarrassing implications for the Ministry of Internal Affairs. It was based, after all, on information which was capable not only of saying that the number plates of the kidnap car were false but also of identifying the car's original number plates as WAB 6031. And these could be traced easily to a Fiat 125p used by Department Four.

It is also remotely possible that the initial report from Bydgoszcz mentioned only the false KZC plates. That would have made it easier for anyone, including General Płatek, to make the mistake of broadcasting the news of the false number plates without detecting the danger of doing so.

So did the authorities now see the original announcement as a mistake? Certain facts suggest that they may have. The original announcement was not reprinted in the Monday newspapers (after a paper-free Sunday). Instead they published only a small part of it combined with the second communiqué broadcast on Sunday evening. This contained a description of the kidnappers and their car, based on Waldek Chrostowski's testimony, and mentioned the continued search for the car with false KZC 0423 number plates without saying that it had been seen following the priest's car out of Bydgoszcz.[5]

Jan Olszewski moved on to another questionable feature of Płatek's testimony. Having asked Adam Pietruszka to look into the car he had seen in the Ministry yard on Sunday morning, how had the General reacted on discovering that the list of cars with Warsaw number plates presented to him later by Pietruszka did not contain the number plates he had seen on the car in question?

Płatek said he had passed the matter on to another channel for investigation. But to whom and when? He had instructed criminal investigations officers in Bydgoszcz to investigate, the General replied, saying that if they were returning the next day they should report the results of their enquiries to him immediately. 'And that's what happened,' Płatek said. 'A piece of paper with the WAB 6031 number plates written on it along with the information that the car belonged to the Ministry of Internal Affairs was handed to me by the Director of Criminal Investigations…'

Olszewski responded with a pertinent question: 'How did you establish that it was Piotrowski's car?'

Płatek's reply: 'I asked for and got hold of the complete list of cars along with their official and unofficial number plates. I had it once I got back from my superior.'[6]

The General was talking here of that hectic Monday evening after he had been told by Colonel Jabłoński that the car belonged to the Ministry. We have already seen from his own account how the General seemed to have known immediately that the car was Piotrowski's. Indeed, he had told the court in his opening statement that he had challenged Piotrowski by saying, 'You were seen in Bydgoszcz with the car.' He had done this, moreover, *before* he went to see General Ciastoń.

So did he already know it was Piotrowski's car or did he really need the documents to prove it? And if it was so easy for him to get hold of the full list of cars in the midst of a departmental crisis, why did he not do so in the early morning quiet of Sunday, when he said he had failed to find WAB 6031 on the list of official number plates?

After further probing questions, the court announced a recess on the ground that the witness was tired. General Płatek's performance had not been impressive, but when the court reassembled after the recess, the proceedings took a turn towards the farcical. The presiding judge, Artur Kujawa, read out a document from Police Headquarters in Toruń recording the investigation from start to finish and ending with a special mention of 'the gigantic involvement of General Płatek'. He then read out a similar document sent by the Bydgoszcz Police Headquarters to the director of the Ministry's Investigations Bureau, Colonel Zbigniew Pudysz, praising General Płatek's 'great role... inspiring and directing the investigation'. It was as if the court deemed it necessary not only to support General Płatek but also to vouch for his good conduct professionally.

Edward Wende for the auxiliary prosecutors expressed astonishment that the presiding judge had seen fit to do such a thing. No such documents could take the place of a witness's testimony, he said, and they could not be believed without their authors being interrogated. Jan Olszewski asked the General whether one was to understand from these documents that he had been in constant touch with Bydgoszcz and Toruń, inspiring and directing operations. The General agreed that he had been.

'In that case,' Olszewski continued, 'could you say when the interrogation took place of Mieszczyński and Pacler, the two officers who knew from the evening hours of 19 October that a car wearing WAB 6031 number plates was to be found outside the church where Fr Popiełuszko was saying Mass?'

Płatek: 'I don't know. Those names never reached me.'

Olszewski: 'So much for the value of those two documents.'[7]

Olszewski's cross-examination continued at length, unrelieved by any revelations or clear, unhesitating testimony from the General. Assiduous probing failed to elicit satisfactory explanations of why the information from the two officers in Bydgoszcz took so long to emerge decisively in the investigation, or why Piotrowski was allowed to go home on Monday night. According to the General, he and his superior (he continued to avoid mentioning General Ciastoń by name) had both concluded that taking a police officer into custody was 'something out of the ordinary' and should not be done without all the circumstances being checked most carefully. The intention, he said, was to arrange a confrontation between Piotrowski and the officers from Bydgoszcz when they arrived.

So why was Captain Piotrowski taken into custody on Tuesday then? Had suspicions grown since the previous evening? Olszewski asked. Płatek's explanation was that the officers from Bydgoszcz had been interviewed that morning, and that there were 'other circumstances, such as the statement and the checking of the car'. Anything less informative would be hard to find. There was no explanation either of why, on Tuesday morning, Colonel Luliński left for Toruń, supposedly on the instructions of General Płatek, or why Leszek Pękala was ordered to leave for the southern city of Nowy Sącz, or why Piotrowski applied for the issuing of four pairs of handcuffs.

None of these mysteries seems to be characteristic of the closing stages of a murder investigation. On the contrary, they raise the possibility that things done in the Ministry in the immediate aftermath of Colonel Jabłoński's revelations about the car could well have been devoted to something other than securing Piotrowski's arrest. There is no direct evidence to support this but none either to discredit it because the authorities provided scant information about what happened.

General Płatek showed no inclination to provide anything beyond a few bare facts and nobody asked him to say more about the main event of Tuesday afternoon, the return to Warsaw from Toruń under anti-terrorist escort of the key witness, Waldek Chrostowski. But Chrostowski, remember, was not taken home until he had been kept waiting under guard for well over an hour at a remote spot on the edge of the former airport at Bemowo, while the officer in charge sent and received radio messages in a second car. One can only surmise that doubts about Chrostowski's safety or his destination persisted until early evening, when he was finally taken to his flat and was able to make his way to St Stanisław's.

What can be said for certain is that when the General was questioned by Jan Olszewski, he sounded more like someone on trial rather than a witness for the prosecution. This was hardly surprising. Two witnesses from the Ministry had already contradicted him and two more were about to do the same once the General left the stand.

Barbara Story had said that Płatek had twice phoned for her boss, Piotrowski, on the day of the crime, 19 October. He said he did not.

Józef Maj, another of the colonels from Captain Piotrowski's section, had denied the General's claim that when he took him the travel permit signed by Pietruszka for 19 October it bore signs of an attempt to alter the date.

And Colonels Luliński and Głowacki, who had passed the crucial information about the kidnap car to the General on Saturday night, were about to follow him to the witness stand and present him with the most fundamental contradiction of all.

At the start of Płatek's third day on the witness stand, 23 January, Edward Wende began his cross-examination with more of a statement than a question: 'According to the mass media,

you were suspended from your duties for reasons of professional negligence.'

This was too much for the presiding judge, Artur Kujawa,
who leapt to the General's defence yet again. 'The witness is not
on trial,' he said. Wende replied that 'yesterday's cross-examination suggested otherwise'. The judge disagreed.

As the General made his way carefully through the final
hours of questioning, the most serious challenge came from
Adam Pietruszka. He told the court that contrary to what Płatek
had said, the number plate WAB 6031 was definitely on the list
of cars kept under glass on a desk in the Department's secretariat. He asked Piotrowski to confirm this.

The bench's reaction to this request was to read out, for no
obvious reason, part of Pietruszka's testimony concerning
Piotrowski's statement that Fr Popiełuszko 'might be in the
Vistula'. Again, the court appeared intent on defending Płatek
rather than helping to answer questions.

When Piotrowski was finally allowed to respond, he said that
while he had wondered more than once during the trial whether
or not he was having hallucinations, it was possible that the
number plate was on the list in the secretariat but he couldn't say
for sure.

As the end approached General Płatek seemed to relax, and
it was then that he said something unusually interesting. Judge
Maciejewski reminded him that he had once said that the
problem of Fr Popiełuszko had been 'a parochial affair'. If that
was so, the judge asked, why was it that 'what was done was
done'?

'I have asked myself that question,' Płatek replied, 'but have
been unable to find an answer. I can't understand what was the
purpose of it. Piotrowski really was in a difficult situation, under
pressure on three levels: there was a problem out in the
provinces, maybe colleagues from outside the Ministry, and he
also sought solutions within the law.'

This, clearly, made little sense but Edward Wende wanted the
General to identify the three levels that had put Piotrowski
under pressure.

'He was under pressure from below, from above and from the side,' the General said. 'That's my own, personal feeling.'

This was the closest General Płatek came to saying anything revealing.

# 31
# Missing Witnesses

The clear and consistent testimony of Colonels Luliński and Głowacki, the two officers that General Płatek had sent to Toruń, was in marked contrast to the confused performance of their former boss. And although the judges seemed convinced that the General was beyond reproach, the account of the two colonels contained serious challenges to his veracity and deserved to have been presented earlier.

Stanisław Luliński retold the now familiar story of how Wacław Głowacki, at his urging, had telephoned General Płatek to tell him about the Fiat with WAB 6031 number plates and, later, KZC 0423 plates.

Asked by the presiding judge if the written report which he and Głowacki delivered to Pietruszka on Sunday mentioned the number plates, Luliński gave a remarkable answer: 'No, they were not included because the information about the plates had been passed on by telephone the previous night and on top of that Toruń provided the details to the Ministry direct in subsequent cryptograms.'[1]

This was the first time anybody had suggested that routine police procedures could have ensured that the vital clue reached the Ministry regardless of whether General Płatek had heard what Głowacki told him over the phone. The General had already testified that at least one and probably two officers had been appointed to collect, file and analyse incoming information.

Luliński said that the information about the number plates had only just reached Toruń from Bydgoszcz when he noticed it at about 11 pm.

Jan Olszewski asked whether the information should have been passed on by Toruń to Warsaw. 'Yes, I think so,' Luliński said. 'Such things were passed on to Warsaw immediately.'

The implication was that not only General Płatek but also the Ministry had been advised separately of the likely true identity of the kidnap car. So why had there been no mention of this information reaching Warsaw by normal police channels? Why did General Płatek have to seek the assistance of Criminal Investigations, as he had claimed? Was it because the information had been suppressed, either in Toruń or in Warsaw?

The court and prosecution were more immediately interested in Luliński's evidence against Pietruszka. But the question of whether the crucial information about the number plates had been received at the Ministry did not go away. It fell to Wacław Głowacki to explain once again why he and Luliński had not referred to the number plates in their written report. 'In my opinion,' he said, 'the [Toruń] office had sent everything to Director Płatek's department, and Płatek already knew about the number plates. After all, we had told him by telephone...'[2]

An argument about witnesses broke out as soon as Głowacki left the stand. Judge Kujawa announced that two witnesses had failed to appear because they were ill: Eugeniusz Mirowski, one of General Płatek's deputies, and Beata Marszczak, the young typist and friend of Piotrowski.

When Kujawa asked what counsel thought should be done about the absence of these two witnesses, Pietrasiński, the lead prosecutor, said he was content to have their testimony read out in court or even do without it altogether. Edward Wende, on the contrary, proposed that they should be summoned to appear and so should four others: the two officers who had noted down the suspect number plates outside the church in Bydgoszcz; Zbigniew Jabłoński, another of Płatek's deputies who

Pietruszka thought could vouch for him; and another Zbigniew Jabłoński, the colonel from the Criminal Investigations Bureau who had confirmed that the car seen in Bydgoszcz belonged to the Ministry.

Wende was supported in part by counsel for Pietruszka and Piotrowski. The prosecutor disagreed. He said that none of these witnesses could throw further light on the facts of the case, which had already been adequately explained.

Adam Pietruszka suggested that the officers from Bydgoszcz, Mieszczyński and Pacler, be allowed to explain how the information about the WAB number plates reached particular units of the Ministry of Internal Affairs and how it was passed on.

The prosecutor immediately objected on the ground that the matter was of no significance. But Pietruszka said that all he wanted to hear was how such pieces of information got through to individual levels of the service and whether he could have obtained the information about the WAB car within a definite time span. Andrzej Grabiński supported Pietruszka's request.

In retrospect, this was a matter of capital significance. It was an important part of the prosecution case, stated quite clearly in its indictment that Colonels Luliński and Głowacki gave General Płatek specific details of the number plates on Saturday night. It was also part of the case against Pietruszka that he allegedly suppressed the fact that the two colonels told him about the number plates on Sunday evening after their return from Toruń. But what if the information passed to the General over the telephone had also reached the Ministry as a result of normal police procedure?

If it did, what happened to it? Why did it not feature in the prosecution's case? Why did the court have to wait until Colonel Luliński's appearance, in the final days of the trial, to be told that such crucial information was usually passed to Warsaw immediately in coded messages? The court never tried to answer these questions, but the fact that Pietruszka, of all people, chose to raise the issue suggests that answers did exist.

If, as Pietruszka had earlier suggested, information about

cars and number plates was pouring in to Deputy Minister Ciastoń's office on Sunday, it is difficult to understand how the SB itself and the SB chief, General Władysław Ciastoń, could not have known about an SB car seen by SB officers stationed outside the church in Bydgoszcz.

One possible explanation is that the information was suppressed in Toruń and never got to Warsaw. If so, someone from Toruń should have been in the dock. It is equally possible, however, that the message did reach the Ministry but went automatically to a variety of addresses, including very senior ones. And in that case, no single person, not even Adam Pietruszka, could be accused of suppressing it. This, perhaps, was what Pietruszka was getting at.

But Judge Kujawa not only rejected Pietruszka's proposal on the grounds that it was 'not pertinent to the present case', he also declined to call either Mieszczyński and Pacler, the two officers from Bydgoszcz or Colonel Zbigniew Jabłoński of the Criminal Investigations Bureau.

This ensured that the men who discovered the vital clue of the car number plates and the man who delivered it in person to General Płatek could never be questioned. Jabłoński was never even on the list of witnesses. As for the two colonels appointed by Płatek to collect and distribute incoming information, Iskra and Będziak, they were listed as witnesses but excused from appearing by the prosecution. So the question of why SB headquarters took three days to act on the information coming from the SB in Bydgoszcz was ignored and never answered.

The court was also deprived of Beata Marszczak's testimony, supposedly because of illness. Many had been keen to see if she could reveal more about her conversation with Piotrowski in the café at Wilanów when he had complained of senior officers who encouraged juniors to 'go for it' but left them in the lurch when things went wrong.

When her previous testimony was read out, Piotrowski told the court that the director who had shouted back at him was Adam Pietruszka. Beata Marszczak's testimony was welcome to the court as long as it further incriminated Adam Pietruszka

As the trial approached its end, it was clear that General Płatek had been protected by the court.

No one, however, was more protected than the man whose name was studiously avoided as far as possible throughout the trial, and who was never asked any official questions, General Władysław Ciastoń, Deputy Minister of Internal Affairs and Head of the SB. General Płatek claimed that he spent a large part if not most of his time with General Ciastoń during the first three days of the investigation (when no progress was made in identifying the guilty trio), but at no time was he asked to reveal to the court what he and Ciastoń did or discussed during the long hours they spent together. If Płatek did spend most of the time with Ciastoń, why was he suspended from duties for not exercising 'adequate supervision' of his department? Was it not Ciastoń who kept him away from his desk?

The court had made it clear in the opening days of the trial that it preferred Ciastoń's name not to be mentioned. Chmielewski was persuaded to withdraw his pre-trial claim that Piotrowski had spoken of Ciastoń having to agree to their operation. And though Piotrowski confirmed that he had indeed named Ciastoń, he too changed his mind and agreed with Judge Kujawa's suggestion that the 'top brass' or *góra* consisted of Adam Pietruszka alone.

General Ciastoń had not been accused. Why then did he need this gratuitous acquittal? And why was he not asked to describe how the crime of the century, as many in Poland liked to call it, was investigated and solved.

# 32

# Closing Polemics

In his closing plea, delivered on 29 January 1985, the lead prosecutor, Leszek Pietrasiński, demanded the death penalty for Grzegorz Piotrowski and 25 years in prison for Leszek Pękala, Waldemar Chmielewski and Adam Pietruszka. However, his speech will be remembered not for its summary of the case against the accused but for its defence of the Ministry and the regime and for its denunciation of their victim, Fr Popiełuszko.

Pietrasiński dutifully reflected the political reaction to the crime enunciated by General Jaruzelski. This had not simply been a murder trial, he said. What he called 'the socialist rule of law' in Poland had also been on trial. The four men in the dock were, indeed, officers of the Ministry of Internal Affairs, he said, but that was not why they had committed the crime; they had committed the crime because they had betrayed the principles of conduct that officers of the Ministry were bound to observe. The crime had been possible, Pietrasiński said, because it was part of a conspiracy inside the Ministry, hidden from colleagues and from superior officers alike. Without Adam Pietruszka, without the travel permit he signed and the 'W' pass he provided, without his support and without his ability as Deputy Director of Department Four to cover up their absence from the office, Piotrowski, Chmielewski and

Pękala would not have been able to do what they did. This, Pietrasiński argued, was obvious, and by being obvious confirmed the truthfulness of Piotrowski's consistent allegations in relation to Pietruszka. 'What Piotrowski said during the investigation and in court about the role of the accused Pietruszka in undertaking, preparing and engaging in violent action against Fr Jerzy Popiełuszko is thus also true.'[1]

Pietrasiński's reasoning was not convincing, but it enabled him to conclude 'that there was no "top brass" or "top level" in the Ministry of Internal Affairs inspiring this crime. That "*góra*", that "top level", turned out to be the accused Pietruszka alone.'

Pietrasiński next turned to Piotrowski's motive for the crime. A great deal of time had been spent arguing over this when Piotrowski was on the witness stand in the early days of the trial, but now the prosecutor took it a stage further. Not only did he review at length the history of the official case against Fr Popiełuszko, with generous quotations from the allegations and charges against him which had never even been tried in court, Pietrasiński then claimed that the priest's alleged crime and that of the men who killed him were on a par because they were both designed to oppose the 'policy of national reconciliation' pursued 'with broad public support' by the Jaruzelski government.

Pietrasiński was sticking to a well-established government line, but he appears to have been authorised to go further. The distinguishing mark of Fr Popiełuszko, he suggested, was hatred.

> It was not for agreement and harmony that he called as a priest; it was not of reconciliation, forgiveness or love of one's neighbour that he spoke, but of struggle against the system, the State and its organs. It was not for peace and quiet, for public order or respect for the law that he called. On the contrary he sowed hatred, he reviled, he insulted, he sneered, he called for social unrest and fanned the flames of such unrest

not only in Warsaw but in other places throughout the country...

The virulence with which Pietrasiński delivered his words, almost as though they were physical blows, indicates the extent, perhaps, to which the priest's words had once wounded the authorities and those who served them. The studied malevolence of this attack surpassed anything ever written or said about Fr Popiełuszko. Never before had anyone suggested that the priest was as guilty as his murderers, or that he had brought his death upon himself. Leszek Pietrasiński did so, however, with all the solemnity of a lawyer denouncing a notorious criminal rather than the victim of a murder.

He fell victim to the accused, who considered it their vocation — as he did — to undertake activities above the law... and who thought — as did Fr Popiełuszko — that they would be protected because of the work they did. However, while Fr Popiełuszko had grounds for thinking that his 'top brass' would show indulgence, officers of the Ministry of Internal Affairs who blatantly break the law could not and ought not to have expected this. By committing a crime, they, like Fr Popiełuszko, struck a provocative blow at the policy consistently pursued by the organs of State, the policy serving the interests of the whole of society...

The extremist attitude and activity of Fr Jerzy Popiełuszko gave birth to a no less damaging extreme, the product of which were the loathsome crimes which are the subject of judgment in this case... This trial has brought together two attitudes with one common denominator. The first is typical of some clergy... who confuse the pulpit with the microphones of Radio Free Europe and scorn the law... The second marks those... who have found it possible to turn against the policy of the State by placing themselves above the law in committing the most serious of crimes... Both of these attitudes must be termed extremist.

Leszek Pietrasiński was repeating what General Jaruzelski had maintained from the start: that the real target of the murderers was not Fr Popiełuszko but the so-called policy of national reconciliation, pursued by the Party and government. At no time had the General betrayed the slightest hint of sympathy for the priest, nor did the prosecutor now.

There is a chance that this speech by Leszek Pietrasiński may one day form part of a study of the rule of law as practised in the declining years of the so-called Soviet Bloc. After all, how many murder trials feature a prosecutor who attacks the victim of the crime and at the same time finds it necessary to defend those who employ and control the secret policemen who commit it? For Pietrasiński, the need to protect the *góra* was so important that he returned to the subject yet again. Repeating that the crime bore all the hallmarks of political provocation, he granted that one could speculate about the intentions of its 'inspirers' but said that the trial had demonstrated that if they existed they were 'not to be found in the Ministry of Internal Affairs'.

Pietrasiński's speech as a whole was an insult to the priest, to what he stood for, and to the nation that admired him. Inevitably, this determined much of what the auxiliary prosecutors would say in reply.

The following day, Edward Wende delivered a speech that reflected widespread national feeling. Scathing in his reaction to the prosecutor's speech and shockingly graphic in reminding the court of the brutal manner in which Fr Popiełuszko had been put to death, he told the court that the Catholic Church, while not aspiring to that which is Caesar's, could not abdicate its right to speak out on moral issues to those in power. In this trial, however, in violation of the presumption of innocence, a principle respected by all civilised codes of criminal procedure, it had been said that Fr Popiełuszko had engaged in criminal activity by allegedly using the pulpit for non-religious purposes.

I was Fr Jerzy's defence counsel and that I shall remain. As an auxiliary prosecutor in the trial of his murderers, I did not think that I would be obliged to speak in defence of their victim. I am obliged to do so out of regard for Fr Jerzy's memory and good name and also because elementary decency requires one to defend a man who can no longer defend himself... I also have the duty to voice a determined protest against the attempt to place an 'equals' sign between the victim of the crime and those in the dock accused of committing it... The public prosecutor's statements which would place the victim of the crime on a par with his torturer and executioner are unheard of in the chronicles of world justice... No sentence was ever passed on the priest and none ever will be. Nobody ever established that the priest was guilty of anything. But the priest is depicted as an enemy and an attempt is being made to continue doing that, after his death...[2]

Wende's impassioned oratory was followed by a strictly academic disquisition by Krzysztof Piesiewicz on the lessons to be drawn from this case for the law of the land. Piesiewicz, who represented Waldemar Chrostowski, presented an unemotional but painstaking analysis of the evidence which pointed persuasively to the conclusion that it was the intention of Piotrowski and his two accomplices from the start to murder Fr Popiełuszko and also Waldemar Chrostowski, should the occasion arise.

That, Piesiewicz said, was the brutal, shocking truth about the people who acted, as one of them had said, like automatons. 'I have a question for the criminologists, political scientists, psychologists and sociologists: how were these automatons made? My question for the prosecutor is: who set them in motion?'[3]

Andrzej Grabiński, the eldest of the auxiliary prosecutors, was brief but to the point. It was wrong, he said 'to sneer at society by shifting the blame onto the victim'.

The multitudes of workers from Warsaw, Gdańsk, Silesia and all corners of Poland, who had honoured the dead priest at his funeral, also refuted the abuse heaped on Fr Popiełuszko during the trial and challenged the attempt to place him in the dock as well. In People's Poland, Grabiński said, workers were 'the ruling class' and their will was binding on all. 'For that reason, one cannot defame the memory of Fr Popiełuszko, for that reason it is wrong to call him an extremist and treat him on a par with his killers.'

Grabiński saw great menace in the crime, which he agreed was a great provocation.

> We know that in some countries police officers place themselves above the law and above government and organise death squads. In this court room we have heard the theoretical justification for the appearance of death squads in our country: the claim that the law is powerless... All of us, the whole of society, have been on the threshold of a great danger. This should be taken into account when discussing what was done by the accused...[4]

Jan Olszewski recalled that one of the accused had said Fr Popiełuszko had worn 'a cross on his breast but hatred in his heart'. He might have ignored the allegation of hatred, he said, had it not been taken up by the public prosecutor who had given it special form by treating as equals the men accused of the murder and the victim.

> One cannot place an 'equals' sign between the man whose weapon was the word and those whose weapon was the noose and the cudgel. There is no provision for any such treatment in the law of any modern civilised country...

Olszewski said that the prosecutor's view of Fr Popiełuszko was based on the charges which the offices of Pietruszka and Piotrowski had helped compile against him, and no doubt also, on that notorious complaint from the Office of Denominational Affairs which had been read out in court and which accused him of taking part in an anti-State conspiracy.

> Fortunately Fr Popiełuszko's sermon which was supposed to

be the prime if not the only evidence of the plot, was also read out in court. That sermon proved to be, as it were, the final word of 'the accused' who could not speak in his own defence in this court. I cannot add anything to that defence. A comparison of the two texts, to all who heard them here, says it all... Let us leave the victim of this murder in peace and turn to the real issues of the trial...[5]

Noting that Piotrowski had concluded in court that Pietruszka alone had sanctioned his operation against the priest, Olszewski wondered why he had been mad enough to go around scattering evidence of his presence in Bydgoszcz, dismissing as unimportant the fact that SB officers on duty near the church had jotted down the car's number plates.

> If the man who does that isn't mad — and the tests say he isn't — he must be totally convinced that everything he does will be effectively covered up by persons affording him protection. In brief, he must really believe in the existence of the 'top brass'. These calculations, anyway, are not entirely without basis. It's true that the perpetrators of this crime were exposed in three days, but we also know that given Piotrowski's way of operating, his participation in the crime could have been established the next day.[6]

For Jan Olszewski, this prompted further questions.

Why did it take three days for details of the report by the two Bydgoszcz officers to reach the operations headquarters in Warsaw? Why did Luliński's and Głowacki's information about the WAB 6031 plates fail to get through to General Płatek while it did reach Pietruszka and Piotrowski, enabling them to change the plates?

Olszewski agreed that the crime was a political provocation but gave his own reason why.

The uniform worn by Chmielewski and the cap badge left on the road next to the priest's car were part, he said, of 'a provocation within a provocation'. The badge was intended to show

348    *The Murder of Fr Popieluszko*

the public that the abduction was the work of the uniformed police, the MO. For the detectives investigating the crime, it was meant to indicate an attempt to stir up anger against the MO and the need to look for the kidnappers in opposition and underground circles. Solidarity was meant to conclude that the authorities were switching to 'direct acts of terror', while the authorities, confronted with a supposed provocation by the underground, would have to adapt their methods to those of the underground. This principle was to be forced on both sides. The crime, Olszewski said, was intended to set in motion 'a mechanism of reciprocal terror'.

Olszewski asked who could profit if Poland thus became a country of poverty, terror and despair. Nobody in Poland, he thought. But in international relations, he said, the weakness of one country was the strength of another. 'Who stood to gain if Poland became weak? That question can be answered by any Polish child who really knows the history of the homeland...' Olszewski concluded by saying that the accused had acted in 'an alien interest'. Everyone knew that he was talking about the Soviet Union.

This would normally have marked the end of the presentations by the prosecutor and auxiliary prosecutors. On the last day of January, the 24th day of the trial, counsel for Piotrowski, Pękala and Chmielewski all delivered their final pleas. Then the presiding judge announced that Pietruszka's counsel, Barbara Marchuk, was ill, and that the court would adjourn for four days.

It was during this generous pause in proceedings that Archbishop Bronisław Dąbrowski, the Secretary of the Episcopate, issued an official protest against the way the press, radio and television were covering the trial. They were being tendentious, he wrote, highlighting attacks on the Church and its representatives by the accused, by some witnesses and by the office of the prosecutor, violating press law by broadcasting the names of Bishops slandered by Piotrowski on radio, and reporting speeches by the auxiliary prosecutors without mention of their defence of the murdered priest or of the Church in Poland. This manipulation of information, the

Archbishop said, meant that the shameful murder of Fr Popiełuszko was treated as a matter of secondary importance and that someone had a particular interest in disrupting relations between Church and State.

The Archbishop's argument was strengthened when the court reassembled. Not only had the recess enabled Barbara Marchuk to return fit enough to put some incisive questions challenging the case against her client, it had also given the lead prosecutor time to prepare a surprisingly detailed rejoinder to the auxiliary prosecutors, which he sprang on them as soon as Marchuk was finished.

Pietrasiński took exception to Jan Olszwski's suggestion that Piotrowski's part in the crime could have been detected in a day. He also rejected the idea that the crime served an 'alien interest'. It was well known, he said, in whose interest lay a socialist Poland, stable and calm, recovering strength and gaining power from a society living together in harmony. Like Olszewski, he chose not to name the USSR.

Pietrasiński next took aim at Edward Wende, who had defended Fr Popiełuszko vigorously and movingly as one of a long list of priests remembered in Polish history for their patriotism and devotion to social welfare. People's Poland, Pietrasiński said, paid due tribute to 'progressive patriots in soutanes' but Wende had not mentioned that one of the priests he had named had been condemned by Pope Leo XIII and the Polish Bishops. Pietrasiński recalled with relish Vatican condemnation of Polish uprisings in the 19th century and its support along with Polish Bishops for the country's partition between Prussia, Russia and Austria in the late eighteenth century, as a result of which two Bishops had been hanged by rioters in Warsaw. In another obvious insult to the memory of Fr Popiełuszko, the prosecutor described the Requiem Masses for these 'traitor-bishops' as 'Masses for the Homeland'.

The Church, certainly, left nobody in any doubt that the murder of Fr Popiełuszko was evil. That was when a priest was killed. It's entirely different, however, when a priest kills. There have been two such cases in Poland recently. Representatives of the Church spoke out publicly in defence of the criminal priests, talking about circumstances and motives. So when a priest kills, the circumstances and internal motives of the culprit are matters of prime importance in the eyes of some representatives of the Church while the actual death of a person does not have so great a significance.[7]

Pietrasiński was talking, presumably, about the case of a Jesuit priest who did indeed kill a fellow Jesuit — but after his release from 13 years in psychiatric hospitals — and the case of Fr Zych, who, as we saw earlier, did not kill anyone.

If Pietrasiński had wanted to provoke the four auxiliary prosecutors, he failed. All spoke briefly and very correctly in reply, pointing out errors of fact and conveying a sense of regret that the public prosecutor should have sunk so low.

Grzegorz Piotrowski's final speech confirmed that the accused and the prosecutor shared the same philosophy and in that sense were on the same side. He criticised the auxiliary prosecutors and spoke at length about the Church, much as Pietrasiński had. He also challenged the prosecution on several points, claiming that premeditated murder had not been proved. He told the court that if the accused had planned to kill the priest, they would have done so differently and more effectively.

Pękala and Chmielewski spoke more briefly with varying degrees of remorse and regret, and asked for lighter sentences. Adam Pietruszka's 'final word', the shortest of all, repeated his plea of innocence, regretted the political damage done by the crime and the trial, and expressed the hope that the court would see fit to acquit him.

Two days later, on 7 February 1985, Judge Artur Kujawa read out the verdicts. All four accused had been found guilty. Piotrowski and Pietruszka were each sentenced to 25 years in prison, Pękala received 15 years, Chmielewski 14.

Jacek Ambroziak's report said the court room was packed.

There were some new faces to be seen but there were no clergy present, no members of Fr Popiełuszko's family, and no Waldemar Chrostowski. It was the latter, on his return to Warsaw, who gave his own verdict: 'There should have been more people in the dock.' This view was widespread throughout Poland among people who never set foot in the Toruń court, but Chrostowski's judgment was based objectively on evidence in that court room.

Chrostowski recognised what the authorities had achieved: they had succeeded, through Pietrasiński's management of the prosecution and Judge Kujawa's conduct of proceedings, in keeping the damage down to only four officers.

But General Zenon Płatek and General Władysław Ciastoń certainly had questions to answer, as did General Czesław Kiszczak, Minister of Internal Affairs.

Piotrowski's implied criticism of Kiszczak during the trial suggested that he had nothing to do with the operation, but the Minister was clearly responsible for the policy of damage control that began as soon as he took over the investigation.

# 33

# Communist Government's Finale

The authorities wasted little time in tidying away whatever legal procedures remained in connection with the murder of Fr Popiełuszko. In March 1985, the Toruń court produced a detailed 'justification' of its verdicts. Anyone reading it may have been puzzled to see that evidence which seemed capable of incriminating both Pietruszka and Płatek was used to convict only the former. But the document received little publicity, and in April the appeals of Piotrowski, Pietruszka, Pękala and Chmielewski were rejected by the Supreme Court.

Thoughts of the Toruń trial were revived briefly in May when it was announced that the Central Committee of the Communist Party had accepted the resignation of Mirosław Milewski, General Kiszczak's immediate predecessor as Minister of Internal Affairs, from membership of its Political Bureau and Central Committee.

Many people had been expecting this since the murder of Fr Popiełuszko, when Milewski still exercised some influence in the Ministry as the Politburo member responsible for Party work there. Viewed as a hardliner, he was naturally suspected of having something to do with the crime. The fact that Milewski was already under investigation over a financial scandal big enough to end his career was still being withheld from the public.

Equally interesting was the announcement in July that General Jaruzelski had recalled General Konrad Straszewski from his post as a Deputy Minister of Internal Affairs and appointed Colonel Zbigniew Pudysz, the Director of the Ministry's Investigations Bureau, in his place. According to the government spokesman, Jerzy Urban, the change was a normal example of the movement of staff and had no connection with Fr Popiełuszko.

General Straszewski had been Director of Department Four until his own promotion and the appointment of General Płatek in his place in December 1981. He must have been familiar with both Pietruszka and Piotrowski.

That was the last official mention of anything remotely connected with the Popiełuszko case for some time. The authorities clearly wanted to put it behind them.

But they knew that the challenge presented by the Church and Solidarity had been reinvigorated by the martyrdom of the priest they each claimed as their own. Cardinal Glemp defended Fr Popiełuszko against allegations raised in court. Talking to journalists days before his departure for the United Kingdom, he said the Church would defend its priests and denied that any were breaking the law. He also denied ever deciding to send Fr Popiełuszko abroad, as claimed during the trial. He couldn't have made him leave Poland against his will, he explained, even though they both knew that his life was in danger. Fr Popiełuszko, he said, was a priest with charisma. People were drawn to him; he did not want to leave them.

Solidarity's verdict, in a statement from Lech Wałęsa, said that the trial had revealed for all to see that the SB had been given a licence to decide for themselves on matters of life and death, a 'horrible truth' that the people of Poland had already known in their hearts. The fact that this was now common knowledge, Wałęsa said, did not necessarily mean that the future would be any easier. He appealed to the authorities to work for genuine national reconciliation on the basis of the agreements of August 1980 when Solidarity was born.

The Solidarity leader could not have expected a favourable

response. The trial had made it clear that the authorities were determined to brazen it out regardless of the embarrassment and shame they had incurred. It came as no great surprise when 'the forces of law and order' went on the offensive.

Just one week after the Toruń trial ended, uniformed and plain-clothes police raided a meeting of Solidarity activists, including Wałęsa, in a flat in the Zaspa district of Gdańsk. Seven men, but not Wałęsa, were taken into custody.

Two days later it was announced that the meeting had been 'illegal' and that three of those detained — Bogdan Lis, Władysław Frasyniuk and Adam Michnik — had been charged with preparing to foment unrest. This was a revealing moment. All three had only recently been released after long spells in prison — Michnik and Frasyniuk about six months earlier and Lis in December. As private citizens, they thought they had every right to meet whomever they liked wherever they liked. But, under Article 282a of the Criminal Code, introduced in the first week of martial law, people could be arrested even when chatting over a cup of coffee on the grounds that they were engaged in 'activity designed to provoke public unrest or riots'. The authorities were claiming, in effect, that they could read people's minds and had the right to take action (though in a manner less drastic than the modern version of the preventive strike).

What the authorities did not even suspect at the time, however, was that in 1989, Lis, Michnik and Frasyniuk would spend the fourth anniversary of their arrest in Gdańsk as members of a large Solidarity team negotiating with the authorities at the historic Round Table talks in Warsaw, and that these talks would lead to the restoration of Solidarity as a legal trade union, to its participation in partially free elections and ultimately to the formation in August 1989 of a government led by one of Solidarity's most respected advisers, Tadeusz Mazowiecki.

When, in the summer of 1985, Lis, Michnik and Frasyniuk were sentenced in Gdańsk to two and a half, three and four and a half years in prison respectively for belonging to a secret organisation and planning a general strike, Generals Jaruzelski and Kiszczak may well have believed that they were faithfully serving their own *racja stanu*. But without knowing it, they were beginning the last four years of Communist government in Poland. They were on the threshold of one of the most momentous political revolutions of the twentieth century, the collapse of Communism in Central and Eastern Europe in 1989, and the disintegration of the Soviet Union itself in 1991.

The credit for these largely unforeseen changes has since been awarded with hindsight to the policies of Western political leaders such as Ronald Reagan and Margaret Thatcher or to the work of the new man in the Kremlin, Mikhail Gorbachev, who became leader of the Soviet Communist Party in March 1985 following the death of Konstantin Chernenko.

Although these politicians exerted undoubted influence on world developments, that influence was not obvious inside Poland in 1985 and 1986 when Solidarity activists were returned to gaol and their leaders, along with the Church, called in vain for the government to reopen talks. The authorities in contrast insisted on the repression of the opposition largely by imprisonment and a refusal to talk. The political changes in Poland began only when the government finally came round to changing its mind.

Why did it change its mind? Maybe because of American economic sanctions. Certainly in part because of the advent of Gorbachev. But there could have been no change if the Poles themselves had not resisted, gone to prison, been sacked, been beaten up on the streets or in police cells for their pains.

When the Toruń trial ended in February 1985, there was no sign of historic and momentous changes on the horizon. While Lis, Michnik and Frasyniuk awaited trial on serious charges, some of their most celebrated colleagues, men who had spent years in prison awaiting trial for allegedly preparing to overthrow the state by force, would be put away for three months or so by magistrates' courts for petty misdemeanours such as leading a demonstration or sporting the name of Solidarity on a briefcase.

It was a repetition of an old routine, completed in both 1985 and 1986 with a system of conditional releases which amounted to amnesties by another name.

There is always a danger that hindsight will embellish or oversimplify the record of even the most recent history. In Poland, though, even in 1985, it was possible to argue that the policy of violent repression, imprisonment and intimidation which had failed to kill off Solidarity in the previous three years could not succeed. Fr Popiełuszko, adapting a simile once used by Cardinal Wyszyński, had described Solidarity as a great tree which, though buffeted and damaged by a storm, puts out new roots and clings tenaciously to the soil. It was a tribute to that faith that his grave rapidly became a shrine to be visited by pilgrims and politicians.

In April 1985, two months after the trial, the British Foreign Secretary, Sir Geoffrey Howe, arrived in Warsaw after visits to Prague and Budapest. In addition to lengthy talks with General Jaruzelski and Foreign Minister Olszowski, Sir Geoffrey found time for a visit to Cardinal Glemp, for a meeting with Solidarity representatives during a reception at the embassy and for a visit to St Stanisław's where he was escorted by Fr Bogucki as he paid his respects at the grave of Fr Popiełuszko. This remarkable occasion ended with cries of 'Long live England' from an enthusiastic and grateful crowd as the embassy car pulled away from the churchyard gates.

General Jaruzelski and his colleagues enjoyed no such moments of celebration. And they had to reckon with the probability that most if not all senior representatives of Western countries visiting Poland would want to talk to the Solidarity opposition as well as to them.

The brief visit in April of the new Soviet leader, Mikhail Gorbachev, to join Communist Bloc colleagues in extending the Warsaw Pact for another thirty years was remarkable only for surprisingly strict security arrangements, which ensured that none of the leaders were exposed to the danger of meeting the Polish public face to face or of reading the Solidarity leaflets scattered on the streets in the centre of the capital. Gorbachev himself, to judge from his banquet speech in Warsaw, was pre-occupied with the danger he saw in President Reagan's 'Star Wars' project rather than the spectre of political change.

In fact, few people saw any reason to doubt that the future of those Communist leaders and the Warsaw Pact was secure although some Western journalists in Poland may have had a more optimistic view of Solidarity's prospects than their readers or listeners at home.

One incident in particular was revealing. One of the men recently gaoled by a magistrate's court was the legendary Jacek Kuroń. Convicted of leading Solidarity's May Day march through the Żoliborz district of Warsaw, Kuroń appealed against the verdict and his three-month sentence. As Karol Małcużyński and I had witnessed at close quarters, he had neither led nor taken part in the demonstration; all he did was appear at the moment of confrontation with the police and negotiate a peaceful end.

On a Saturday afternoon towards the end of May, I was in court to see Kuroń acquitted on appeal, so I was late for dinner at the home of the British Ambassador, John Morgan. The news I brought from the court room appeared to shock one of the guests, Major Wieslaw Gornicki, reputedly General Jaruzelski's closest aide. But the guest of honour, the late pub-lishing tycoon Robert Maxwell, who was visiting Warsaw to see the General in connection with a proposed biography, took it in his stride. He admired my devotion, he told the table in his remarkably deep and fruity voice, but Solidarity was now a thing of the past and his paper would no longer be saying anything about it. Maxwell, clearly, was trying to please the General, but as anyone who stayed in Warsaw for more than a weekend would have known, none of the State-controlled papers, not even *Trybuna Ludu*, the Party daily, could get by for long without mentioning the 'former Solidarity'.

By the first anniversary of Fr Popiełuszko's murder, the Masses for the Homeland at St Stanisław's were still drawing large congregations and his grave, which was always guarded by volunteers throughout the night, had already been visited by extraordinary numbers of people from Poland and abroad. It would also become a place of political statement, visited by leading foreign politicians who talked to representatives of Solidarity. The precedent set by Malcolm Rifkind in November 1984 and followed the next year by Sir Geoffrey Howe would prove to be no small factor in developments to come.

There was one notable exception. Willi Brandt, then Chairman of the West German Social Democratic Party, visited Warsaw in December at the invitation of General Jaruzelski to mark the fifteenth anniversary of the Polish-West German Treaty, which he had signed when he was Chancellor. Brandt declined an invitation to visit Lech Wałęsa in Gdańsk, to the great disappointment of the Solidarity opposition, and did nothing to displease the General in three days in Warsaw. He did not visit Fr Popiełuszko's grave and did not talk to the usual Solidarity representatives — although he apparently met a number of Catholic intellectuals, some of whom were connected with Solidarity. Brandt's visit only encouraged Jaruzelski's hope that he and his regime could be welcomed back into respectable European society.

Having recently given up the post of Prime Minister and assumed the role of head of State as Chairman of the Council of State, the General had returned the previous week from a trip intended originally to take in Libya, Tunisia and Algeria, but which suddenly included a brief stop in Paris and an unexpected visit to President François Mitterrand.

The official media in Warsaw said the General had been received by the President and that their meeting marked a turning point in Franco-Polish relations. Reports from Paris, however, suggested that General Jaruzelski's car was refused entry at the front gates of the Elysée Palace and sent to the back door. The General, it was said, had gatecrashed but was not turned away.

This small but embarrassing coup followed by Brandt's visit may have encouraged Jaruzelski, but his regime still appeared to operate in the spirit of martial law. In November 1985, a Gdańsk University student, Marcin Antonowicz, died in hospital in his home town of Olsztyn two weeks after being picked up by the police late one night and sustaining a wound to the base of his skull. The official explanation — reminiscent of the Przemyk case — was that the young man had been drinking and had banged his head on the roadway when trying to escape from the police vehicle.

Another dispiriting development took place in the academic world. By early December of 1985, six university rectors and some seventy pro-rectors, deans or department heads had been sacked from their administrative appointments (although not their teaching jobs) under new powers granted to the Minister. As the government spokesman, Jerzy Urban, explained, those who operated against the socialist state could not count on the State placing the education of young people in their hands.

The authorities also had some notable success in the hunt for leaders of the Solidarity underground. In the summer of 1985, they caught Tadeusz Jedynak from the Jastrzębie coal fields of the south. In January 1986 they arrested Bogdan Borusewicz from Gdańsk. As a result, the national underground leadership — the TKK or provisional coordinating commission — was reduced to just two men, Zbigniew Bujak from Warsaw and Marek Muszyński from Wrocław. Five months later, on the last day of May, came the news that Bujak, who had eluded capture since the first day of martial law, had been arrested in a flat in Warsaw. Two other members of the Warsaw underground leadership — Konrad Bieliński and Ewa Kulik — were picked up on the same day.

For Solidarity, this was the worst possible news. For the authorities, the capture of Bujak, perhaps the greatest legend of the resistance, was a triumph. Communist delegates meeting in Warsaw applauded when the news was brought to them by General Dankowski, a Deputy Head of the SB, who predicted that underground activities would be paralysed. In fact they were not, for as always happened, replacements came forward to fill the gaps left by those behind bars. Wiktor Kulerski, Bujak's closest colleague in the Warsaw underground, joined the national leadership.

The prospects, however, were daunting. With three national leaders of the Solidarity underground now in custody, the authorities were in a position to bring them to trial and find them guilty of preparing to overthrow the State system by force. They had acted swiftly when bringing the murderers of Fr Popiełuszko to trial. Why not act as quickly now when the official media were intensifying claims that Solidarity was working for Western intelligence centres intent on destabilising Poland?

In the event, they did what they had done before. In July, the traditional month for amnesties, a law was passed providing for the release of 'some' political prisoners on the assumption or on a pledge that they would not return to 'the path of crime'. Political prisoners were released, among them Bogdan Lis and Adam Michnik. The authorities, clearly, were engaged in a pretence, for they knew that these two would never promise not to 'return to crime' because they didn't believe they had committed a crime in the first place. When the Minister of Justice told a newspaper that even Zbigniew Bujak could be released if only the authorities could feel sure that he would not return to crime, it looked as though they could all be set free.

On 8 September, the Bishops called for the release of all political prisoners, insisting that they should not be forced to compromise their rights or convictions. On Thursday, 11 September, it was announced that General Kiszczak had asked the Prosecutor General to arrange the release of all political prisoners by the coming Monday.

The next evening, following advice from Jacek Kuroń, reporters and photographers assembled at Zbigniew Bujak's home at the end of a long lane in Milanówek, southwest of the city. As Bujak's mother-in-law sustained her guests with tea, bread, butter and ham (his wife was away mushrooming), four of us went into the darkness to wait. Eventually the tall figure of Bujak, still wearing the goatee beard of his disguise, came striding up the middle of the lane. He shook hands with each of us as we introduced ourselves. 'Znam Pana,' he told me; 'I know you.'[1]

When I left Poland four days later at the end of my BBC assignment, there seemed to be grounds for believing that things were improving. While there was scepticism and caution among those now free, there was also confidence in the ultimate outcome. Adam Michnik, for instance, had told me that he believed in the formula preached by the Pope and by Fr Popiełuszko about defeating evil with good.[2]

> I simply think that by doing good to those who persecute us, we somehow, by that very fact, increase the sum of humanism in public life. For defeating evil with good means answering lies with truth and answering the use of force with resolution, while renouncing force oneself... I do believe that evil can be defeated by good... that one can replace totalitarian dictate with a system of dialogue... The fight for dialogue which we are now conducting amounts in fact to the building of democracy that will exist in Poland after we overcome the totalitarian system. That we will win is perfectly obvious to me.

It did seem possible that the release of political prisoners was a step towards that end, but they were not the only ones to benefit from the July law. A week after I left Poland, three of the SB men convicted at the Toruń trial the previous year had their prison terms reduced. Adam Pietruszka's sentence of 25 years was cut to 15, Leszek Pękala's 15 years dropped to 10, and Waldemar Chmielewski's 14 years went down to eight. Grzegorz Piotrowski's 25-year sentence remained untouched.

In December 1987 — fifteen months later — the same law of July 1985 was used to reduce their sentences further. Pietruszka's dropped to ten years, Pękala's to six years, and Chmielewski's to four years and six months. Piotrowski's sentence was cut to fifteen years.

By this time, after three separate visits to Poland, I could see that the authorities had indeed made some tactical adjustments, imposing stiff fines on opposition activists rather than imprisoning them, but there was no sign that they would ever sit down and negotiate with Solidarity.

# Epilogue

It was in the summer of 1988 that the changes began. I was in Australia when I noticed a small news brief in the paper about resumed strikes in Poland. Soon afterwards, Tadeusz Jedynak, a former member of the national leadership of the Solidarity underground, arrived in Australia to visit fellow Poles. When I interviewed him in Canberra, he repeated what Solidarity and the Church had stated consistently since martial law had been imposed in December 1981: that General Jaruzelski would have to agree to negotiations with Solidarity.

By happy coincidence, on the very day the interview was published, General Kiszczak announced the government's readiness to talk to Solidarity. Not everyone believed the Polish authorities were serious. Jedynak, however, left immediately for Poland. And in Warsaw, Karol Małcużyński set off for Gdańsk to see what Lech Wałęsa thought.

When the Round Table talks began on 6 February 1989 with a plenary session in the Namiestnikowski Palace, chaired jointly by General Kiszczak and Lech Wałęsa, the scene was set for a conference of great consequence, for which Solidarity had assembled a team of more than 230 negotiators and experts.

Even some of the journalists reporting from the scene couldn't believe what was happening. Yet when the Round Table finished deliberations on 4 April it had been agreed that Solidarity was to be restored as a legal union, free to publish its own daily paper and to take part in partially free elections to a new, two-chamber parliament on Sunday, 4 June.

The Communist Party ensured a secure majority for itself in the Sejm by the established practice of selection before the election, leaving to the voter the task of approving the officially chosen candidates. But 35 per cent of seats were open to competition by opposition candidates. And every seat in a newly constituted 100-seat Senate would be freely contested.

It has since been suggested that the results of voting on Sunday 4 June came as a surprise. They did not. On the Friday before the vote, I phoned Warsaw from Canberra to ask Janusz Onyszkiewicz how he saw Solidarity's prospects. He told me then, with a hint of apprehension, I thought, that it looked as though Solidarity would win every seat it was contesting except one, a Senate constituency in Szczecin, which would probably go to a millionaire independent. There was a second round of voting where necessary on 18 June, but Solidarity's moral victory, precisely on the scale Onyszkiewicz had predicted, was already clear after the first round.

Once again, however, the news from Poland was overshadowed by an act of violence elsewhere: the Tienanmen Square massacre in Beijing. Inevitably, perhaps, reports of Communist brutality, in which as many as 3000 pro-democracy students were said to have lost their lives at the hands of the People's Liberation Army, took precedence over a stunning victory for freedom and democracy in Poland secured by peaceful means.

The implications of that victory, however, were far from clear. Back in Warsaw for the opening session of the new parliament, I watched General Jaruzelski and Lech Wałęsa, neither of whom had stood for election, take their places on the front bench of the chamber, in a gesture of hopeful reconciliation. The date was 4 July 1989, the day *Gazeta Wyborcza*, Solidarity's Election Newspaper, reported on its front page the apparent demise, under Gorbachev, of the notorious Brezhnev Doctrine of 'limited sovereignty' with which the Kremlin had justified armed intervention to crush the Prague Spring of 1968.

A new freedom of action seems to have provided the answer

to how the election results should be reflected in the allotment of political power. After much argument about the method of choosing a President, General Jaruzelski was eventually elected by a dramatic joint session of Sejm and Senate, but by only one vote. The Communists' secure hold on power was a thing of the past.

President Jaruzelski appointed General Kiszczak to form the next government. But that was not to be. On 7 August, Lech Wałęsa issued a statement which essentially said 'no' to a Kiszczak government and invited the Peasant and Democratic Parties, old allies of the Communists, to join Solidarity in forming a government. On 24 August, Tadeusz Mazowiecki became Prime Minister, accomplishing what *Gazeta Wyborcza* had suggested weeks earlier in its famous, front-page headline: 'Your President, Our Prime Minister'. The coalition government, led by Solidarity, included the Communist Defence Minister, General Siwicki, and General Kiszczak, Minister of Internal Affairs.

By the time I returned again to Warsaw early in 1990, the Communist Party, officially known as the Polish United Workers' Party, had dissolved itself and its members had become Democratic Socialists. At the same time, however, documents from the Ministry of Internal Affairs were being systematically burned at Konstancin, south of the capital. Among scorched remains recovered from the site were SB reports on the activities of Catholic priests, the work clearly of the department once run by General Zenon Płatek.

Real changes at the Ministry of Internal Affairs began in March 1990 after Krzystof Kozlowski, Deputy Chief Editor of the Catholic weekly, *Tygodnik Powszechny*, and a member of Wałęsa's team at the Round Table talks, was appointed Deputy Minister in March 1990. It was Kozlowski, who, in the process of taking over his new job in the Ministry, discovered an unexplained cache of jewellery and articles made of gold, among them coins and a couple of gold bars.

Further enquiries uncovered a previously unpublished report which revealed that from 1968 to 1971, the Ministry's

Intelligence Department, Department One, headed at the time by Mirosław Milewski, actively cooperated in the criminal activities in Western Europe of three brothers by the name of Janosz, whom it described as gangsters.

The report, commissioned by General Kiszczak in the spring of 1984 and compiled by General Władysław Pożoga, the Director of Intelligence and a Deputy Minister, was delivered to the Communist Party's Central Committee in the autumn of 1984. It said that in an operation code-named *Żelazo* (Iron), the brothers acquired a considerable hoard of gold, silver, precious stones and jewellery, as well as other expensive valuables, by a variety of criminal methods, including insurance fraud, housebreaking and robbery with violence, and that Milewski's Department One, in exchange for helping the brothers smuggle their ill-gotten gains into Poland by car or train, received 50 per cent of the swag. The Party leadership, which received the report in the autumn of 1984 — when Fr Popiełuszko was murdered — decided against criminal action, keeping the report to themselves and delaying the announcement of Milewski's departure, without any hint of his disgrace, until the following May.

There was no such hesitation in 1990 on the part of the new managers at the Ministry. On 6 October, Milewski and four former officers of Department One — two Generals and two Colonels — were placed under provisional arrest on suspicion of large-scale corruption in the *Żelazo* affair. So too were two of the brothers. The news was sensational; not only did it provide an alternative reason for Milewski's fall from grace, it also suggested the possibility that the priest's murder was part of a political struggle resulting from the *Żelazo* investigation.

The news came at a pivotal political moment. President Jaruzelski had resigned and in the coming election Lech Wałęsa would defeat Tadeusz Mazowiecki for the presidency.

The possibilities of the conspiracy were absorbing but were not to be confirmed either way. Milewski and his six alleged accomplices were released from prison three weeks after their arrest. Investigations supposedly continued but in July 1991 the case against them was dropped. The official explanation was twofold: lack of evidence and the lapse of time. More than ten years had passed since the alleged crimes were committed, which made it impossible to prosecute the charges in court.

Great expectations were not entirely discredited, however, for on 8 October 1990 two other retired Generals from the Ministry of Internal Affairs, Zenon Płatek and Władysław Ciastoń, had been placed under arrest as a result of renewed investigations, prompted largely by Adam Pietruszka, into the murder of Fr Popiełuszko.

According to Pietruszka, Kiszczak had told him when arrested in November 1984 that he had to let himself be locked up 'for a while' to stop the investigation going deeper, meaning higher. In the interests of the Ministry, he was told later, it was his duty to function as a 'dam', keeping the waters of suspicion and incrimination away from his superiors. Kiszczak had thanked him personally for this, he said, and promised he would be let out 'shortly'. Five years later, with no prospect of release, Pietruszka wrote to the Prosecutor's Office and investigations were resumed.

By the time Płatek and Ciastoń went on trial in Warsaw in June 1992, it appeared that Piotrowski, Chmielewski and Pękala had joined Pietruszka in incriminating their former superiors. According to the indictment, Płatek and Ciastoń had initiated, controlled and directed the abduction and murder of Fr Popiełuszko. They had been constantly in charge of the operation by means of the radio communications linking Piotrowski's car to Płatek's office; and when the crime was completed, they had tried to cover it up.

The indictment quoted Pietruszka as saying he had heard Ciastoń telling Płatek: 'Popiełuszko must be silenced, so do what you have to. But in the event of something happening, I, officially, know nothing about it.' A similar allegation was made against Płatek. Having been told on Saturday night that local SB officers had reported the presence of the Department Four car outside the church in Bydgoszcz, he had ordered Pietruszka to change the number plates of the car, then parked in the Ministry yard, telling him: 'And remember, I know nothing about it.'[1]

Both Piotrowski and Chmielewski were said to have told investigators that it was Ciastoń who had decided that if the priest died, they should 'get rid of the body'. Piotrowski had phoned Ciastoń from the Ministry as soon as they got back to Warsaw after the murder and told him what had happened. During the Toruń trial, of course, Chmielewski had tied himself in knots, insisting that they had not entered the building. The investigation was also said to have confirmed that a full list of all car number plates used by any department was to be found on the desk of each department head. This meant that Płatek had lied when he told the court in Toruń that he was unable to find WAB 6031 on the list of car number plates kept under glass on his desk.

If any of these allegations were proved in court, a conviction would be possible. But again, the omens were not good.

One of General Ciastoń's defence lawyers was 79-year-old Władysław Siła-Nowicki, a former Solidarity adviser who said he wouldn't be defending the General if he did not believe he was innocent. One of the Popiełuszko family's lawyers, Edward Wende, insisted repeatedly that the case was incomplete, that it should be sent back to the prosecutor's office for the collection of further evidence, that there should be more people in the dock, and that more documents still described officially as state secrets should be made available.

As for the prosecutor, he was a replacement for the man who had initiated the investigation but had been removed from the case the previous December for reasons never satisfactorily explained. Pleading not guilty, both Ciastoń and Płatek announced that they would exercise their right to silence, refusing to answer any questions.

When the star witnesses took the stand — Waldemar Chmielewski and Leszek Pękala, both already at liberty, Adam Pietruszka and Grzegorz Piotrowski — their testimony, to judge from press reports, did not live up to the promise of what they had said during the investigation. On 24 September 1992, the court let the two Generals out of prison on bail. They had been behind bars for nearly two years.

Almost two years later, on 19 August 1994, following numerous adjournments and intermittent hearings, during which a long parade of frequently forgetful witnesses from the old regime had presented deeply conflicting testimony about the crime, and convincing evidence of lasting rivalries and hatreds inside the security services, Generals Ciastoń and Płatek were acquitted.

The outcome, however, did not put to rest suspicions and doubts aroused by the original investigation and the trial in Toruń. How could it, when a prosecutor formerly involved in the case testified that the Toruń trial had been stage-managed and conducted appallingly; when the testimony of Pękala and Chmielewski tended to confirm that on returning to Warsaw after the murder Piotrowski had phoned someone from his office to report on their operation? Pękala thought it was Ciastoń. Piotrowski, typically, said he was in such a state at the time he might have phoned Jaruzelski.

General Kiszczak told the court that those behind the murder of Fr Popiełuszko were to be found outside the Ministry of Internal Affairs, very probably in 'the hierarchy of State power'. He also revealed that close surveillance, including bugging, of Mirosław Milewski and Stefan Olszowski, Foreign Minister at the time of the crime, failed to produce evidence that they had any connection with it. In one respect, the General agreed with Edward Wende and his colleagues that the full story of the murder of Fr Popiełuszko had yet to be revealed and that there was room still waiting to be filled in the dock. Ciastoń and Płatek were innocent, he said; the investigation had not paid enough attention to a possible KGB connection. General Kiszczak spoke as if he had forgotten that he had been in charge of the first investigation but said nothing then about the KGB.

Most disappointing of all was the failure of the Warsaw trial to elicit any explanation as to why it took so long for the crucial information identifying the kidnap car as a Department Four vehicle to get from Bydgoszcz to the Ministry in Warsaw. Even when the three key officers in Bydgoszcz at the time took the witness stand, the trial got no closer to the truth; the testimony of the former SB chief, the former head of the local Section Four, and the former overall police chief, a General, was a model of confusion and advanced memory loss.

The Warsaw trial did little to cast new light on the origins of the crime, but it did produce one penetrating comment from one of General Kiszczak's former deputies, General Władysław Pożoga. Asked about various statements attributed to him in a recently published book, Pożoga said he agreed with only one: that if the death of Grzegorz Przemyk in 1983 had been investigated properly, and if policemen from the station on Jezuicka Street in Warsaw's Old Town had been tried for causing his death, maybe Fr Popiełuszko would never have been murdered.

It was Fr Popiełuszko who stated publicly from the altar that Grzegorz Przemyk — with whose funeral this book began — had been murdered.


In 1995, the year after the acquittal of Ciastoń and Płatek, Adam Pietruszka was released from prison. He was fifty seven.

On 21 March 1996, the Warsaw Appeals Court overturned the acquittal of Ciastoń and Płatek.

The retrial of Ciastoń, seventy five, began on 30 October 2000, four years later. Płatek, seventy four, was too ill to appear.

Grzegorz Piotrowski, at the age of fifty, left prison, in Opole in southern Poland, on 16 August 2001.

On 8 December 2002, Wladyslaw Ciastoń was acquitted once again, for lack of evidence. The Polish News Agency, PAP, reported that General Wojciech Jaruzelski had welcomed the verdict with satisfaction because, he said, it confirmed that there was 'no inspiration from above' in the case of Fr Popiełuszko. 'That murder', he said, 'quite apart from being morally appalling, was aimed primarily against those in power at the time and personally against me.'

# Endnotes

The author's sources, apart from his own notes and records, are all Polish. All translations from the Polish, whether from interviews or printed matter, are his own. Among the printed sources to which the author is indebted are:

Solidarity information bulletins and opposition statements, plus underground journals and publications generally delivered unsolicited to the author's office in Warsaw; key excerpts from pre-trial interrogations delivered unsolicited and in person in 1985 by a young lady never seen before or since; four books to which I am profoundly indebted for their record of essential documents: Peter Raina, *Ks. Jerzy Popiełuszko, Męczennik Za Wiarę I Ojczyznę* (*Fr Jerzy Popiełuszko, Martyr for Faith and Homeland*), Warmia Diocesan Publishing House, Olsztyn, 1990; Fr Bronisław Piasecki, *Ostatnie Dni Prymasa Tysiąclecia* (*The Last Days of the Primate of the Millennium*), Dom Polski, Rome, 1982; *Proces O Zabojstwo Ks. Jerzego Popiełuszki* (the reports from the murder trial in Toruń of Jacek Ambroziak, published by the Press Bureau of the Polish Episcopate in nine editions of its regular *Pismo Okólne* (*Circular Letter*), 1985, and later collected in one volume); and Krystyna Daskiewicz (Professor of Criminal Law at Poznan University), *Uprowadzenie I Morderstwo Ks. Jerzego*

*Popiełuszki (The Abduction and Murder of Fr Jerzy Popiełuszko)*, Kantor Wydawniczy SAWW, Poznań, 1990. I am equally in debt to Fr Grzegorz Kalwarczyk's eloquent account of how Fr Popiełuszko's body was taken back to Żoliborz. Any excerpts translated from the documents contained in the books above are identified in the notes by the authors' names: Raina, Piasecki, Ambroziak and Daszkiewicz. I have chosen to rely on Daszkiewicz's record of the early days of the trial, when Ambroziak's version was not verbatim.

*1 - Death of a Schoolboy*
[1] *Homilie* (The sermons of Fr Jerzy Popiełuszko), pp. 71-74, published underground by Słowo, 1985.
[2] Ibid.

*2 - The Priest*
[1] Raina, Part One, p. 28.
[2] Author's interview with Fr Przekaziński, Warsaw, autumn 1986.
[3] Author's interview with Dr Jarmużyńska-Janiszewska, Warsaw, autumn 1986.
[4] Przekaziński interview.

*3 - Solidarity*
[1] Author's interview with Fr Przekaziński, Warsaw, 1986.
[2] Lad Boży, Włocławek, 1 May 1983, quoted by Raina, Part One, p. 35.
[3] Raina, Part One, p. 110.
[4] Kevin Ruane, *The Polish Challenge*, BBC Publications, 1982.
[5] Ibid., p. 23.
[6] Piasecki (book), pp. 145-149.
[7] Ibid.
[8] Ruane, p. 146.
[9] Piasecki, pp. 80-81.
[10] Ruane, p. 232
[11] An English translation of Kukliński's interview published in *Kultura* in April 1987 is to be found in *East and West, Writings from Kultura* (ed. Robert Kostrzewa), Hill and Wang, New York, 1990.
[12] Andrzej Kępiński and Zbigniew Kilar, *Kto Jest Kim w Polsce Inaczej* (*A Different Who 's Who in Poland*), Vol. 2, Czytelnik, Warsaw, 1986.
[13] Ibid.

*4 - Martial Law*
[1] The Primate's account, broadcast by Radio Józef on 9 December 2001.
[2] Author's translation from a collection of the Primate's sermons,

published by the Warsaw Archdiocese in 1988 under the title *A Wolanie Moje Niech Do Ciebie Przyjdzie* (*And Let My Cry Come Unto Thee*).
[3] Radio Józef, as above.
[4] *Homilie* (The sermons of Fr Jerzy Popiełuszko), p. 7. The readings included passages by the Primate and the Bishops already quoted in this chapter.
[5] Ibid., p. 18.
[6] Reading and sermon in *Homilie*, pp. 27-30.
[7] Piasecki, p. 100. The late Primate's words, in an address in March 1981, were about the nation, not Solidarity. 'The nation is like a mighty tree which has its roots cut but puts out new ones. This tree may pass through storms and they may tear off its crown of glory, but it still clings tenaciously to the soil and stirs hope that it will be reborn.'
[8] Raina, Part One, p. 81.

*5 - Warnings and Dirty Tricks*
[1] The Solidarity leaders under arrest were: Andrzej Gwiazda (Gdańsk), Seweryn Jaworski (Warsaw), Marian Jurczyk (Szczecin), Karol Modzelewski (Wrocław), Grzegorz Palka (Łódź), Jan Rulewski (Bydgoszcz) and Andrzej Rozpłochowski (Katowice). The four from KOR were: Jacek Kuroń, Adam Michnik, Zbigniew Romaszewski and Henryk Wujec, all from Warsaw.
[2] All extracts from the diaries are in the author's translation and are taken from Zapiski 1980-84, the first ever edition published by KOS in October 1985 for the Committee for the Defence of the Rule of Law.
[3] Peter Raina's excellent book

contains a list of 47 actors who took part in the Masses for the Homeland. Among them were Halina Mikolajska, Maja Komorowska, Andrzej Łapicki, Zbigniew Zapasiewicz, Daniel Olbrychski, Andrzej Szczepkowski, Kazimierz Kaczor and Piotr Fronczewski.
[4] *Listy do Ksiedza Jerzego Popiełuszki (Letters to Fr Jerzy Popiełuszko)*, NOWA, 1985, pp. 5-[6] Author's translation.
[5] Raina, pp. 88-91 and 99-102.

### 6 - A Night in Gaol
[1] Zapiski, p. 86.
[2] Raina, Part One, p. 121.
[3] Ibid., pp. 122-125.
[4] Quotations from the sermons are in the author's translation, either from his own recordings or from *Homilie*, p. 97.
[5] Raina, Part One, p. 136.
[6] Ibid., p. 137.

### 7 - Torment by Interrogation
[1] Raina, Part One, p. 155.
[2] Ibid., pp. 156-157.
[3] Details first published in *Praworządność (The Rule of Law)*.
[4] *Praworządność*, No. 4, 6 November 1984.

### 8 - Indictment and Amnesty
[1] Letter quoted in editors' footnote to Fr Popiełuszko's diary.
[2] *Homilie*, p. 122.
[3] Ibid., p. 126.
[4] Letters, op. cit., p. 88.
[5] Copy of the letter in the author's possession.
[6] Author's translation from his own recording.

### 9 - The Final Weeks
[1] *Homilie*, p. 127.

[2] Raina, p. 206.
[3] Raina. pp. 209-212.
[4] Author s translation of Urban's article.

### 10 - Department Four
[1] Testimony quoted in this chapter is taken mainly from Jacek Ambroziak's court room record of the trial as published by the Church (see above) and from typewritten excerpts of pre-trial interrogations of the accused and of witnesses. Author's translation.
[2] Chmielewski and Pękala interrogations, 27 October 1984.
[3] Ibid.

### 11 - On the Gdańsk Road
[1] Toruń trial, 17 January 1985, Ambroziak, *Pismo Okólne* 4/85, pp. 66-67.
[2] Toruń trial, 8 January 1985, as in Daszkiewicz, p. 306.

### 12 - Bydgoszcz
[1] Wilk's account of the journey and later developments recorded on a home video reconstruction of Fr Popiełuszko's trip, undertaken by Fr Bogucki and friends including Jacek Lipiński, and shown to the author in autumn 1986.
[2] Recording in author's possession.

### 13 - Kidnapped
[1] Toruń trial, 17 January 1985, Daszkiewicz, p. 91.
[2] Toruń trial, 3 January, Daszkiewicz, p. 57.
[3] Toruń trial, 8 January, Daszkiewicz, p. 69.
[4] Toruń trial, 17 January, Daszkiewicz, p. 92.
[5] Toruń trial, 21 January, Daszkiewicz, p. 104.

*14 - The Murder*
[1] Trial, 28 December, Daszkiewicz, p. 42.
[2] Trial, 8 January, Daszkiewicz, pp. 69-70.
[3] Trial, 3-4 January, Daszkiewicz, pp. 61-62.
[4] During interrogation on 25 October, Chmielewski said the train passed 50 metres away.
[5] Trial, 28 December, Daszkiewicz, p. 45.
[6] Ibid., Daszkiewicz, pp. 46-47.
[7] Trial, 3 January, Daszkiewicz, pp. 63-64.
[8] Trial, 9 January, Daszkiewicz, pp. 73-74.
[9] Ibid., Daszkiewicz, p. 74.
[10] Trial, 28 December, Daszkiewicz, p. 47.
[11] Trial, 4 January, Daszkiewicz, p. 64.

*15 - Removing the Traces*
[1] This narrative is based on testimony given before and during the Toruń trial.

*16 - First Announcement, First Arrest*
[1] Details of Chrostowski's ordeal, his return to Warsaw and his help in the investigation are based on the author's interviews with Chrostowski in Warsaw in 1985 and with Edward Wende in Canberra, Australia, in 1988.
[2] Ibid.

*17 - Behind the Scenes*
[1] This narrative is based on testimony given before and during the Toruń trial.

*18 - Covering Up*
[1] Text of anonymous ransom demand received by Bishop Miziołek, published in *Praworządność*, Nos 6 and 7, 10 February 1985.
[2] Marszczak pre-trial interrogation, 20 November.

*19 - The Party Line*
[1] *Praworządność*, Nos 6 and 7, 10 February 1985, p. 7.
[2] *Nowe Drogi*, Supplement 4/1984, pp. 93-96.
[3] Ibid., pp. 96-97.
[4] Ibid., pp. 182-186.

*20 - Kiszcak's Half-Truths*
[1] Interrogations, 26 and 27 October. Author's translation.
[2] Ibid., 27 October.
[3] Raina, Part One, pp. 250-251.
[4] *Praworządność*, Nos 6 and 7, 10 February 1985, p. 17.

*21 - Return to Żoliborz*
[1] Raina, Part One, p. 265.
[2] Ibid., p. 263.
[3] Ibid., p. 271.

*22 - The Funeral*
[1] Raina, Part One, pp. 297-303.
[2] Author's own recording.
[3] Author's own recording.

*23 - Recriminations*
[1] Author's translation of his own copy.

*24 - Nailing Pietruszka*
[1] Trial, 4 January, Daszkiewicz, p. 140.
[2] Interrogation, 5 or 6 November.

*25 - Płatek's Excuses*
[1] Copies of interrogations in author's possession.
[2] Copy of indictment in author's possession.

### 26 - Góra

[1] When Karol Małcużyński and I tried to see Minister Urban in the hope of negotiating a change in arrangements, we got no further than the lobby telephone, over which one of the spokesman's assistants was bold enough to tell us that we were wrong to imagine they would let the BBC into the court.

[2] Trial, 28 December, Ambroziak, *Pismo Okólne* 1/85, p. 35.

[3] Interrogation, 7 November. Author's copy and translation.

[4] Trial, 2 January, Ambroziak, *Pismo Okólne* 2/85, p. 6.

[5] Interrogation, 6 November. Author's copy and translation.

[6] Trial, 7 January, Ambroziak, *Pismo Okólne* 3/85, p. 11.

[7] Trial, 8 January, Ambroziak, *Pismo Okólne* 3/85, p. 36.

### 27 - Piotrowski Attacks

[1] Trial, 9 January, Ambroziak, *Pismo Okólne* 3/85, p. 50.

[2] Ibid., p. 53.

[3] Ibid., p. 55.

### 28 - Pietruszka's Defence

[1] Trial, 11 January, Ambroziak, *Pismo Okólne* 3/85, p. 85.

### 29 - Płatek

[1] Trial, 21 January, Ambroziak, *Pismo Okólne* 5/85, p. 19.

[2] Ibid., pp. 19-20.

[3] Ibid., p. 20.

[4] Ibid., p. 22.

[5] Ibid., pp. 25-26.

[6] Trial, 22 January, Ambroziak, *Pismo Okólne* 5/85, p. 31. This was a revealing answer. In his first two sentences (according to Ambroziak's record Platek used impersonal verbs, concealing the source of his information. Sentence three can only have been based the two Bydgoszcz plain-clothes officers saw when the cars departed from outside the church, but Płatek never admitted seeing their report. He suggests here that Głowacki had told him, but Głowacki never testified that he did so.

[7] Ibid., p. 31.

[8] Ibid., p. 31.

[9] Ibid., p. 35.

### 30 - A Witness Not on Trial

[1] Trial, 22 January, Ambroziak, *Pismo Okólne* 5/85, p. 46.

[2] Ibid., p. 48.

[3] Ibid.

[4] Ibid.

[5] When the author took a serious interest in the matter, he was informed that the archives of Polish TV news had no record of the announcement of the abduction it had broadcast on the evening of Saturday, 20 October 1984. But the BBC Monitoring Service's Summary of World Broadcasts - Part Two published the text of the announcement, not only mentioning the false plates, but even spelling them out as KZC 0423.

[6] Ambroziak, *Pismo Okólne* 5/85, p. 49.

[7] Ibid., p. 51.

### 31 - Missing Witnesses

[1] Ambroziak, *Pismo Okólne* 5/85, p. 64.

[2] Ibid., p. 68.

### 32 - Closing Polemics

[1] Quotations, in the author's translation, come from the text of Pietrasiński's main speech transmitted by the Polish News Agency, PAP,

and reprinted in Ambroziak, *Pismo Okólne* 6/85, pp. 17-30.
[2] Ambroziak, *Pismo Okólne* 6/85, pp. 33-35.
[3] Ibid., p. 48.
[4] Ibid., p. 52.
[5] Ibid., pp. 53-54
[6] Ibid., pp. 56-57.
[7] Ibid., *Pismo Okólne* 7/85, p. 24.

### 33 - Communist Government's Finale

[1] Author's interview for *The Listener.*
[2] Author's interview for *The Listener.*

### Epilogue

[1] *Gazeta Wyborcza*, 29 June 1992.

# Index